TREASURES OF THE
GREAT NATIONAL
GALLERIES

TREASURES OF THE GREAT NATIONAL GALLERIES

AN INTRODUCTION
TO THE PAINTINGS
IN THE FAMOUS MUSEUMS
OF THE WESTERN WORLD

BY

HANS TIETZE

PHAIDON PUBLISHERS INC
DISTRIBUTED BY
GARDEN CITY BOOKS · NEW YORK

PRINTED IN GREAT BRITAIN

Text printed by The Pitman Press, Bath
Monochrome Illustrations printed by Clarke & Sherwell Ltd, Northampton
Colour Plates printed by Hunt Barnard & Co. Ltd., Aylesbury

CONTENTS

CONTENTS

BUDAPEST
The Museum of Fine Arts
and
BRUSSELS
The Museum of Fine Arts
p. 126

MUNICH
The Picture Gallery
and
DRESDEN
The Picture Gallery
p. 133

MILAN
The Brera
and
VENICE
The Academy
p. 143

THE VATICAN
The Picture Gallery
and
NEW YORK
The Metropolitan Museum of Art
p. 150

THE PLATES

INDEX
of Painters and Paintings
p. 417

PREFACE

*I*N THIS BOOK *the leading National Galleries of the world are set side by side, and examined from the point of view of their historical evolution and their artistic individuality. Such an attempt to grasp these famous collections as spiritual entities, and not merely as fortuitous accumulations of art treasures, has never previously been undertaken. Indeed, even the histories of the individual collections have not aroused much attention, although there have been some valuable researches into the history of a few of them, and occasional comprehensive accounts. It is hoped that this book will show how historical circumstances and national tendencies have affected the incomparable artistic treasures of all nations which these Galleries contain.*

This representation is naturally incomplete, and there is one missing even among the leading Galleries—the Hermitage in Leningrad, which, though equal in rank to the others, has had to be omitted because it has proved impossible to obtain worthy photographs for the illustrations. On the other hand, some additional material has been added in the form of Galleries which are either National Galleries but not of the first rank, or of the first rank but not National Galleries, or whose development was influenced in a particular direction by special circumstances. Apart from the completeness afforded by their inclusion, they also help to clarify the concept of a National Gallery as a cultural institution of the first importance.

The original intention was to illustrate this book exclusively with pictures which play a leading part in the history of their Gallery, or are especially characteristic of it, but this intention has not been completely fulfilled. The most popular pictures and those most in accord with contemporary taste may equally claim to be represented in a selection devoted to illustrating the combined harvest of time and the garnering of what, at any given moment, has been held to be the highest achievements of art. They are the pride of the nation which owns them and the responsibility of all mankind.

New York, March 30, 1954

BIBLIOGRAPHICAL NOTE

THE best comprehensive accounts dealing with the history of single Galleries are the ones for London (Sir Charles Holmes and C. H. Collins Baker, 'The Making of the National Gallery', London, 1924), for Madrid (Enriqueta Harris, 'The Prado', London and New York, 1940), and for Dresden (Hans Posse, 'Die Gemäldegalerie in Dresden', 1937). There have also been some exhaustive researches into archives, such as the second part of the Memorial volume on the Vienna Gallery, A. Lhotsky's 'Die Geschichte der Sammlungen', Vienna, 1941–45, or Corrado Ricci's 'La Pinacoteca di Brera', Bergamo, 1901. On the other hand, there are several collections where there has hardly been any serious attempt to go beyond a brief summary in the Catalogue and no real effort has been made to relate the history of the institution to the history of the country or to the main intellectual currents of the time.

I. Thomas Gainsborough: *Portrait of Mrs. Siddons*. London, National Gallery

INTRODUCTION

I T MIGHT, perhaps, be wise to begin by defining what we mean by the words 'National Gallery' or 'National Museum' since the terms themselves can refer either to the ownership of the collection or to its contents. The name may mean—as it usually does in Italy and France—that the institution is the property of the State, distinguishing it from similar institutions which belong to a province, a city, or some other public or private body. On the other hand, the name may—as is most common in German usage—have the meaning 'national' as opposed to 'international'. The Germanisches Nationalmuseum in Nuremberg was founded in the Romantic era for the purpose of collecting examples of German art and culture, and the Nationalgalerie in Berlin was created in 1861 as an extension of the much older international collection, with the object of providing a home for German art of the nineteenth century.

These two meanings have given rise to another, deeper, meaning, describing a collection of pictures which is not merely the property of the whole nation but is able—and intended—to express the peculiar relationship of the nation to the art of the past, and to show that relationship effectively. Such a collection represents the nation in a field in which every other nation seeks to outdo it and as a rule there is only one gallery in each country which bears this distinguishing label.

This book is limited to those galleries which, in my opinion, have attained the highest international rank and at the same time fulfil most completely their function as national representatives. Generally speaking the two things coincide, although there are several collections which are called National Galleries and were founded with this express purpose, but are too poor or too young to have, as yet, developed their characteristics fully. With time, given fortunate circumstances and the necessary work, they may be able to fulfil their purpose, overcome their initial difficulties, and take their place alongside their older sister-institutions. Foundations such as the National Galleries of Australia, Canada, Ireland and Scotland are only on the threshold of their careers, and the same may be said of their counterparts in Belgium, Sweden, Hungary, Czechoslovakia, and elsewhere.

The artistic potential of a nation is expressed not only in its creative activity but also by the way in which it prizes and, as far as possible, acquires great works of art regardless of their origin. It goes without saying that a nation's own creative impulse is the most immediate and important expression of its aesthetic aspirations, but even the secondary activity of collecting affords opportunities for the development of a national character and for the creation of something which clearly distinguishes its own collections from those of other countries. My purpose in writing this book is to define this individual quality in the great National Galleries.

To collect objects of any kind presupposes the recognition of values above and beyond the immediate uses for which the objects were designed, and art-collecting is unthinkable unless aesthetic values are recognized as self-sufficient. Classical antiquity, in its later periods, had arrived at this point and works of art were collected on the largest scale, purely as works of art; but in the Middle Ages aesthetic values were subordinated to others. There can be no doubt that during the Middle Ages objects of the highest artistic value were produced, and there were people of the most profound sensibility, fully capable of appreciating them. Yet artistic quality was not a value in itself, but only something additional to the purpose of the object. This purpose was to adorn the House of God and its Services, or to fulfil a didactic or decorative function in a princely residence, and, therefore, such objects were gathered together in ecclesiastical or secular treasuries. Beauty was something which helped these objects to achieve their ends more completely, but, in the eyes of contemporaries, their essential worth had nothing to do with aesthetic charm, and was due solely to the fact that they enshrined sacred relics, were used in the celebration of church services, were made of precious metals, or showed the exalted rank of their owner; in fact, any reason except that they were works of art, the only reason why today we admire and collect them.

Two closely related movements prepared the ground for a change of attitude and helped to revive the practice of art-collecting. These were the transition from a natural economy to a money economy, and the break-up of the feudal system which gave place on the one hand to the absolute monarch and on the other to the rising merchant classes in the newly important towns. Historians of European civilization have always recognized the collections of the Dukes of Burgundy and of Berry as signs of the coming Renaissance. A new epoch in the history of art was heralded by these French and Burgundian pioneers who began to collect in a new spirit, acquiring objects simply because of their artistic worth; and, at the same time, artists began to think increasingly in terms of artistic values, even though, as yet, there was no question of art for art's sake. Such a transformation does not come about in a day or a year, or even in a century, and many traces of the earlier approach lingered on, some of them even into our own days, but in spite of this we may say that a new spiritual factor came into human life at that point in time. For the first time since antiquity things could be appreciated without any reference to their normal functions and they could be put in a special category of values, aesthetic and historical in type.

Art-collecting, as distinct from the earlier piling up of treasures, was surrounded from the very beginning by all the related activities which have accompanied it ever since: dealers, connoisseurs, forgers, all these appeared as soon as there was scope for them, that is to say, as soon as collectors existed.

The first art-collectors all belonged to the ruling classes, for there were no other people who could afford the luxury of acquiring objects which had no purpose but that of arousing pleasure and interest. The princely pioneers in this field, the Dukes of Burgundy and Berry, or the early Medici, set an example which, furthered by the whole trend of the times, produced a new kind of refinement in living. To collect works of art became not merely a legitimate pursuit but a mark of social distinction, and, by a familiar sociological process, it became a duty among the upper classes and especially among ruling princes. As so often happens, rivalry speeded up the tempo and in the sixteenth and seventeenth centuries the patronage of the arts, including collecting, became a matter of prestige. No architect of the period, drawing up plans for an ideal palace, would ever have omitted to provide for a gallery, the possession of which was not a matter for the prince's personal taste but as much an obligation as the possession of an expensive mistress, of a well-run stud and of sumptuous palaces and gardens.

Of course, such princely collectors included men who acquired works of art with passion and knowledge, and who, therefore, were much more successful than those who collected simply as a routine duty. Gifted collectors, such as Lorenzo de' Medici, Philip II of Spain, the Emperor Rudolf II, King Charles I, were as much shining exceptions as the true collectors among modern millionaires. They brought together collections which were simply astounding in their quality and their quantity, and these collections, which originated in the interest and tastes of one member of the family, subsequently became part of the dynastic heirlooms, to be kept intact and increased whenever the opportunity arose on account of their prestige value. Thus they became permanent establishments which not only reflected the glory of the royal house, but equally and at the same time conferred honour upon the nation as a whole: in the guise of dynastic treasuries they grew into National Galleries.

The history of individual galleries will serve to show the different forms taken by this process in various places. On the whole, it follows the same pattern as the change in the role of the prince himself, from the absolute ruler of the Baroque era step by step into the principal servant of the state in the Age of Enlightenment. Princes inherited the idea that it was part of their duty to patronize the arts, but the new spirit of the time laid on them the further duty of making the results of their patronage useful to their subjects. This transition, too, was gradual and was aided by social, economic and cultural tendencies. The established dynastic principle of self-glorification seemed to be best served by opening the collections, grown famous in their seclusion, to distinguished strangers; the increasing number of such visitors led to the opening of the collections at regular times and in this way, by easy stages—and especially in places where tourist trade was important—the general public came to be admitted regularly. This happened first in Florence, where the splendid collections of the Medici passed to the Tuscan State in 1737; Dresden followed a little later and in 1768 Goethe, then a young student, awaited the opening hour with passionate eagerness. The tendency was so strong that even where such collections had always remained closed to the public, public opinion began to press for a change. In 1747 the Parisian art critic, La Font de Saint Yenne, pressed for the piled-up and invisible treasures of the Louvre to be opened to the public, and in 1777 John Wilkes, in the first debate in the House of Commons to be devoted to such artistic matters, protested against the transference of the Raphael Cartoons from Hampton Court, where they could be seen by the public, to Buckingham Palace, which was inaccessible.

A few years later, in 1789, the Italian art-historian Luigi Lanzi expressed the same idea in an article on the Uffizi: "The Grand Duke has opened the Gallery to everyone, since it belongs in fact to everyone." The nationalization of the art collections founded by ruling houses began to come within measurable distance, and this took place in two ways—by moral force and by legal expropriation.

The claims of the public were in accord with the economic theories of the eighteenth century, which held that works of art of earlier periods should serve not merely to delight but also to stimulate contemporary production. This point of view was not altogether foreign to earlier patrons of the arts, for they also hoped to call new masterpieces into life by assembling old ones. When Lorenzo de' Medici set up antique statues in the garden of San Marco it was with the intention of raising contemporary sculpture to the same level as painting had then attained, and this concern for present-day needs set the standard for all later Medicean patronage. The Grand Duke Cosimo (who died in 1574) linked the family collections with the Court workshops which carried on all the applied arts, and, at about the same time, that great collector the Emperor Rudolf II surrounded himself with a whole army of decorative artists. Their productions were still intended for the use—and therefore for the greater glory—of the Court, but these Court workshops were the cradle of a national decorative style. Under Louis XIV of France this system was organized down to the last detail by Colbert's comprehensive and far-sighted patronage. The King's extensive acquisitions, the founding of Academies in France and for French artists in Rome, the creation of State workshops for Gobelins tapestries and for porcelain—all were part of a unified system. The artists were stimulated by the classic models provided for them and they were able to transform these models in their own works, while the craftsmen were affected by this atmosphere and gave of their best. Both continued to work for the glory of the King, but their productions went beyond this limited goal: the great tradition of French art in the nineteenth century and the uncontested superiority of French decorative art in the same period were firmly based on the lead gained in Louis XIV's time. From this enlightened Court patronage the whole nation eventually derived both reputation and profit.

Even apart from the practical advantage, the art of the past became a powerful factor in the national life. The classicism of the late eighteenth century was by no means simply a rediscovery of the antique world, but derived from a number of sources, including an awareness of a certain exhaustion of creative power and the need to renew it by getting back to fundamentals. On the one hand, an increased feeling for humanity and for nature, on the other, the growth of national sentiment were the two forces which were to dominate the complex scene of the nineteenth century. Classicism and Romanticism are not successive stages of a single development but go hand in hand, in spite of deep contradictions in the nature of their inner impulses and effects. Interest in classical antiquity and in the forms of art inspired by it reached new heights, and at the same time the relics of the national past became the objects of enthusiasm and reverence.

This coming-of-age of the peoples and their heightened self-consciousness converted the ordinary man's vague claim on the princely collections into an assumption of full legal possession and moral responsibility for it. Princes, who had once boasted of being the State, gave place to a State created by the nation, and patronage of the arts, which had been a princely prerogative, passed to their successor. Once again it was Florence which pointed the way to the future, for, when the great line of the Medici was on the point of extinction, the last representative of the family, the Grand Duchess Anna Maria Luisa, came to an agreement with her successor to the sovereignty of Tuscany. This was in 1737, and it provided that the art treasures gathered by her forebears over the centuries should remain for ever in Tuscany, as the property of the State. This was a completely logical action, for it meant that when the family died out, the works of art which had for so long contributed to their fame should not pass to the new rulers—for whom they would at most represent a material profit—but should be 'an honour to the nation and a benefit to the public'.

As one might expect, the decisive step was taken as a consequence of the French Revolution, when the collections of the deposed Bourbons were immediately made into public property. Not only were the French the first people in Europe to take their destiny into their own hands, but even more, they were the first to be hammered, by events unparalleled in their gravity and speed, into a nation conscious of its own individuality. Their example and influence affected all Europe, and one result of the now greatly heightened national sentiment was the creation of National Museums in many capitals. These new National Galleries were either transformations of existing Court collections, such as the Louvre, or entirely new creations, as in Amsterdam and, above all, in London; for even the Rijksmuseum was based on the older collections of the House of Orange, while the National Gallery in London came into existence solely through an act of national will, created by public funds for the public use and without help from the ruling house. The stupendous collections of the Stuarts had been precipitately scattered after the Civil War; and the parts re-assembled by Charles II, as well as the additions he and his successors made, remained specifically Crown property. Following the Anglo-Saxon principle of self-help, the English people created their own Gallery independently. Three-quarters of a century earlier, in 1753, Sir Hans Sloane's collections had been acquired by Act of Parliament and opened to the public to become the kernel of the British Museum and the first public museum in the modern sense.

The foundation of the National Gallery marks the triumph of the new principles which had gradually undermined the customs surviving from earlier times. In spite of their greater accessibility to the public, some of these heirs of Royal zeal in collecting retained much of their former courtly character—Vienna and Madrid, for example—and there was even a newcomer to their ranks in the Hermitage at St. Petersburg, which maintained an atmosphere of regal exclusiveness, just as the splendour of the setting in Vienna gave many visitors to the Kunsthistorisches Museum the feeling that they were the Emperor's guests. Here, as also in Madrid, far-reaching and revolutionary changes had to take place before Court collections were transformed into true National Galleries.

Long before the question of their legal ownership was fully resolved, great collections of this kind had in fact become national institutions, and were thought of as such; even in the courtly phase of their existence they had served ideals which went far beyond their original purposes. Riedel, the Keeper of the Dresden Gallery, in the first printed Catalogue of the Gallery (1765) states the new aims: to honour the memory of the greatest artists and to improve the public taste. This combination of educational and purely idealistic aims, so characteristic of the Age of Enlightenment, conferred an outstanding position upon the major collection in every country, irrespective of its original owners. Just as Princes had competed for the best Raphael or the best Dürer, so now the nations took up the rivalry in a field in which to be left behind was tantamount to cultural inferiority. "I wish, Sir," said John Wilkes in his speech of 1777, "the eye of painting as fully gratified as the ear of music is in this island, which at last bids fair to become a favourite abode of the polite arts." An internationally famous Gallery became an object of national pride and a cultural obligation.

It is plain enough that this development is very closely bound up with the rise of the idea of nationality: nations must first become conscious of their own individual characteristics before they can develop a passionate interest in their own possessions and performances, or regard them as patents of nobility and proofs of superior civilization. It was only then that they began to create such symbols or to acquire them for themselves by taking over existing ones and endowing them with a new meaning; without counting the cost, they made their capital cities splendid supported scientific and cultural institutions, set about the creation of National Galleries and Museums which were simultaneously fulfilments of educational and aesthetic aims and symbols of the nation. Several of these galleries were founded with this ambitious goal specifically in mind, while others were taken over more or less complete; whatever its origin, such a collection can attain to heights which few others can reach. They reign in splendid isolation and hardly anywhere is there a case where more than one collection or group of collections occupies this special place in the affections of a nation. Once this is accomplished, the people guard their creation with jealous vigilance, disputing the slightest alterations—even the cleaning of pictures—and refusing to part with their possessions even in times of the greatest financial stress. None of the terms imposed on the French by the Allies in 1815 aroused such opposition and resistance as the return of works of art to their original homes, and yet this was not a question of an old inheritance but simply the short-lived spoils of a victorious army. After the collapse of Austria the Government toyed with the idea of selling some of their art treasures to meet the desperate need for money. Nothing came of it, and even in this emergency there was never any question of touching the really important collections but only relatively unknown works stored in depots. The sale of important pictures from the Hermitage by the Russian Government was a measure decided upon because of the impossibility of getting much-needed foreign exchange in any other way, and it seems that they later tried to call the whole thing off: national art treasures have become as much an inalienable symbol as a consecrated crown once was.

Like any other privilege this carries responsibility with it, and a National Gallery should not merely surpass other institutions by reason of its possessions but should always bear in mind its duty to represent the nation's highest aspirations in this field, the expression of a people's faith in the arts, its veneration of them, and the desire not to be inferior to any other country in this.

The struggle for the first place among the major Galleries has resulted in a tremendous wealth of important works of art being garnered together in them. Taken as a whole their possessions represent the cream of what, through the ages, has been held to be the best of its kind by competent judges. A good deal has not stood the test of time and has sunk into oblivion—usually no farther than the cellars of the museum, from whence it may at any time be resurrected by a change in taste. A high proportion of the artistic heritage of European civilization, weeded out by efforts which have sometimes extended over centuries, is preserved and exhibited in these collections. The National Galleries serve an international public.

In this book eight of the leading Galleries are characterized in some detail. Seven of them were involved in the recent war, since the Prado also suffered in the prelude to the World War. Their buildings were damaged, and some of them destroyed, and the contents preserved from damage or even annihilation only by the precautions taken by the curators, and for part of the Berlin collections these precautions were unfortunately vain. This must be a matter of the deepest concern to everyone who cares for the arts. Since the end of the war the means of destruction have become so much more potent, the speed with which the blow could fall in the future has become so much greater, that it is open to question whether there is any hope of saving these treasures if occasion arises. The least part of their value lies in the millions they would fetch on the market; their real worth lies in the intellectual labour which they embody and in the spiritual pleasure stored up in them. To create these possessions the nations contended one with the other, and each land has built its own memorial in the Gallery which enshrines its history and its way of life.

THE PICTURE GALLERY IN VIENNA

THE PICTURE GALLERY of the Kunsthistorisches Museum in Vienna can lay claim to the first place among the great national Galleries, not so much because its beginnings go right back to Renaissance times (a distinction which it shares with the Uffizi, the Prado, and the Louvre), but rather on account of the way in which it has preserved its original form so much more tenaciously than its sister institutions. The changes which took place in the nineteenth century, and above all after the collapse of the Austro-Hungarian Empire, affected it only superficially and left it unchanged in essentials so that even today the Gallery is principally a monument to the dynasty which ruled over Austria for so many centuries. The selection of 'Art Treasures from Vienna', exhibited in many European cities and in America a few years ago, was generally regarded as being the Hapsburg pictures.

Because of this origin, the Vienna Gallery, as we know it, is only the fragment of a greater whole, which has suffered somewhat by being separated from the rest of the collections of which it once formed part, for the old Imperial Collection included bronzes and manuscripts, tapestries and armour, drawings and goldsmiths' work, coins, medals and cameos, curiosities and marvels of nature, all of the highest quality and in enormous numbers. Only in the nineteenth century was this family treasure broken up and the individual parts arranged systematically in the Kunsthistorisches Museum and in two Treasuries. The Picture Gallery, like the other separate parts, became an independent entity and the factors which had conditioned its origin became apparent. It is too one-sided to give a truly balanced picture of the development of all the different styles, and schools that are much better represented in quite average Museums are but thinly represented in Vienna and sometimes are not there at all. On the other hand, other schools are so incomparably well represented in the Gallery that it alone, after the fall of the Hapsburgs, can give an overwhelming impression of the riches, the power and the far-reaching ambition of the dynasty. Several art-loving members of the family assembled the collection, and in the seventeenth century it was decreed to be indivisible and inalienable. It shows a definite family taste, with a definite bias in favour of certain art-forms and a no less significant prejudice against others; above all, it gives the clearest possible picture of the changing fortunes of the dynasty and their Empire. These traits also explain the national character of the Gallery, for, in the six and a half centuries of Hapsburg rule over Austria, the country formed the family as much as the family formed the country.

The oldest parts of the present Gallery are connected with the name of the Emperor Maximilian I, at once 'the last of the Knights' and a politician of considerable astuteness, among whose many-sided and usually shrewd enterprises the patronage of the arts held an important place, though it, too, was a curious mixture of mediaeval superstition and modern dynastic propaganda. The Emperor had the right instinct when he singled out Albrecht Dürer from his contemporaries in Germany for the Imperial patronage, even though the only use he made of his opportunity was to commission the illustration of some ponderous allegories, nowadays almost incomprehensible. The portrait of Maximilian by Dürer which belongs to the Gallery (Plate 4) does not come from the Emperor's collection, but it gives a good idea of his personality. The official reticence of the portrait is enlivened by a certain intimacy, still more apparent in the study from life—in the Albertina in Vienna—which, according to the inscription, was drawn by Dürer in 1519 in the Emperor's private apartment at Augsburg. The ability to carry his high-sounding dignities easily and unaffectedly makes Maximilian the ancestor of the Hapsburg Princes and the Hapsburg patrons of art.

His interest in the arts found a timely expression in the person of his daughter, Margaret of Austria, for many years the Emperor's able Regent in the Netherlands. She was one of the leading Renaissance collectors and may have been the original owner of the Vienna portrait of Maximilian, if it was in fact the picture Dürer offered her at Malines. She does not seem, according to Dürer's own account, to have been very favourable to him, for she had already felt the cosmopolitan impact of the Renaissance, overriding local and national interests.

This Renaissance desire for encyclopaedic breadth reached a climax in Maximilian's great-grandson, the Emperor Rudolf II. Not only was he the first Hapsburg collector on the grand scale, he was one of the most impassioned collectors of all time. The descriptions by contemporary travellers of his collections in his favourite residence, the Hradschin Castle in Prague, read like fairy-tales. If the measure of true love is willingness to sacrifice everything for it, then Rudolf proved the depth of his love for art, for, towards the end of his life, he became so utterly absorbed in his passion for collecting that he neglected his duties as a ruler and was forced to abdicate. The extent of his collections was as boundless as his passion, for they were not confined to works of art but embraced everything in the far-reaching Renaissance idea of a Cabinet of Curiosities; whatever was rare, curious or out of the way, in nature or in art, was included in this motley collection. Yet Rudolf had a remarkable sense of quality, as well as an inordinate desire for quantity. His favourite painters were Dürer and Bruegel, and many of their finest works, now the pride of the Vienna Gallery, were originally his.

The most important of his Dürers, *The Feast of the Rose Garlands*, painted in 1506 for the German colony in Venice, later on, after years of neglect and oblivion in the Imperial palace in Prague, passed into private hands and is now the property of the Czechoslovak National Gallery. In spite of all its sufferings it is still one of the noblest ruins in the history of art, still splendid in the less damaged parts. On the other hand, some of Rudolf's Dürers, brought to Vienna immediately after his death in 1612, are in a good state of preservation. The *Adoration of the Trinity* (Colour Plate II), the only one of Dürer's large altarpieces to have come down to us in good condition, was painted in 1511 for the chapel of the Old Men's Hospital at Nuremberg and was transferred to the Imperial collection in 1585 in spite of strong civic opposition; only the original frame remained in Nuremberg, being replaced in Vienna by an exact copy. Other works by Dürer from Rudolf's collection are the *Martyrdom of the Ten Thousand*, painted in 1510 for the chapel of Schloss Wittenberg; the *Madonna with the Pear*, which, to judge from the innumerable replicas, must have been extremely popular in the Baroque period; and the portrait of the merchant and humanist Johann Kleeberger of 1526, one of the painter's last works. There were others; and it may be remarked in passing that Rudolf also owned one of the finest collections of Dürer's drawings, now in the Albertina in Vienna.

Rudolf was no less successful as a collector of Bruegel's works, although the old Inventories do not make it quite clear which of the masterpieces that now form some of the treasures of the Vienna Gallery originally belonged to the Emperor. They certainly included the *Massacre of the Innocents* and the *Tower of Babel* (Plate 9) and probably also the *Children's Games* (Plate 8). There was a time when Bruegel was regarded simply as a jester, but nowadays we look upon him as a philosophical interpreter of the world and we can imagine Rudolf sitting in front of his pictures, brooding over the ways of the world. This ageing eccentric also had a weakness for erotic themes, to which Vienna owes two famous Correggios, the *Ganymede* and the *Io* (Plate 18), and the same tastes were reflected in the works of Rudolf's Court painters, works in which the Gallery is all too rich.

The splendour of the Hradschin Gallery was short-lived. Immediately after Rudolf's death an important part of the collection was transferred to Vienna, the seat of his successors, and the Thirty Years War completed the ruin of the Hradschin; after lootings by Saxons and Bavarians there followed the taking of Prague in 1648 by the Swedes, who carried off about five hundred objects from the Gallery on the grounds that the Bible commands the Israelites to take away the goods of the unbeliever. The majority of the pictures passed into the possession of Queen Christina, but only a few of them stayed for very long in Sweden, for she took the finest with her to Rome after her abdication and conversion to Catholicism and, later still, they formed part of the basis of the celebrated Orleans Collection. Today they are scattered all over the world and almost every major museum prides itself on the possession of one or more of them.

Because of the rapid dispersal of his collections Rudolf can hardly count as the founder of the Hapsburg treasures: these laurels are shared by two other members of the family, the Emperor Ferdinand II and his younger son, the Archduke Leopold Wilhelm. By his will of May 10, 1621, Ferdinand made the family possessions indivisible and inalienable, thereby establishing them legally as an entity, while the Archduke Leopold Wilhelm brought the basic elements together. His long period as Governor of the Netherlands, then the centre of the international art market, gave him plenty of opportunity for collecting and, in addition, he made valuable purchases in Italy and Germany. An important source of supply offered itself in the collections of King Charles I and the Duke of Buckingham, both of which came up for sale during his stay in Brussels, and from which he acquired such gems as Titian's *Ecce Homo* (Plate 15), Andrea del Sarto's *Lamentation over the Dead Christ* and Rubens's *Garden of Love*, a homage to Titian, whose treatment of a similar subject Rubens had admired and copied.

Archduke Leopold Wilhelm surrounded himself, during his stay in Flanders, with a court of artists who painted for him and advised him in his purchases. His principal advisers were, first, Anton van der Baren, the flower painter, and, later, David Teniers the Younger, to whose pictures we owe our knowledge of the original arrangement of the Gallery in the Archduke's palace in Brussels. To some extent these Gallery-pictures still betray something of the character of an over-full Cabinet of Curiosities, yet real connoisseurship and sensibility were predominant. The Archduke may well have possessed these qualities himself, for a glance at his collection shows that it was formed by a very personal taste. Some years before his death he brought this enormous collection—1,397 pictures, 343 drawings and 542 pieces of sculpture—to Vienna and bequeathed it to his nephew, the Emperor Leopold I, as a part of the family possessions. As far as the older masters were concerned, the Archduke had a marked preference for the great Venetians of the High Renaissance, and—perhaps as a result of the influence of his Flemish advisers—a noteworthy interest in the Flemish Primitives; but at the same time he was a zealous patron of contemporary or near-contemporary artists, for we hear of his portrait being painted by dozens of artists. His tastes are still traceable in the Vienna Gallery, for it is to Archduke Leopold that it owes Venetian masterpieces from Antonello da Messina and Mantegna, by way of Giovanni Bellini, Giorgione (Plate 11), Palma Vecchio and Lotto (Plate 16), up to Titian (Plates 13, 15, 17) and Tintoretto (Plate 14); it is rich, too, in the Flemish Primitives—Jan van Eyck, Hugo van der Goes, and two large panels by that rare painter Geertgen tot Sint Jans (Plate 1)— and it was from the Archduke that several new Bruegels came to join those already there—the *Peasant Wedding* (Colour Plate IX), the *Return of the Herd* (Plate 7), and probably also the *Return of the Hunters*. Many of the pictures by Rubens, Jordaens, and Van Dyck (Plate 19) came from Leopold Wilhelm. The Flemish 'Little Masters' are very well represented, particularly, as is natural, his Court painter and expert, David Teniers; yet there is an almost total absence of Dutch pictures. Apparently, Leopold Wilhelm, in his double capacity as a Prince of the Church and Governor for the Catholic Emperor, was not inclined to favour the Protestant painters of the Dutch Republic, but in any case their artistic aims might not have found much favour in the eyes of such a connoisseur, even had his background been quite different.

After the incorporation of Leopold Wilhelm's munificent bequest, the Austrian Hapsburgs felt no desire to increase their collections for some while, yet the collection grew in the next few years for two reasons. The first of these was the relationship with the Spanish Hapsburgs, with whom the Viennese branch of the family was connected not only by blood but also by numerous intermarriages. Naturally, the Vienna Hapsburgs were curious about the appearance of their Spanish cousins and nephews—and still more about the looks of their brides—and as it happened that a certain Diego Velazquez was the Court painter in Madrid, it came about that there are more of his portraits in Vienna than anywhere else outside the Prado. They got there on account of their family interest and not because they were valued as works of art; indeed, the portraits of Maria Anna, Baltasar Carlos (Plate 25), Philip Prosper, and Margarita Teresa (Plate 26), which we admire so much, were so little esteemed that the Emperor felt himself obliged to send his own Court painter to Madrid in order to get a really trustworthy likeness of his bride. This painter was named Duchatel—and that is all we know about him.

The second major event in the history of the collection during the Baroque era was its organization into a Gallery, properly so called. At the beginning of the eighteenth century the collection was increased by the addition of a number of pictures gathered together from various Imperial residences, and the whole was then installed in a building near the Hofburg which had been specially adapted for it. It was called the Stallburg, and contemporary engravings and miniatures give us an idea of the appearance of the Gallery, with each of the rooms forming a decorative ensemble regardless of the historical continuity of its contents. In order to obtain this decorative effect the pictures were cut down or added to, altered in shape or overpainted—in short, underwent the sort of treatment that flatly contradicts all our modern ideas on museum conservation. To the highly self-confident men of the Baroque era, works of the past were means like any other which could be made to serve their own artistic, and above all, decorative ends.

The installation of the Gallery in the Stallburg was a foretaste of the increased centralization and more systematic organization of the Age of Enlightenment. The Empress Maria Theresa made a number of important purchases for the Gallery, for she bought several altarpieces by Rubens from Jesuit churches, which came into the market when the Society of Jesus was expelled from the Austrian Netherlands. These included the *St. Francis Xavier preaching* and the *St. Ignatius Loyola exorcizing Devils* (Plate 21) which had by turns adorned the high altar of the Jesuit church in Antwerp, but still more important was the acquisition of the *St. Ildefonso Altar* (Colour Plate X), Rubens's splendid masterpiece of 1630–32 painted for the Jesuit church in Brussels. It would have been damaging to the prestige of the Empress, as her Minister, Prince Kaunitz, pointed out to her, if works of this rank were to fall into the hands of the foreign princes who were trying to obtain them, instead of passing into the possession of the ruler of the Netherlands. The Emperor Joseph II, no particular friend to the Church, followed his mother's example when, in 1781, he bought Caravaggio's *Madonna of the Rosaries* (Plate 22) from the Dominican church in Antwerp. This picture, painted in 1607, had been given to the church by a group of artists which included Rubens.

At about this time the Imperial castles were once more ransacked for any good pictures which might have been overlooked on previous occasions, and a few did in fact come to light which have since become popular favourites, such as Raphael's *Madonna of the Meadow* (Plate 12), Moretto's *St. Justina* (Plate 10), Bruegel's *Peasants Dancing*, Rubens's intimate portrait of Hélène Fourment ('*Het Pelsken*', Plate 20) and some of Holbein's portraits; they may well have been Imperial property for a long time, but they are not recorded in any Inventory before their incorporation into the Gallery. The Gallery itself now moved from the Stallburg into the Belvedere, the former residence of Prince Eugene of Savoy and one of the gems of Austrian Baroque architecture.

The extension of the collection and the move to a new building mark the transition into an organized museum. Christian von Mechel, of Basle, who was responsible for the arrangement and for the first printed Catalogue, undertook to hang the pictures by Schools. He was a friend of Winckelmann, whose new, historical, attitude to the art of the past he shared. The decorative keynote of the Baroque arrangement gave way to the rationalism of the Enlightenment, and in 1781 the Gallery became a public Museum.

The Gallery stayed in the Belvedere for nearly a century, so long in fact that it became generally known as 'the Belvedere Gallery', but in the last quarter of the nineteenth century it was transferred to Hasenauer's pompous edifice on the Ringstrasse, specially built as the Kunsthistorisches Museum. Through all this period the contents of the collection remained practically unchanged although they suffered a loss when the Emperor Joseph II consented to an exchange with his brother, the Grand Duke of Tuscany, which brought a few Italian pictures of the High Renaissance to Vienna, where they were superfluous, at the cost of precious works like Bellini's *Allegory* (Plate 51) and Dürer's *Adoration of the Magi* (Plate 30). Clearly, the Director in Vienna was no match for his Florentine colleague in artistic judgment. Most, but not all, of the pictures taken to Paris during the Napoleonic Wars came back in 1815. Some compensation for these losses was afforded by the pictures which continued to turn up in the Imperial residences—for example, Tintoretto's *Susanna* (Plate 14)—or works taken over from suppressed convents, like Rueland Frueauf's huge altarpiece and Conrad Laib's *Crucifixion* of 1449 (Plate 2), heralds of an increased interest in early Austrian art which was not to be fully developed until somewhat later. An important increase in numbers came about through an administrative decree, which, however, did not prove lasting. In 1816 and again in 1830 a number of pictures from abandoned Vene-

II. ALBRECHT DUERER: *The Adoration of the Trinity.* Vienna, Kunsthistorisches Museum

tian churches and official buildings of the Republic were assembled in a depot, from whence they were taken to Vienna and divided between the Imperial Gallery and the State Academy of the Fine Arts, and although the Treaty of 1866, which separated Venice from Austria, specifically provided that Italy should have no claim on these pictures, yet, after the First World War, the Italian Armistice Commission did claim them and, under pressure, got them. The Vienna Gallery, so rich in the Venetian School, thereby lost a good deal of not very important material along with much that was valuable, for example Cima da Conegliano's *Madonna under the Orange Tree*, now an ornament of the Accademia in Venice.

Apart from such more or less ephemeral additions, the Vienna Gallery was regarded as complete in the nineteenth century, and it rested on its laurels at the very time when changes in society provided many opportunities for making important new acquisitions—the time when the National Gallery in London was built up from nothing and the Berlin Gallery from not much more. It might even be said that this quiescence was part of the specifically Austrian character of the Gallery, for the Austrian ruling house was beginning to show signs of decay and from the time of the alliance of Hapsburg and Lorraine onwards took less interest in the collections, not really having the inclination to make sacrifices for their increase.

Even the great event of the nineteenth century, the move into the Kunsthistorisches Museum, was in a certain sense a termination: the decorative richness of the building—which to modern taste is too heavy a frame for its contents—made alterations difficult and extensions practically impossible. The collections here assembled were to be regarded as complete and definitive. Because of the luxury of their setting and by their refusal to compete with others they were to testify to the greatness and splendour of the dynasty which had brought them together and had high-mindedly made them available to their subjects, and up to the very last moment they remained what they had always been designed to be— a means of dynastic aggrandisement.

After the fall of the Hapsburgs in 1918, the Gemäldegalerie was taken over by the Austrian Republic along with the other former Imperial collections and the new regime contented itself with measures which took into account the change in taste and the new aims of the collections. Far the most important acquisition during these years was Dürer's *Venetian Girl* of 1505, and such acquisitions were only possible in the financial straits of the new Republic by extensive barter of material from their huge depots. Further important additions came from the Estense and the

Benda and Figdor Collections. The two latter belonged mainly to a category which was to be systematically cultivated from now on, for, with the addition of the material formerly in the State-maintained Oester-reichische Galerie (including two panels by Michael Pacher) a whole new collection of early Austrian painting was created which, incidentally, has lately been turned over to the Oesterreichische Galerie. In the space of thirty years this hitherto entirely neglected School has taken its rightful place in the history of German painting at the end of the Middle Ages. This development corresponded to the separation of modern Austria from the other lands which had been joined with it under the Hapsburg rule. The Hapsburgs had united many peoples under their sceptre and their ambitions had ranged across a large part of Europe: to them it would have seemed senseless to confine their interests to the German Provinces, but for the reduced and impoverished new state it was an avowal.

The reorganization of the collections was interrupted by the Second World War, which sent the Vienna treasures underground to safety like all others in Europe. The pictures returned unharmed from the salt mines in Alt-Aussee, but the Museum buildings were so badly damaged by bombs that they have not yet been completely repaired, and so a selection from the temporarily homeless pictures was exhibited in a number of cities in Europe and America. However much these travels called attention to them and to the other Viennese treasures, it gives reason for satisfaction and rejoicing that this migratory existence is now over and that the pictures have returned safely to their home.

Among the sporadic new acquisitions of these sad years there was at least one outstanding masterpiece—Jan Vermeer's *The Artist in his Studio* (Plate 23), once the pride of Count Czernin's collection. For the Vienna Gallery it is at once a welcome addition and a stranger, a representative of a School or, rather, a trend of style, which was almost entirely lacking before.

This brings us back to where we started: to the special character of the Vienna Gallery, reflecting the aesthetic interests of the dynasty which ruled Austria for nearly half a millenium. They reigned during that time over the German Empire, ruled for many years over the Southern Netherlands and over large parts of Northern Italy, and they had the closest ties with Spain. To them France was always the rival and the hereditary enemy, and England was always outside their sphere. In consequence, the Gallery is rich in German pictures (although it is only very recently that particular attention has been paid to works produced in Vienna and in other Austrian centres); it has an abundance of masterpieces of the Italian

and Flemish Schools, though Dutch painting was rejected; and it possesses
a Spanish section which is unique outside the Prado on account of its
portraits by Velazquez. French and English painting is represented only
by a few accidental examples, most of which were bought by some
ambitious later Director. This political aspect is not the only peculiarity
of the Gallery for it is relatively poor in all early phases of stylistic development and correspondingly rich in ripe or even over-ripe styles. The
founders and owners were great lords, not interested in the involved
struggles and occasional gaucheries of an art which is striving to find itself,
but quick to recognize the finished performances of a mature style. As a
result of this the Vienna Gallery contains fewer sketches and small
cabinet-pictures than other collections of its rank, but it has more highly-
finished masterpieces of a decorative type. The Gallery itself was a kind of
decorative whole, intended to show the power and the greatness of the
Hapsburgs to the best advantage. A decided family taste is manifest in all
the acquisitions over hundreds of years; the principal creators of the
Gallery—Rudolf II, the Archduke Leopold Wilhelm, the Empress Maria
Theresa—shared the same likes and dislikes and bought works of more or
less the same type. All of them loved Dürer, Titian, and Bruegel, and,
so far as later painters were concerned, Rubens and Van Dyck as well.
Their one-sidedness makes the Vienna Gallery, which has remained their
finest memorial, unique for the study and appreciation of these masters.

The Picture Gallery in Vienna

NOTES ON THE ILLUSTRATIONS

BRUEGEL, Pieter, The Elder (*c.* 1530–1569)

The Return of the Herd Plate 7
Panel, 46 × 62½ in. (No. 709)

Signed: Bruegel MDLXV. From the collection of Archduke Leopold Wilhelm.
Belongs to a series illustrating the months; in the same series are two other pictures in Vienna, the *Harvesters* in the Metropolitan Museum in New York and the *Haymaking* latterly in Prince Lobkowitz's collection at Castle Raudnitz in Bohemia.
The haunting mood of late autumn, of cattle coming home out of the cold, is created by a seemingly naive simplicity in the rendering of nature, which conceals all pictorial devices. A wealth of acutely observed detail is set into a panoramic landscape without diminishing the impression.

Children's Games Plate 8
Panel, 46½ × 63½ in. (No. 708)

Signed: Bruegel 1560. An encyclopaedic description of children's games common in Holland at that time, rendered in minute detail with humour devoid of sentimentality. The scene is set with stage-like clarity.

The Tower of Babel Plate 9
Panel, 45 × 61 in. (No. 715)

Signed: Bruegel MCCCCCLXIII. From the collection of Archduke Leopold Wilhelm.
Bruegel shows building still in full swing with masons showing their plans to the king, in the foreground group; building gear is illustrated in great detail elsewhere in the picture. But the vastness of the undertaking and the feverish activity presage the chaotic end.

A Peasant Wedding Colour Plate IX
Panel, 45 × 64¼ in. (No. 717)
Cut at the bottom.

From the collection of Archduke Leopold Wilhelm.

This late work, like its companion piece, the *Peasant Dance*, shows us a different Bruegel, one who can build up a composition with large figures according to the mannerist principles of his time. The simplicity of the forms and the brilliance of the colour create the impression of stained glass. The fashionably dressed, bearded guest on the extreme right is probably a self-portrait of the artist.

CARAVAGGIO, Michelangelo (1573–1610)

Madonna of the Rosaries Plate 22
Canvas, 143½ × 98 in. (No. 496)

Probably painted in Naples in the summer of 1607; in 1617 the painter Finsonius took it to the Netherlands, where a group of artists, Rubens and Jan Bruegel the Elder amongst them, presented it to the Church of the Dominicans in Antwerp. In 1781 it was bought by Emperor Joseph II.
The Virgin, with the aid of St. Dominic, is distributing rosaries to the people surging towards her. It is significant that this picture, clearly intended for the altar of a church, was not erected in Italy. The sharply contrasted light and shade together with the emphatic naturalism in depicting ordinary people, especially in details such as the soles of their feet, were bound to arouse opposition.

CORREGGIO, Antonio (Allegri)
(1489?–1534)

Jupiter and Io Plate 18
Canvas, 64½ × 29¼ in. (No. 64)

Belonged originally to the decoration of a room in the Castle at Mantua, together with the *Ganymede* in Vienna, the *Leda* in Berlin (Plate 151) and the *Danae* in the Borghese Gallery in Rome. In 1601 it was sold to Rudolf II by Pompeo Leoni. Jupiter in the form of a cloud, embraces Io, whose sensuous rapture emphasizes the presence of her invisible lover.

(20)

CRANACH, Lucas, The Elder (1472–1553)

Stag Hunt of the Elector Frederic the Wise
Plate 6

Panel, 31½ × 45 in. (No. 1452)

Amongst the hunters are the Elector and Emperor Maximilian. Hunting pictures, like sporting pictures today, were popular in aristocratic circles of the sixteenth century.

DÜRER, Albrecht (1471–1528)

Emperor Maximilian I Plate 4
Panel, 28¼ × 24½ in. (No. 1443)

Signed with monogram and the date 1519. A long inscription bears the Emperor's titles and dates relating to his life.
A preparatory drawing, done from life in Augsburg on June 28, is in the Albertina in Vienna. The mixture of proud nobility and human warmth is brilliantly expressed.

The Adoration of the Trinity
Colour Plate II

Panel, 53 × 48½ in. (No. 1445)

Signed in monogram on the tablet next to the self-portrait of the artist. It also bears a detailed inscription of 1511.
Painted for the Chapel of All Saints in the Zwölfbruder Haus in Nuremberg. The old man's head on the extreme left represents the donor, Mathias Landauer. It was bought by Emperor Rudolf II in 1585. This painting is the only one of Dürer's large altarpieces which has come down to us in a well preserved state. In its monumentality the influence of Italy is manifest.

DYCK, Anthony van (1599–1641)

Portrait of an Officer Plate 19
Canvas, 45½ × 41 in. (No. 1034)

The sitter has been identified tentatively as Ferdinand Gonzaga, son of Duke Vicenzo of Mantua. The proud pose of the officer, clad in rich armour, is surely inspired by Titian's portraits.

EYCK, Jan van (died 1441)

Portrait of Cardinal Nicolas Albergati
Plate 3

Panel, 13½ × 10¾ in. (No. 624)

Probably painted in 1431, when Albergati visited the Netherlands as Papal Legate. The

preparatory silverpoint study from life is in Dresden. The combination of great accuracy of detail with an understanding of the character as a whole is one of Van Eyck's great achievements.

GEERTGEN tot Sint Jans (c. 1465–1495)

The Finding of the Remains of St. John the Baptist Plate 1
Panel, 67¾ × 54¾ in. (No. 644)

Originally the reverse of the *Mourning over Christ*, forming the right wing of the High Altar of the church of the Johannites in Haarlem. In 1604, already sawn apart, it was in the possession of the Governor of Haarlem. In 1635 it was in the collection of Charles I and later in Archduke Leopold Wilhelm's collection. In a very good state of preservation. The painting shows in the main scene the burning of St. John the Baptist's remains, in the background the burial of his trunk and head, in the middle distance the rediscovery of his unburnt remains by members of the Johannite Order and at the back on the extreme right the brothers receiving these remains. In spite of its numerous scenes, a dignified restraint, so characteristic of early Netherlandish art, permeates this picture.

GIORGIONE (1477?–1510)

The Three Philosophers Plate 11
Canvas, 47½ × 55¾ in. (No. 16)

Archduke Leopold Wilhelm's collection. An early mention of this picture makes it one of the few secure works by the artist. The scene, which has so far not been explained satisfactorily, is set in a magically evocative landscape. Sebastiano del Piombo's share in this picture, suggested as early as 1525, cannot be established.

HOLBEIN, Hans, The Younger (1497–1543)

Portrait of Jane Seymour, Third Wife of King Henry VIII Plate 5
Panel, 25¾ × 18¾ in. (No. 1481)

One of the earliest pictures Holbein executed in the service of the King. With great care and diligence he renders details of jewellery and dress without sacrificing the penetrating psychological characterization. Giving up of spacial depth becomes increasingly characteristic for Holbein's English style.

LAIB, Konrad (active *c.* 1440–1460)

The Crucifixion   Plate 2

Panel, 70½ × 70½ in. Inscribed: "d Pfenning. 1449. Als ich chun."

Originally the central panel of an altar. The inscription "d Pfenning," previously interpreted as the signature of an unknown artist, has not been explained satisfactorily so far. The painting on gold ground shows the Crucifixion amongst a crowded scene. This picture, in which connections with North Italian painters can be recognized, is one of the keyworks of painting in the alpine countries in the fifteenth century.

LOTTO, Lorenzo (*c.* 1480–1556)

Virgin and Child with SS. Catherine and James the Great   Plate 16

Canvas, 44¾ × 59⅜ in. (No. 214)

There is something of the simplicity of popular art in the arrangement of seated and kneeling figures in a serene landscape and in the brightness of the colours, characteristic for the middle period of this Bergamese artist.

MORETTO DA BRESCIA, Alessandro (*c.* 1498–1554)

St. Justina   Plate 10

Panel, 78 × 53⅞ in. (No. 218)

The saint, adored by an unknown donor, is standing in a landscape.
By omitting all symbols usually associated with the saint, the religious content of the picture is conveyed through its contemplative atmosphere.

RAPHAEL (1483–1520)

The Madonna of the Meadow   Plate 12

Panel, 44½ × 34¾ in. (No. 29)

According to Vasari this was painted in Florence as a present for Taddeo Taddei. From his palace it came into the collection of Archduke Ferdinand Karl in 1662 and was brought from Ambras to Vienna in 1773.
A characteristic example of Raphael's Florentine Madonnas, carried out before he developed his 'monumental style' in Rome. How to compose within the limits of a steep pyramid was Raphael's main problem at this period.

REMBRANDT (1606–1669)

Portrait of the Artist's son Titus   Plate 24

Canvas, 27¾ × 25¼ in. (No. 1269)

There is great tenderness in the representation of this boy just growing into manhood. The fall of light emphasizes the boy's concentration on his reading.

RUBENS, Peter Paul (1577–1640)

The Ildefonso Altarpiece   Colour Plate X

Panel, 138 × 92⅜ in. (No. 834)

In the central panel the Virgin gives the chasuble to St. Ildefonso.
The wings show Archduke Albert and his wife Isabella with their patron saints. Commissioned by the Infanta Isabella for the altar of the Brotherhood of St. Ildefonso in the church of St. James on the Couden-Berg in Brussels, it was painted in 1630–32. In 1777 it was bought by the Empress Maria Theresa. It is one of the religious keyworks, and after its recent cleaning glows again in its original colours.

'Het Pelsken' (Portrait of Hélène Fourment with a fur)   Plate 20

Panel, 69¼ × 38 in. (No. 829)

Mentioned in Rubens's will as 'Het Pelsken' ('The Little Fur') and left to the sitter. Traceable in Vienna since 1720.
An intimate creation of Rubens's late period and probably inspired by Titian's related composition, also in Vienna, which Rubens had copied.

St. Ignatius Loyola Driving out the Devil   Plate 21

Canvas, 210½ × 155½ in. (No. 865)

This picture and the *Miracle of St. Francis Xavier*, also in the Vienna Gallery, were painted for the Jesuit church in Antwerp, whose high altar they decorated in rotation. It was bought by Empress Maria Theresia, when the order was dissolved in Belgium in 1776. Both these paintings were executed by the workshop with the aid of Rubens's sketches, the artist himself adding final touches, a common practice in a busy workshop of the Baroque period.

TINTORETTO, Jacopo (1518–1594)

Susanna and the Elders   Plate 14
Canvas, 57⅝ × 76¼ in. (No. 239)

Tintoretto painted this subject repeatedly. The present version is the most important. The nude figure of Susanna, radiating white light, is placed in a garden landscape, which in spite of a truly Tintorettesque indication of depth, still has the effect of a tapestry. The prying Elders are well hidden even from the onlooker.

TITIAN (c. 1485–1576)

Nymph and Shepherd   Plate 13
Canvas, 59 × 73⅝ in. (No. 186)

Archduke Leopold Wilhelm's collection.
A work of Titian's late period, but harking back to Giorgione in subject matter. The broken colour so characteristic of Titian's late style spreads a harmonious shimmer over the figures and the landscape.

Ecce homo   Plate 15
Canvas, 94½ × 141¾ in. (No. 178)

Signed: Titianus Eques Ces. F. 1543. Painted for a Flemish merchant living in Venice; in 1620 it came into the Duke of Buckingham's collection and it was bought from his estate for Emperor Ferdinand III.
The striking representation had already caused early critics to recognize several individual portraits in the painting, such as Aretino as Pilate. In this influential composition the surging backwards and forwards of the crowd is conveyed with every means at the artist's disposal.

Portrait of Jacopo de Strada   Plate 17
Canvas, 49¼ × 37⅜ in. (No. 182)

Signed: Titianus F. There is a later inscription giving the dates of the sitter. From vivid contemporary reports we know that the portrait of this antiquary of the Courts of Bavaria and Austria was painted in 1567–8, and thus belongs to Titian's latest works. In Archduke

Leopold Wilhelm's collection. Strada's lively pose and the construction of the background in layers, are an exception in Titian's *œuvre*.

VELAZQUEZ, Diego (1599–1660)

Portrait of Infante Baltasar Carlos   Plate 25
Canvas, 50½ × 39 in. (No. 616)

Probably a present from the Spanish court. First exhibited in 1816. At an early age the young prince, son of Philip IV of Spain, was betrothed to the Archduchess Maria Anna, daughter of Emperor Ferdinand III, who later became his father's second wife.

Portrait of Infanta Margarita Teresa
     Plate 26
Canvas, 50½ × 39½ in. (No. 615)

Painted in a rose-coloured dress at the age of 3. In the imperial collection from an early date, it was first hung in the gallery in 1816. It is the most popular of Velazquez's child portraits. The still life of the vase of flowers has been much admired.

VERMEER, Jan (1632–1675)

The Artist in his Studio   Plate 23
Canvas, 51⅛ × 43¼ in.

Signed J. Ver-Meer. Mentioned in the inventory of the estate of Vermeer's widow. In 1813 it was bought by Count Czernin as a Pieter de Hooch and remained in his family till 1942.
The most recent interpretation of the subject matter suggests that the artist has not meant to portray reality but his daydream of good living and the enjoyment of fame. The map on the wall, which shows the seventeen Netherlandish provinces before their partition, suggests that Vermeer, a Catholic, is looking back longingly to a past that seemed rosier to him. At the same time the map has the function of emphasizing the picture plane. The pictorial means are close to those employed in the *Woman reading a Letter* in Amsterdam (Plate 138).

THE UFFIZI IN FLORENCE

THE UFFIZI, like the Vienna Gallery, is the product of the cultiva-
tion of the arts by a long-established dynasty—so much so that in
Florence the family name became a synonym for the active patronage of the arts. Yet while the Hapsburg collections may be compared
to a flower garden coaxed from rather reluctant soil, the Medici collection
grew naturally out of its native earth. One was so international that later
concessions to local art scarcely affected its essential character, the other
is so predominantly Tuscan that contributions from other lands are no
more than parallel examples. The Hapsburgs were constantly preoccu-
pied with the expansion of their domains and attempted—prematurely—
to create a state which was not based on nationalities. The Medici, who
sprang from Florentine merchant stock, looked no farther than the narrow
confines of their homeland and believed their highest task to be the
material and spiritual advancement of that land, which was never more
than a petty principality compared with the Austrian Empire at the
height of its fortunes when it included large parts of Italy and of the
Netherlands. Austrian art, in spite of occasional hopeful beginnings,
scarcely ever rose above a purely local importance; Tuscan art occupies
so great a place in the world's art that we do not think of it as a local or
even a national phenomenon, but rather as the possession of everyone
who cares for the arts. This exceptional quality of Tuscan art from the
fourteenth to the sixteenth century—in some ways comparable to Dutch
painting of the seventeenth century or French painting in the nineteenth
—determines the unique character of the Uffizi.

The acknowledgment of Florentine Renaissance art as a common
European heritage and the recognition of the Uffizi as the repository of
this treasure depend upon one other special circumstance. Florence was
not only the birth-place of modern, post-mediaeval art, but was also the
birth-place of art history. Not only Giotto, the father of modern art, but
also Vasari, the father of art-historical writing, was a Tuscan who lived
and worked in Florence; and, obviously, that was no coincidence. The
extraordinary achievements of local masters were the object of civic pride
earlier here than anywhere else, and as a result of this the chronicles of
the city, and other literary sources, devoted more space to them than is

the rule with documents of that period; in turn, this recognition of art and artists in the life of the community had a stimulating effect on further creative effort. Here, earlier than anywhere else, artists were counted among the leading citizens; here, earlier than elsewhere, information on their lives and works was collected. It seems perfectly understandable that it was here that Vasari wrote his classic book, still unsurpassed by any of its imitators, for it was here that art was a part of ordinary life. Ecclesiastical and secular corporations competed among themselves to secure the services of the best artists, many of whose most important works were created for the community, so that the history of Florentine painting could be written in broad outline without mention of the works commissioned or owned by private collectors. This wealth of masterpieces accessible to everyone—in contrast to Venice, where a considerable part of the best work was in jealously guarded private collections—kindled the general interest and produced those notices in contemporary literature which have already been mentioned.

When we read how a great work of art like Cimabue's *Rucellai Madonna* was carried in triumph from the artist's house to Santa Maria Novella, or observe the interest taken by the Florentine public in artistic competitions, or the circumstances under which Leonardo's and Michelangelo's wall-paintings for the Council Chamber came into existence, and we compare them with those obtaining in, say, Venice for a similar commission, we can hardly avoid the impression that Florentine art rested upon a broader social basis. Where else would a Government have patronized the arts by choosing the two best artists available and allowing them complete freedom to paint whatever they wanted, in the way they wanted, without conditions or instructions? Here the arts could develop without tutelage but assisted by powerful patronage.

Nor was there any other place where the ruling house was so complete a symbol of energetic patronage of the arts. As soon as the Medici had established their hold over the city they began their successful efforts on behalf of the arts. Their activity as collectors depended on their financial dominance as bankers and merchants and can be traced right back to the last years of Cosimo de' Medici, who might well have been called the Father of the Florentine Collections as well as *Pater Patriae*. Many of his descendants followed his example. His grandson Lorenzo Il Magnifico was very proud of his own treasures and loved to show visitors round himself. Even though the collection suffered severe losses when the Medici were temporarily expelled in 1494 and again in 1527, and their houses were plundered by the mob, yet the collections went on growing until the second Cosimo, the first Grand Duke, housed them in a specially adapted building. The *Galleria*, which as early as 1589 had a special show-place for the cream of the works in the *Tribuna*, was never definitely separated from the *Guardaroba*, which, in Renaissance usage, included all the objects and furnishings necessary for the decorative purposes of a Court. There was not yet an Art Gallery in the modern sense of the word, but a kernel of works brought together by inheritance or by later acquisition, and this became the basis of the later Gallery, eventually presented to the Tuscan State as a public museum by the last representative of the house, Anna Maria Luisa, in 1737.

The collecting activities of the Medici were, in general outline, very much the same as those of other princely families, but their great superiority lay in the systematic care they took of the works in public buildings and their encouragement of new productions. The elder Cosimo's cabinet in the Casino Mediceo has always been compared to an Academy, and in Lorenzo we find the idea of a productive patronage still more strongly developed: he placed antique statues before the eyes of young artists in order to inspire them to similar greatness. In a city like Florence, where art was a part of everyday life, the ruler had to bear its claims in mind and when Titian passed through Florence and offered to paint the portrait of the Grand Duke, Cosimo had to refuse the offer in the interests of the local artists. The other side of the sense of obligation towards the art of the country can be seen in the measures taken to prevent important works leaving the country, for as early as 1602, under the Grand Duke Ferdinand I, the sale or export of such works was forbidden by law. In the eighteenth century this law was renewed and extended, and when the State collections were reorganized under the Grand Duke Leopold I and his son, measures were taken to provide for the pictures from suppressed convents, and abandoned churches and public buildings.

Thus a number of factors combined to form the Uffizi Gallery and its unique collections. There is not much left now of the collection brought together by Cosimo as evidence of the power and wealth of the family, but the Uffizi was greatly enriched in the seventeenth century by the collection of two other members of the family, Cardinal Leopold and Giovanni Carlo de' Medici, brother of the Grand Duke Ferdinand II, which passed into the family possessions in 1640. Shortly before that date, in 1631, the extraordinarily rich collections of the extinct Della Rovere family in Urbino made a notable addition to the Medici treasures. The highly advantageous exchange with the Vienna Gallery in 1793 has already been mentioned in the preceding chapter (p. 16).

Yet another fortunate circumstance was the role of the Uffizi as a haven of refuge for masterpieces of Tuscan art. A good proportion of the pictures which, in the great days of this School, had adorned churches and convents, guild halls and secular buildings, now came to be sheltered here, and in many cases these pictures were not just examples of painting in the three great centuries, but were *the* examples—the classic productions of the School. Many of them are well attested in the rich, local art literature and fully described by Vasari or his successors, Borghini and Baldinucci. This means that in the Uffizi we find the cream of those works of art on which is based our picture of the development of style in an all-important period, while many another famous Gallery has to be content with mediocre or controversial examples. No other collection can illustrate the history of Italian art so systematically as the Uffizi.

The tendency towards system is another, additional, element in the collection. Grand Duke Cosimo had the celebrated collection of portraits assembled by Bishop Paolo Giovio of Como copied on a small scale as a series for his own Gallery, and to them he later added further examples. In the second half of the next century the collection of self-portraits of artists began to take shape, and in 1681 a special wing was built to house them. To be invited to contribute to this unique assemblage came to be regarded as a mark of distinction for a painter. Another field of collecting systematically pursued was that of drawings, and Vasari was a pioneer in this as in so much else: his 'Book' of drawings by many of the artists whose Lives he had written was, unfortunately, later split up, but a considerable number of the drawings was secured for the Uffizi in 1778. Later the Cardinal Leopold enjoyed the advice of Filippo Baldinucci, the first man to make systematic use of drawings as an aid to the study of paintings. After the Gallery had become a public museum Luigi Lanzi helped with its arrangement on historical principles, such as he had laid down in his History of Painting. In 1795 a further innovation was made —the placing of a label with the dates of birth and death of the painter on every picture, thus making a princely Cabinet of Curiosities into a means of educating the public in the history of art. We can see, too, that the forces which determined the character of the Gallery never became set in a rigid formula: pictures were hung in the *Tribuna*, where the cream of the collection was exhibited, and were then sent back to one of the Medici Palaces or Villas. In particular there was a continual coming and going between the Uffizi, the seat of the Gallery since 1581, and the Pitti Palace, the Medici residence since 1550, and this exchange was facilitated by the existence of the long corridor over the Arno which links the two buildings.

From the end of the eighteenth century the Academy of Fine Arts was incorporated in this gigantic store of works of art, and pictures from abandoned churches were taken there, and from thence to the Uffizi, which in its turn transferred surplus works to the Academy. This elasticity in the organization of the Florentine collections was turned to good use after the First World War when Dr Giovanni Poggi, then Director of the Florentine Museums, divided up the total treasures between the three institutions and one or two subsidiary galleries according to a clear plan, and the credit for bringing out the individual character of each institution is due to him. By taking over masterpieces of Tuscan painting from the Academy, and by similar exchanges with the Pitti, the Uffizi became a lucid and impressive demonstration of the special place of Tuscan painting in Italian and in European art. The Academy retains the great mass of local works and the Palazzo Pitti keeps the memory of the old princely collection, where masterpieces of painting are treated as mere decoration, and decoration is raised by the incomparable quality of its elements to the grandest heights of splendour. The Academy is content to be of practical use. The Uffizi holds a discreet balance between richness and modesty, calculated to throw the essence of this ancient and splendid collection into sharper relief.

If we seek to arrange in chronological order the varied factors which decided the history of the collection, we must first remember that there is now very little in Florence which can be traced back to the theoretical founders, Cosimo and Lorenzo de' Medici, and of that little least of all is in the Uffizi. Their famous Library, with the Vatican the earliest in Europe, is still preserved, but the collection of pictures suffered irreplaceable losses when the family fell on evil days. The Inventories dating back to the time of Lorenzo afford an insight into the original richness of the collection, yet they are neither complete nor do they give a true picture of all the services these great patrons rendered to the arts. From other sources we learn of the pictures by Filippo Lippi which Cosimo gave to Pope Eugenius IV, and from first-hand knowledge we know the small altarpiece by Rogier van der Weyden in the Staedel Institut in Frankfurt, with the donor portraits hinting at Cosimo. Signorelli's *Pan* (Plate 150), which was one of the glories of the Berlin Gallery until its destruction in 1945, was probably the picture painted for Lorenzo which Vasari describes. On the other hand, there are the major works which came to the Uffizi from Medici Villas—such as Botticelli's *Spring* (Plate 45) and his *Birth of Venus* (Colour Plate XI)—that are not mentioned in these Inventories.

The history of the collection becomes consistent only in the time of the Grand Duke Cosimo, who enlarged the Pitti Palace and converted it into the family residence, building the Uffizi as a home for the Government Offices. At about the same time as the Hapsburgs, the Medici declared their treasures to be an inalienable family possession, and in both cases this establishment of the collections on a legal basis was a symbol and a symptom of the rise of absolute monarchy. In the Uffizi some rooms were set apart from the offices of government and reserved for the art treasures, making the collecting of works of art into a sort of State function. The most highly valued pictures, those by such painters as Raphael and Andrea del Sarto, as well as the antique statues, were assembled in the *Tribuna*, and the original arrangement was described in a pamphlet commemorating the marriage of Maria de' Medici and Henry IV of France. The seventeenth century brought the bequests of the last Duke of Urbino, Francesco Maria II, a monument of princely patronage in the Renaissance, and the collections of Cardinal Leopold de' Medici and other members of the family, which were representative of the international Baroque ideal. It is a striking fact that Cardinal Leopold and the Hapsburg Leopold Wilhelm resembled each other closely, and were contemporaries sharing the same tastes. The last of the Medici, the Grand Duchess Anna Maria Luisa, conveyed the family art collections to the Tuscan State and prohibited their ever leaving it, while her successor Francis Stephen of Lorraine (afterwards the Emperor Francis I of Austria), to whom the collections were State business rather than a matter of family pride, was yet so mindful of them as to forbid the export of major works of art from Tuscany, to arrange for the use of suppressed convents as depots and to further the systematic publication of the contents of the Gallery in book form.

Napoleon's victories resulted in the removal of the most important pictures and statues to Paris in 1801, from whence the greater number— 56 pictures, not by any means the total taken—were returned to Florence after Waterloo. During the following century a number of administrative measures were taken, some of them of considerable importance, such as the creation of a separate Museum for sculpture and applied arts in the Palazzo del Podestà (the Bargello) and the Museum in the convent of S. Marco, where the works of Fra Angelico are twice as effective in the place where he lived and worked. The suppression of several convents in 1886 enriched the Uffizi and other Florentine Galleries, while the beginning made in 1858 on a general Inventory of the works of art in Tuscany prepared the way for their transfer to public ownership. On the whole, this period was marked by attention to detail—in spite of some considerable additions—rather than by a broad vision such as directed the reorganization following the First World War.

The Second World War was a much more dangerous affair to the collections than the First had been. Some of the works were hidden for safety in various Villas outside Florence, but others were looted by the retreating Germans and taken as far as the Tyrol before the liberation of Italy brought them home, when works of art were once again carried in triumph through the streets of their own city. The losses and the damage suffered by the pictures were not serious, but the damage to their home was such that the complete re-opening of the Gallery has had to be undertaken step by step. In the Tuscan Schools the stress is now more than ever laid on the historical continuity of the School, and this basic element of the Gallery is set off against the international element introduced into the Gallery in the seventeenth century. The interplay of these two factors is what gives the Uffizi today its place among the great picture galleries of the world. The clearest evidence of the unique character of the collection can be found in the history of the pictures selected for illustration.

The Uffizi

NOTES ON THE ILLUSTRATIONS

ALBERTINELLI, Mariotto (1474–1515)

The Visitation   Plate 47
Panel, $91\frac{5}{8} \times 57\frac{1}{2}$ in. (No. 1587)

Painted in 1503 for the Church of the Visitation in Florence. It was justly praised by Vasari as an unusually original achievement by the artist, who usually contented himself with imitating Fra Bartolommeo. A sculptural effect is achieved by the simplicity of the composition.

BELLINI, Giovanni (*c.* 1430–1516)

Religious Allegory   Plate 51
Panel, $28\frac{3}{4} \times 46\frac{3}{4}$ in. (No. 631)

This painting came from Vienna in 1783 in exchange for another picture. None of the various interpretations of the subject has achieved universal recognition. This mystery has doubtlessly increased the attraction of the picture, which in feeling seems to foreshadow the mood of Giorgione's paintings. In fact the picture was attributed to Giorgione till late into the nineteenth century. For a painting of this period—it was painted about 1480–90—the abandoning of conventional form in a religious composition is unique.

BOTTICELLI, Sandro (1444–1510)

The Birth of Venus   Colour Plate XI
Canvas, $68\frac{3}{8} \times 109\frac{1}{2}$ in. (No. 878)

Painted for Lorenzo di Pierfrancesco de' Medici, then 15 years old. Together with its companion piece, the *Spring*, it passed to Giovanni de Medici and from him to Cosimo, first Grand Duke of Tuscany. Earlier interpreters were content to see in the picture an illustration of Poliziano's allegorical poem 'Giostra'. Recently, however, E. H. Gombrich, without denying inspiration by Poliziano, presupposes a neoplatonic programme in keeping with the spirit of the times. The sweet melancholy of the painting and its linear grace combined to cast an irresistible spell over the nineteenth century.

The Adoration of the Magi   Plates 41–42
Panel, $43\frac{3}{4} \times 52\frac{3}{4}$ in. (No. 882)

Presented to the church of Santa Maria Novella in Florence, by a certain Guaspero di Zanobi del Lama, who as a compliment to the ruling family requested that the personages in the painting should have the features of various members of the Medici family. Cosimo, Piero and Giovanni are represented as the three kings, Lorenzo is seen as the young man on the extreme left and Guiliano as the young man on the right, in sharp profile. The painting came to the Uffizi in 1796 from the Medici Villa Poggio Imperiale.

The Madonna of the Pomegranate
     Plates 43–44
Circular panel, diam. $56\frac{1}{4}$ in. (No. 1607)

Still in its original frame. Through the circular shape—as always a sign that the picture was originally destined for private devotion—the angels are more intimately linked to the main group, whose centre is formed by the play of hands around the symbolic pomegranate.

The Three Graces (detail from the *Spring*, No. 8360)   Plate 45

According to Gombrich, this painting too is based on a humanist programme, whose general trend of thought is found in a letter of 1477–8 from Marsilio Ficino to the young patron.

BRONZINO, Agnolo (1503–1572)

Portrait of Maria de' Medici   Plate 49
Panel, $20\frac{3}{4} \times 15$ in. (No. 1572)

The sitter is the eldest daughter of Cosimo I (1540–57). Probably painted when she was twelve to fourteen years old. A typical portrait by Bronzino, who conscientiously observes the features of his sitter, rendering them with cool objectivity.

CARAVAGGIO, Michelangelo (1573–1610)

The Young Bacchus   Colour Plate III
Panel, 37⅜ × 33½ in. (No. 5312)

Till 1925 the picture was in the depot of the Uffizi. It was first recognized by Marangoni as one of Caravaggio's earliest works executed in Rome. By limiting the subject to a single half-length figure, by rendering every facial contour and every still-life object with great intensity, and by employing strong local colours, Caravaggio created a revolutionary picture.

CIMABUE (c. 1240–1302)

The Virgin and Child Enthroned with Angels and Saints   Plate 27
Panel, 154¾ × 99 in. (No. 8343)

Painted for the monks of Vallombrosa, for the High Altar of the Badia di Sta. Trinita in Florence.
This powerful composition closes a line of development which goes back to the Byzantine tradition. The artist's striving for creation of space opens the way for Giotto's revolutionary art. With sure instinct, Florentines have always placed Cimabue at the beginning of the new art.

DÜRER, Albrecht (1471–1528)

The Adoration of the Magi   Plate 30
Panel, 37⅜ × 45 in. (No. 1444)

Signed with Dürer's monogram and dated 1504. This painting, probably commissioned by Frederick the Wise, remained in the church of the Castle at Wittenberg till 1603, in which year Christian II presented it to Emperor Rudolf II. By an exchange with the Vienna Gallery it came to the Uffizi in 1792. Out of the many solutions which Dürer found for this subject, the present one, with its loose composition, is perhaps the most attractive.

FROMENT, Nicholas (c. 1450–1490)

The Raising of Lazarus   Plate 39
Central panel of a triptych. 69 × 52¾ in. (No. 1065)

Signed and dated: Nicolaus Frumenti absolvit hoc opus XV Kl. Junii MCCCCLXI. (18th May, 1461).

Seems to have been intended originally for the Osservanti of the Mugello near Florence. At the dissolution of the monastery it came to the Academy and in 1841 to the Uffizi. The harsh realism of the scene of the miracle and the typically northern calm of Christ and his surroundings are elements alien to Florentine art of this period, but obviously excited great interest there.

GENTILE DA FABRIANO (c. 1360–1427)

The Adoration of the Magi   Plate 29
Panel, 118⅛ × 111 in. (No. 8364)

Fully signed and dated May 1423. Painted for the chapel of Palla Strozzi in the sacristy of Sta Trinita, where Vasari saw the panel and described it in detail. From the Academy it passed to the Uffizi in 1919. This Umbrian composition with its emphasis on gracefulness and meticulous rendering of all accessories makes an interesting contrast with Florentine and other interpretations of this subject. Many characteristic ones can be seen in the Uffizi (Botticelli, Dürer, Leonardo da Vinci, Mantegna).

GHIRLANDAIO, Domenico (1449–1494)

The Virgin and Child Enthroned with Angels and Saints   Plate 37
Panel, 74¾ × 78¾ in. (No. 8388)

Painted for the High Altar of the Ingesuati, outside Florence. When this church was destroyed during the siege of the city, in 1529, the painting was transferred to the church of San Giovanni (Calza) within the city itself. In the Uffizi since 1867.
Vasari, in a long description of the panel, mentions as its most noteworthy feature, that Domenico has here for the first time rendered the gold ornament of the armour in colour. This remark shows how striking such naturalism seemed then, whereas today we appreciate more the festive simplicity of this painting.

GIOTTO (1266?–1336)

Madonna and Child Enthroned, with Angels and Saints   Plate 28
Panel, 82½ × 52½ in. (No. 8344)

The date of the picture is in dispute, but is certainly earlier than 1315. In contrast to the Sienese conception, which was derived from Byzantine tradition and is shown in Cimabue's

III. CARAVAGGIO: *The Young Bacchus*. Florence, Uffizi

painting (Plate 27), Giotto's style, in the plasticity of each figure and the simple objectivity of construction, is entirely Florentine, making this picture, more than any other, a starting point of subsequent developments.

GOES, Hugo van der (died in 1482)

The Adoration of the Shepherds   Plate 31
Panel, 99½ × 119½ in. (No. 3191–3)

Painted about 1476 for Tommaso Portinari, an agent of the Medici in Bruges, it was sent to Florence and set up on the high altar of St. Egidio. From the Arcispedale of St. Maria Nuova it came to the Uffizi in 1900. This picture, particularly its naturalist rendering of the shepherds, had a great influence on Florentine painters of the last quarter of the fifteenth century and witnesses the wide range of artistic interest in Florence.

LEONARDO DA VINCI (1452–1519)

The Adoration of the Magi   Plates 32–3
Panel, 95½ × 97 in. (No. 1594)

Commissioned in March 1481 by the monks of the conventual church of San Donato di Scopeto in Florence for their High Altar, it never got beyond the underpainting stage. The lack of colour gives it the appearance of a tentative drawing and fully brings out the daring of his centralized space composition. In the expressive force of the heads, already admired by Vasari, a vision becomes reality.

LIPPI, Fra Filippo (1406–1469)

The Coronation of the Virgin   Plate 38
Panel, 78¾ × 113 in. (No. 8352)

The monk pointing to an angel is the painter himself. The scroll reads: *Is perfecit opus.*
Painted for the High Altar of the nuns of St. Ambrogio for 1200 lire. In 1813 it came to the Academy and in 1919 to the Uffizi. Most participants in the holy gathering have youthful faces and the whole picture has an air of childlike naivety.

MANTEGNA, Andrea (1431–1506)

The Circumcision   Plate 55
Panel, 33⅞ × 16½ in. (No. 910)

Wing of a triptych, which has the *Adoration of the Magi* as its central panel.

In 1587, the triptych, whose original destination is not known, belonged to Don Antonio de' Medici and became part of the family collection in 1632. The reliefs in the lunette, the *Sacrifice of Isaac* and *Moses with the Tables of the Law* are Old Testament prefigurations of the ritual act.

MICHELANGELO, Buonarroti (1475–1564)

The Holy Family   Plate 48
Circular panel, diam. 47½ in. (No. 1456)

Painted in 1504 on the occasion of the marriage of Angelo Doni and Maddalena Strozzi, whose portraits Raphael painted in the following year. Hung in the Tribuna of the Uffizi as early as 1625.
The heroic main group, with its strong movement, is like a freestanding sculpture and greatly influenced painting of the following period. The young men in the background, whose significance has never been explained satisfactorily, are the precursors of the *ignudi* on the Sistine ceiling. Formally and in subject matter no regard is paid to the usual conception of this religious theme, a fact which aroused much opposition amongst later critics.

PERUGINO, Pietro (1445–1523)

Portrait of Francesco dell'Opere   Plate 53
Panel, 20⅞ × 16½ in. (No. 1700)

The inscription on the back reads: 1494 de luglo. Pietro Perusino pinse Franco del Opere. It came from the Palazzo Pitti in 1853.
This develops further a Flemish portrait type, e.g. Memling portraits (compare Plate 226).

PIERO DELLA FRANCESCA (1416?–1492)

Portrait of Federigo da Montefeltro   Plate 36
Panel, 18½ × 13 in. (No. 1615)

Painted at the same time as its companion piece, the portrait of Federigo's wife, Battista Sforza, on the occasion of Piero's stay in Urbino. It passed in 1631 to the Medici through the Rovere inheritance and in 1773 it came to the Uffizi. On the back of both paintings are representations of allegorical triumphs. In spite of the strict profile pose, as on a medal, the sitter appears bathed in light. The discovery of how to render atmosphere is Piero's most stimulating contribution to Italian art of his period.

POLLAIUOLO, Antonio (1429–1498)

Hercules and Antaeus   Plate 35
Panel, $6\frac{1}{4} \times 3\frac{3}{4}$ in. (No. 1478)

Came from the Palazzo Pitti, together with its companion piece, *Hercules killing the Hydra*. A work characteristic for the artist, who was also a goldsmith and sculptor. His passionate interest in anatomical studies ranks him with contemporary scientific investigators.

PONTORMO, Jacopo da (1494–1556)

Portrait of Cosimo de' Medici   Plate 46
Panel, $34\frac{1}{4} \times 25\frac{5}{8}$ in. (No. 3574)

Painted for Goro da Pistoia, secretary to the Medici. It was later in the so called Cell of Cosimo in the convent of San Marco and came to the Uffizi only in 1912. An idealized portrait of the founder of the dynasty and medicean art-collecting.

RAPHAEL (1483–1520)

The Madonna of the Goldfinch   Plate 54
Panel, $41\frac{3}{4} \times 29\frac{1}{2}$ in. (No. 1447)

Painted as a wedding picture for his friend Lorenzo Nasi. When Lorenzo's house was destroyed by a landslide on November 17, 1548, the painting was smashed into several pieces, but was immediately carefully put together again.
It belongs to the group of Raphael's Florentine Madonnas in which he occupies himself with the problem of linking two to three figures within the firm geometrical form of the pyramid. This is the starting point for the development of High Renaissance composition.

SARTO, Andrea del (1486–1531)

The Madonna of the Harpies   Plate 40
Panel, $81\frac{1}{2} \times 70\frac{1}{8}$ in. (No. 1577). Dated 1517

Painted for the nuns of San Francesco in Via Pentollini, and bought by Grand Duke Ferdinand. The painting owes its name to the harpies which decorate the pedestal. In its humanization of the divine this is an important step beyond earlier interpretations of the same theme.

TITIAN (c. 1485–1576)

Portrait of Francesco Maria della Rovere, Duke of Urbino   Plate 50
Canvas, $44\frac{7}{8} \times 39\frac{3}{8}$ in. (No. 926)

Signed: Titianus F.
Begun in 1536, it was completed in 1538. In 1631 it came to Florence by inheritance. A drawing, also in the Uffizi, shows the Duke full length. Perhaps the picture was originally planned in that form and was executed in its present format to conform with the portrait of Duchess Eleanora Gonzaga. The three commander's batons in the background refer to the three military commands held by the Duke, whom Titian represents as a typical aristocratic condottiere of the High Renaissance.

The Venus of Urbino   Plate 52
Canvas, $46\frac{7}{8} \times 25\frac{5}{8}$ in. (No. 1437)

Painted in 1538, for Guidobaldo Rovere, later Duke of Urbino, it came to Florence in 1631 by inheritance.
In the lengthy correspondence with the patron, there is only mention of a nude; no hint indicates the mythological character of the painting. In this typical 'bedroom picture' the youthful model is brought into direct contact with the onlooker. This is not so in the other paintings of this subject, which Titian executed both before and after this picture.

VERROCCHIO, Andrea (1435–1488)

The Baptism of Christ   Plate 34
Panel, $69\frac{5}{8} \times 62\frac{5}{8}$ in. (No. 8358)

Painted in 1476 for the monks of Vallombrosa in S. Salvi in Florence. When the monastery was dissolved in 1808 it came to the Academy and in 1919 to the Uffizi.
The tradition that the young Leonardo da Vinci, then Verrocchio's pupil, painted one of the angels was already noted by Vasari. Modern scholarship, however, takes it to mean that Leonardo's assistance extended over the whole panel, for the hardness of the two main figures, which one would expect from a sculptor like Verrocchio, is softened by painterly sensitivity.

PARIS: THE LOUVRE

L ONG BEFORE THE LOUVRE existed as a State museum open to the public, the rulers of France had been collecting pictures and other works of art, and they were—as has already been emphasized in the Introduction—among the pioneers in this field. Charles IV, who lived at the end of the fourteenth century, and his brothers, Louis of Anjou, John, Duke of Berry, and Philip, Duke of Burgundy, were collectors on so grand a scale that the Inventories of their possessions still make astounding reading, and the remnants of their collections arouse admiration. The collections themselves have long been dispersed, and for this reason the real history of art patronage in France begins with Francis I, early in the sixteenth century.

This second start is a part of the general Renaissance movement which spread from Italy over the greater part of Europe, the victorious advance of which was paralleled by political events. The northern conquerors, overrunning Italy year after year, returned to their homelands the captives of the new spirit in art and learning—the spirit they had encountered in Italy. This conquest of the conquerors was particularly important in the case of France, for the commanders of the French armies not only brought home works of art as booty, they also brought the artists themselves. Thus Leonardo da Vinci was invited to France by Francis I, there to spend the remainder of his eventful life. The Cardinal of Aragon, who visited him at Cloux in 1517, saw there three of his pictures—a *John the Baptist*, the *Madonna and Child with St. Anne*, and a portrait of a woman, generally identified with the *Monna Lisa* (Colour Plate XII). Thus it seems that the most popular picture in the Louvre can be traced right back to the origin of the collection. Over forty years ago it was stolen from the Louvre and remained undiscovered for more than two years. The thief was an Italian house-painter, Vincenzo Peruggia, who did occasional work at the Louvre. On August 21, 1911, at 8 o'clock in the morning he took the picture out of its frame, put it under his workman's blouse, and marched through a back door. When two years later, in Florence, Mr Peruggia offered the smiling Gioconda to an art-dealer, he was arrested, and the picture was surrendered to the French Ambassador. Peruggia declared he had taken this Italian picture to Italy, being a

Lombard and a patriot. He was sentenced to seven months imprisonment. Both the other pictures by Leonardo were also in other hands for a time, returning to the French royal collection only in the seventeenth century.

Andrea del Sarto was another of the celebrated Italian painters invited to France by Francis I, for whom he painted the *Charity* soon after his arrival; the *Holy Family*, his other masterpiece in the Louvre, was bought from Florentine dealers. Other purchases on the part of the King were Raphael's *Belle Jardinière*, which, according to a rather dubious tradition, was originally commissioned by Filippo Segardi of Siena in 1507, while Vasari tells us that the *St. Margaret* was always destined for the King himself or for his sister, Marguerite de Valois. Francis also acquired Fra Bartolommeo's *Annunciation* and Sebastiano del Piombo's *Visitation*, and, as his interest in Italian art became generally known, everyone seeking the royal favour presented him with masterpieces of this School; masterpieces which included Raphael's *Holy Family of Francis I* and his *St. Michael*, both presented by members of the Medici family. Cardinal Bibbiena gave him the portrait of Joanna of Aragon, painted by Giulio Romano and perhaps retouched by Raphael, while Titian's portrait of the King himself (Plate 63) seems to have been the gift of Pietro Aretino. This portrait appears to have been painted about 1530 from a medal, perhaps one of Benvenuto Cellini's, yet it sparkles with life and is so far in advance of anything accomplished by the King's own court painters that it is easy enough to see why the King adopted the new ideas so enthusiastically and thus introduced a lasting new strain into French taste. The so-called School of Fontainebleau was dominated by Italians, or at any rate by Italian taste.

Not much is known about the collections of Francis I under his immediate successors. The second half of the sixteenth century is a stormy period in French history, complicated by political strife and dynastic quarrels, and although new acquisitions were surely made, they were so sporadic that they can be reckoned as part of the new chapter which began for a relatively peaceful France with Henri IV and his Queen, Maria de' Medici.

The Queen showed herself worthy of her forebears. She prepared the way for a new artistic current, which, however, did not flow from her own Italian homeland, but from the North. During her regency for her son Louis XIII, she commissioned Rubens to paint an allegorical cycle for the Luxembourg Palace. It was painted between 1621 and 1625, transferred to the Louvre in 1815, and has been exhibited in a specially designed Gallery there since 1900. This cycle represents the chief events in the life of the Queen in the grandiose manner of the full Baroque style (Plate 67) and with the mastery of Rubens's maturity. In his own lifetime it is probable that the triumph of the Flemish master was more a personal than an artistic success. He was admired in France as an accomplished courtier, as a skilful diplomat, as a learned humanist with all the details of archaeology at his fingertips, even as a virtuoso who could carry out such a gigantic commission in so short a time, but scarcely at all as a painter of genius, destined to exert the greatest influence on French painting. The time for that was not yet ripe. Classicism, under the leadership of Poussin, was to hold the field uncontested, and, as a complete expression of the French genius, was to have the support of the King, who, from about the middle of the seventeenth century, came to regard the patronage of the arts as part of his official duties.

Louis XIII was not himself very interested in art and his sole attempt at patronage, the invitation to Nicolas Poussin to decorate the Grande Galerie of the Louvre, came to nothing. True, Poussin tore himself away from his beloved Rome and went to Paris for a while, but he never succeeded in overcoming the hostility, both intellectual and climatic, of his unaccustomed surroundings. He did not paint the Gallery, and of all the works which he executed for the King, only the *Last Supper*, painted for the Palace at Saint-Germain, now remains in the Louvre. Yet what the King rejected as patron of the arts was taken over, as in so many other instances, by his great Minister, Cardinal Richelieu, who brought together an important collection in his palace, much of which later ended up in the royal collection—for example, the *Allegories* from Isabella d'Este's *studiolo* by Mantegna (Plate 61), Costa and Perugino, which the Duke of Mantua relinquished to the Cardinal in 1627. The greater part of the Mantua pictures went, however, immediately afterwards to an even greater collector, Charles I of England, who could outdo even Richelieu, and it was not until later that more pictures from the Mantua collection found their way to France. In the meanwhile, an exchange between the Kings of England and France gave the former the Leonardo *John the Baptist*, while the French King gained Hans Holbein's *Erasmus of Rotterdam* (Plate 66), among other pictures.

The reign of Louis XIII's successor, Louis XIV, marks the highest point of the French Monarchy and its most complete identification with the life of the nation. No one did more than Louis XIV to give France the cultural and artistic leadership of Europe, and the foundation of the huge royal collections was part of this policy. Following the example set by Richelieu and by Richelieu's successor, Cardinal Mazarin, who had guided his earliest steps, the King deliberately made the patronage of the arts into an instrument of policy and of international propaganda. Living artists were supported and at the same time every opportunity was taken to acquire the works of the old masters whenever they came on the market. The result was that in 1709–10, shortly before the King's death, the royal collection contained 1478 pictures, 930 of them French, 89 Florentine or Roman, 102 Venetian and 178 of the Lombard School.

The most important event in the international art market, which took place shortly after Louis's accession to the Throne, was the dispersal of the world-famous collection of Charles I. At the two public sales of the collection, in 1649 and 1653, Cardinal Mazarin and the banker Jabach, who originally came from Cologne, were among the most eager bidders. The pictures acquired by Mazarin, including those which he later bought from Jabach, passed to the King in 1661, and ten years later the King was able to buy 5542 drawings and paintings from Jabach, who had got into financial difficulties, at a nominal price. These two major additions made a notable increase in the royal collections. Among the Mazarin pictures there were many which are still among the principal ornaments of the Louvre—Giorgione's *Concert Champêtre* (Plate 62), Correggio's *Jupiter and Antiope* and his *Mystic Marriage of St. Catherine*, Raphael's *St. Michael*, *St. George*, and his portrait of Balthasar Castiglione (Plate 64), and Sebastiano del Piombo's *Holy Family*. Many of the Titians in Mazarin's collection had belonged to Charles I, and before that to the Gonzaga in Mantua: these included the *Madonna with the Rabbit*, the *Entombment*, the *Supper at Emmaus*, the so-called *Allegory of D'Avalos*, the *Woman at her Toilet*, and several portraits, incontestably the finest of which was the *Man with the Glove*. On the other hand, the *Pardo Venus* came from Spain, having been given to Charles I by Philip III of Spain in 1623, on the occasion of his informal visit to Spain as Prince; Jabach bought the picture at the sale of the King's collection and then relinquished it to Mazarin, from whose heirs it passed to Louis. At this time too, another much-travelled picture came to rest in France again—Leonardo's *St. John the Baptist*.

Mazarin's collection was particularly rich in the Italian masters, but Jabach owned relatively few Italian pictures, but several of the Holbein portraits in the Louvre came from him. The chief contribution from Jabach, however, was his collection of drawings which are still the foundation and backbone of the Louvre Print Room.

A gallery such as that now possessed by Louis XIV was as important a factor in Colbert's carefully thought out system of cultural propaganda

as the Academies he founded in Paris and Rome. Agents were kept busy
to increase the collection, and purchases and gifts brought in a wealth of
pictures by seventeenth-century masters such as the Carracci, Albani,
Domenichino, Trevisani and so on; Paolo Veronese's gigantic *Feast in
the House of Simon*, for instance, was presented by the Venetian Republic.

Among the Flemings, van Dyck was particularly well represented,
with fourteen pictures listed in 1681, but Rubens was less so, although the
Kermesse (Plate 70) came in 1685 to join the *Tomyris and Cyrus* and the
Vierge aux Innocents. Louis XIV's collection was above all rich in French
pictures, with four splendid Poussins from Mazarin's collection and
thirteen, including some of the finest, from Richelieu's and still others
from various sources, so that at the end of his reign the King possessed no
fewer than forty-one pictures by the great classicist (Plate 76). In addition,
there were fourteen by Claude Lorrain, twenty-six by Lebrun, seventeen
by Mignard, not counting the decorative paintings and the innumerable
sketches and studies by the court painters, which automatically became
Crown property. During the whole of the reign the classicists officially
retained their dominant position but for many years the colourists had
been steadily undermining them. The notorious 'battle between drawing
and colour' finally broke out on the occasion of a meeting of the Academy
in 1668, with Raphael and Poussin as the declared ideals on the one side,
and Titian on the other. It soon grew into a war of pamphlets, in which
the moderns (i.e. the colourists) possessed a powerful advocate in the
person of Roger de Piles, the 'discoverer' of Rubens, who claimed that
the Medici gallery was the best place in which to study his outstanding
qualities. Towards the end of the century the colourists had gained a
decisive victory and Rubens was a confirmed favourite, especially of the
collectors. Even the absolute monarch living on in Versailles, who had
formerly disposed of Flemish painting by referring to it as a theatre of
apes, had to bow to the change in taste, acquiring the *Kermesse* (Plate 70),
with all the sensuous charm and free handling of the paint which made it
the epitome of all that the classicists abhorred.

It was at about this time that a painter of Flemish extraction was born
in the town of Valenciennes, which, by the turn of political events, had
just become French, while he himself was destined to become a symbol of
the French genius in painting. Antoine Watteau began in the style of
Teniers, Ostade and Wouverman; in Paris in 1709 he copied the *Kermesse*
and experienced a decisive influence from Rubens. From then on the
Netherlandish influence grew in French art, the more so since the
indefatigable Roger de Piles had meanwhile been to Amsterdam and

discovered Rembrandt as well. The *Self-Portrait* of 1660 (Plate 71) was the first Rembrandt to enter the royal collection, and from that moment Rembrandt was a powerful factor which reached its highest point in Fragonard's colour and in Chardin's naturalism: the dominance of the bourgeoisie in French art and culture was in preparation.

Meanwhile, the official patronage of the arts was declining both from the point of view of the support of living artists and of the buying of pictures by the old masters. The period of the Regency and the reign of Louis XV—so important for the dominance of the applied arts—was best pleased by decorative talents, and the independent and outstanding artist was neglected. The French royal collections never possessed a picture by Watteau, and no more than two by Chardin, including the *Saying Grace at Table* (Plate 75). The Watteaus went to Sweden, Russia, and above all to the palaces of Frederick II of Prussia.

On the other hand the eighteenth century was important in quite another way, since the development of official collecting in Paris started then. The public began to take an interest in the royal pictures and began even to demand access to them. Since the time of Louis XIV they had been deposited in some of the rooms in the Louvre, which served as a sort of *Garde Meuble*, from which pictures could be withdrawn for the decoration of the royal residences as occasion required. For this purpose, the pictures—like those in the Stallburg in Vienna—were cut down or altered as necessary. In 1747 the critic La Font de Saint Yenne made himself the spokesman of those who wished to see the art treasures made generally accessible, and three years later a selection was in fact exhibited to the public twice a week in the Luxembourg, in conjunction with the Gallery of Maria de' Medici. This precursor of the Louvre, limited almost entirely to works of the French classicists of the seventeenth century and their counterparts in other Schools, was not systematic nor did it last for long. In 1779 the Luxembourg was needed for other purposes and the pictures went back into store in the Louvre. It was not until near the end of the reign of Louis XVI that the idea of a public gallery began to take more definite shape. The Comte d'Angiviller, *Directeur des bâtiments* from 1774 and active under one or another title in this position until the end of the monarchy, was determined to set up a proper museum in the Louvre and to this end he had begun as early as 1778 to adapt several of the rooms there. First of all, however, he wanted to fill in the gaps in the royal collections. One opportunity was offered by the economic recession and there were others offered by the suppression of convents during the Age of Enlightenment, both in France and in Belgium. At the same time d'Angiviller bought at the big auction sales which were then frequent in Paris, and from a sale in 1777 he got Rembrandt's *Emmaus*, while another in 1784 yielded Rembrandt's portrait of Hendrickje Stoffels, Ruisdael's *Sunset*, and Rubens's portrait of Hélène Fourment. Still others came from dealers or private collectors and particular attention was paid to the Netherlandish Schools, previously neglected. Yet all the efforts made by those responsible for the royal collections to introduce greater system were in vain, and it was left for the Republic to provide a public museum in the Louvre.

As early as 1791 Barrère introduced a motion making the Louvre a building reserved to the arts and sciences, and all the pensioners and hangers-on who had ensconced themselves in it were evicted. In the following year pictures from the former royal palaces began to pour in, and a committee of six was set up to decide which of the works of art from suppressed convents or confiscated from émigré aristocrats were worthy of the national collection. This national museum was opened to the public on the anniversary of the fall of the monarchy, August 10, 1793.

The first museum of the French Republic contained 537 pictures and 124 other objects. They were not arranged according to Schools or on any other system, but simply as decorations, and even the choice of the pictures did not differ much from that shown about fifty years earlier, since they consisted almost entirely of works by the representatives of the official style—Poussin, Lesueur, Claude Lorrain, Charles Lebrun and like-minded artists in other Schools.

The new institution had a multitude of difficulties to overcome, including the disinclination of the local authorities at Versailles and the other former palaces to part with their possessions and the competition of Alexandre Lenoir's *Dépôt des Petits Augustins*, where that passionate patriot and antiquary was attempting to bring together all the monuments of the nation's past. Then there were the prejudices of the members of the Committee, who regarded all pictures earlier than the seventeenth century as mere antiquities, unfit for a museum of art, and at the same time regarded all works which reflected the refined elegance of the banished *ancien régime* as vain and frivolous baubles. In this way, on account of aesthetic or moral prejudices, many a masterpiece was rejected.

Events moved rapidly in these years and the structure of the museum soon changed; it became the Central Museum of the Fine Arts, and was known successively as the Musée Napoléon, the Musée Royal and the Musée National du Louvre. This Museum was destined to become a sort

of encyclopaedia of the artistic genius of the human race, arranged by
nations and periods. The overwhelming series of military successes furthered the idea of assembling all the great masterpieces of the past in one
place, so that both instruction and enjoyment could be had on a scale
never possible either before or since. In his final report for 1815, Baron
Vivant-Denon, the leading spirit in the enterprise and an astounding
organizer, could justly remark that 'unheard-of circumstances had
brought about an enormous monument, no less unheard-of circumstances
destroyed it again.' Napoleon's Museum remained thus a short-lived
grandiose dream.

The idea of centralization is highly characteristic of the period itself,
for similar attempts to gather together all the scattered art treasures of a
dynasty or a people into one place were in progress in Vienna, in Naples
and in Amsterdam, and it was at about this time that the Pope created
the great central museums of antique sculpture in Rome. The destruction
of the old social order and the Church in France, followed by the conquest
of most of Europe by the armies of the Republic or of Napoleon, made the
repetition of such experiments possible to an exceptional degree—so
exceptional, in fact, as to justify the experiment at least in part. It would
not be fair to condemn it out of hand as sheer looting, on the same
footing as some of the events of our own days. The Central Museum was
the expression of a powerful tendency of the time and very few people
then felt that works of art would suffer by being uprooted from their
native soil. Among these few none was more emphatic in his protests
than the French scholar Quatremère de Quincy, while on the other hand
numerous prominent representatives of even the plundered countries
expressed their admiration of the overpowering spectacle afforded by
this unique agglomeration of masterpieces. Merely to mention the
numbers makes this clear: in 1804 the Museum contained 472 Italian
pictures and 591 of the Northern Schools, this latter number including
no less than 54 pictures by Rubens, 32 by Rembrandt, 15 by Holbein and
33 by Cranach.

This assemblage was fed from every possible source. French ecclesi-
astical property yielded Jan van Eyck's *Madonna with Chancellor Rolin*
(Plate 58), formerly in the Collegiate church at Autun, and the *Deposition*
by the Cologne painter known as the Master of St. Bartholomew, from
the Val de Grâce in Paris; property confiscated from émigrés included
Rembrandt's *Venus and Cupid*, Paris Bordone's *Vertumnus and Pomona* and
Frans Hals's *Descartes*. It was only now, too, that the Mantegnas from
Mantua acquired by Richelieu (Plate 61) came into the Museum's

possession, and still more pictures were given to the Museum or bought by it.

Fine as many of these single acquisitions were, they pale before the stream of works of art brought back by the victorious armies. It began in 1794 with the conquest of Belgium and continued with the invasions of Holland, Italy, Germany and Austria. Gradually a system was developed. Competent experts followed the armies and the peace treaties contained stipulations regarding the transfer of works of art. For example, the Peace of Tolentino cost the Pope a hundred masterpieces, carefully selected, and even though the prevailing taste was still for works of the late sixteenth and seventeenth centuries, yet even so, works of the fifteenth and even fourteenth centuries began to be included in the loot. Seroux d'Agincourt's 'Histoire de l'art par les monuments' had drawn attention to the importance of the earlier Schools and the Romantics began to champion them against the later Schools.

A further point of importance is that the idea of centralization in the Louvre was counterbalanced by the opposite idea of distribution, for there already existed two branch institutions—the Musée des Monuments Français and the Musée Spécial de l'École Française, at Versailles. The former collected French art of the Middle Ages and Renaissance up to the early seventeenth century, continuing the programme followed by Lenoir's *Dépôt des Petits Augustins*, and developing into the germ of the Musée Cluny. At Versailles the average level of French painting was gathered together, leaving it to the Louvre to assemble the best examples of all Schools, including the highest points of the French. The gigantic quantities of pictures were somewhat reduced after the restoration of Catholic worship by the return of many of them to their original homes, and by the division of many others among the new provincial museums. Many of these newly founded museums were in the recently annexed provinces and those in Brussels and Milan are good examples.

After the fall of Napoleon the works of art went back to their homelands, or, to put it more accurately, in the Treaty of Paris of 1814, which followed the first defeat of Napoleon, there was no mention of them and they remained in Paris, giving Louis XVIII grounds to maintain that they now belonged to France with more reason than that of mere conquest. In 1815, however, after Waterloo and the final defeat of Napoleon, these matters were taken more seriously, especially at the insistence of Canova and other artists who pressed for the return of looted works of art. They were returned—sometimes rather unceremoniously—and the French not only accepted this consequence of defeat with a very bad grace but they raised so many difficulties that in many instances the repatriation of works of art could be carried out only by sheer force. Even some foreigners did not take to the idea of returning these works, and Sir Thomas Lawrence, for example, was of the opinion that every artist must regret the breaking up of a collection which, situated in so central a place in Europe, had been made available to the public with unprecedented liberality. Attempts to lay hands on the works of art which had always been in French possession, as reparations, were frustrated by the determined opposition of the Duke of Wellington and Lord Castlereagh, but most of the looted works—though not all—did get returned. Some of the pictures, especially those which had been sent to the provinces, could not be found when the time came, and others were so big that the cost of returning them, in the absence of Army transport, seemed too great. In addition, a disproportionately large number of Italian primitives—such as Cimabue, Giotto, Gaddi, Gozzoli, Mantegna and others—were left in Paris because the representatives of the Allied Powers did not regard them as of any value and therefore made no fuss about them. Notwithstanding these exceptions, the proud Musée du Louvre was a wreck by the time the restitution was completed, and various stopgaps were called in to fill the empty walls, such as the Medici cycle from the Luxembourg and works by Lesueur and Claude Vernet.

Following on the splendours, the storms and the collapse of the Napoleonic era the Louvre underwent a period of quiet and neglect. Understandably enough, Louis XVIII took no particular interest in a museum which was so pointed a reminder of Imperial glories, and he turned his attention to the Luxembourg, which, during his reign, was organized as the museum of contemporary French art (1818) and was to become priceless as a reserve for the Louvre, for it was decided that no work should enter that great national treasure-house until its creator had been dead for twenty years. The need for living artists to be kept separate from the old masters was realized almost everywhere at about the same moment, but nowhere else was so satisfactory a system of shielding both from unfavourable criticism evolved as in Paris, where the reserve grew enormously from generation to generation and was claimed from time to time for the Louvre. After their period of quarantine, as it might be called, the works which had stood the test of time were taken into the Louvre, for twenty years from the death of an artist is about enough to cancel out the overvaluation of his contemporaries and the undervaluation of the next generation, and the later men could now join the glorious company of their predecessors, as equals.

Louis Philippe, who reigned from 1830 until 1848, was principally interested in the museum at Versailles, dedicated to the glory of France in all ages and containing a huge quantity of historical pictures and portraits, without distinction between Bourbon, Napoleonic or even Republican connections. During this period only a few crumbs fell to the Louvre, yet Louis Philippe, known as the Bourgeois King on account of his parsimony, was able to make a few worthwhile acquisitions for astonishingly low prices. His favourite School was the Spanish, until then but little regarded. During the Napoleonic period many pictures had found their way to France from Spain, unofficially rather than officially, brought back by generals who had served in Spain and acquired works of art there. The most successful of these collectors was Marshal Soult, whose enormous collection of Spanish pictures was to reveal itself as an almost inexhaustible source. As early as 1817 he sold the *Immaculate Virgin* painted by Murillo in 1665 for Santa Maria la Blanca in Seville, to the Louvre and later he repeatedly offered his collection to the King; but at prices that Louis Philippe considered too high.

By comparison with this interest in Spanish art, the lack of interest in French painting in its most French phase, the eighteenth century, is very striking. A few pictures trickled into the Louvre, including Watteau's diploma work for the Academy, the *Embarkation for Cythera* (Plate 77), yet on the whole the French critic Bürger-Thorez remarked with justice that nowhere in the world was French art less valued than in France.

All this was changed when the Second Republic, and then the Second Empire, added their contributions to the Louvre. In 1848, the year of the Revolution, both the structure of the building and the arrangement of the pictures were re-organized: Frédéric Villot was the first to hang them according to Schools, and in 1849 the Comte de Nieuwerkerke was appointed Director-General, holding office until the fall of Napoleon III. In 1851 the Louvre was re-opened with the completely remodelled Galerie d'Apollon as its centre.

Napoleon III took every opportunity to imitate his great-uncle and he also chose to rival him as a patron of the arts; he it was who gave Paris the splendid external form we love and admire, and he spared no costs to enrich the Louvre. In 1852 he outbid the Emperor of Russia, the Queen of Spain and the National Gallery for Murillo's *Immaculate Conception* at the sale of Marshal Soult's collection, paying the then fabulous price of 586,000 francs for it. Still more grandiose was his purchase—for four and a half million francs—of the enormous Campana Collection of pictures, sculpture and jewels, the owner of which had used his position as Director of the official pawnshop in Rome to make countless advantageous purchases. The collection was exhibited as a whole in Paris in 1862, before being divided between the Louvre and 67 provincial museums. This transaction provided the Louvre with a number of Italian pictures of the fourteenth and fifteenth centuries, but it was less satisfactory in that the repeated regrouping of the material led to the dismembering of several works which should have been organic unities, and, as a result, several parts of one and the same altarpiece are today scattered over several different museums.

At about this time the Louvre was enriched from another quarter, when the masterpieces of French art of the first half of the century came triumphantly out of the Luxembourg into their final home in the Louvre. David, Géricault, Delacroix, Ingres, all helped to lay the chief accent on the French School; and at about the same time Bürger-Thorez's admonitions and the propaganda conducted by the brothers Goncourt began to bear fruit. The Second Republic had already acquired Boucher's *Diana* (Plate 73), Aved's portrait of Mirabeau, and a few pictures by Chardin, and now the Second Empire followed with Rigaud's *Robert de Cotte*, Poussin's *Apollo and Daphne* and some more Chardins. The first of the French Primitives appeared in the Louvre in 1863, the *Martyrdom of St. Denis* (Plate 59).

The newly awakened activities of the Louvre inspired many benefactors, but of all the gifts made to the museum none was more splendid or more welcome than the La Caze Collection, rich in works of all Schools, but particularly in French pictures of the eighteenth century. From La Caze there came Ribera's *Club-foot* and his *Madonna*, Velazquez's *Queen Maria Anna*, eleven sketches by Rubens, Rembrandt's *Bathsheba* (Plate 72), Frans Hals's *Gipsy Girl* (Plate 69 B) and a number of good Italian and Flemish pictures, but the great gain consisted of nine paintings by Watteau, including the splendid *Gilles* (Colour Plate XIII), fifteen excellent Chardins and ten Fragonards, as well as many other works, so that the most noticeable gaps in the Louvre were filled at one stroke.

The improvement that began under the Empire continued under the Third Republic, which passed a law in 1895 increasing very considerably the funds available to the National Collections. More and more of the great French painters of the nineteenth century entered the Louvre, the masters of Classicism and Romanticism being followed by the Barbizon School—Millet and Rousseau—and by Courbet (Plate 78), whose major works were acquired in the eighties. The struggle against the admission of the Impressionists was long and violent. When, in 1890, a group of

artists and amateurs offered to present Manet's *Olympia* (Plate 84) to the
nation and, in 1894, the painter Caillebotte bequeathed his choice
collection of Impressionist pictures, the official guardians of taste were
outraged and very nearly refused the gifts. However, in the end they
were accepted in part and Manet's *Olympia* entered the Louvre in triumph
in 1908 after a suitable period of waiting in the Luxembourg, and most of
the Caillebotte pictures followed in 1929.

The Louvre became ever more of a national treasure house, where the
mutabilities of taste were finally stilled. In 1897 the *Société des Amis du Louvre*
was founded and ever since then it has been an indispensable helper
in raising money for important purchases and a channel for the stream
of gifts and bequests. Pictures came in singly or in whole collections.

At the same time as this flood of acquisitions the officials of the Louvre
worked at a systematic building up of the collection; they had the services of an outstanding staff and a school of their own which ensured the
services of suitable younger men for the future. The French section was the
greatest gainer from all these efforts, for its acquisitions included the
noble *Pietà* of the fifteenth century from Villeneuve-lès-Avignon (Plate
60), Jean Cousin's *Eva Prima Pandora*, François Clouet's *Pierre Quthe*,
Poussin's *Inspiration du Poète*, Lenain's *Peasants Eating*, Ingres's *Turkish
Bath* (Plate 82), Delacroix's *Death of Sardanapalus*, Corot's *Trinità de'
Monti*, Courbet's *Atelier* and many others.

The other Schools show a similar development over the same space of
time, and here too the keepers of each department sought to fill up the
gaps. For the later Italian Schools there was little to do, since the in-
herited riches were so great that there was practically nothing to add,
and the new acquisitions were almost exclusively from the earlier periods.
Much the same situation prevailed among the Flemish and Dutch
Schools. The most important German pictures were the altarpiece by the
Master of the Holy Kinsmen and Dürer's youthful *Self-portrait*. The first
El Greco was a gift of the art critic Théodore Duret in 1893; the *St.
Ferdinand* followed it in 1903 and the *Crucifixion with Fray Covarrubias* in
1908. Dr. Carvallo later presented an *Immaculate Virgin* by Valdés Leal,
a painter hitherto unrepresented in the Louvre.

Carvallo was not the only foreigner to enrich the Louvre. He was a
Turk, and Baron Schlichting was a Russian, and to them we may add
the names of the Polish Count Potocki and the Americans Walter Gay
and Michael Friedsam; all of them felt that the Louvre was not just the
French National Gallery but in a certain sense belonged to every lover
of the arts. The Louvre owes this unique position to its close ties with a

creative activity in the arts which has developed organically over more than two hundred years and has become a model for other countries in the process. It is only just to say that French painting from Poussin to Cézanne, and perhaps since Cézanne, has been the great teacher to which we all, irrespective of national loyalties, pay homage. Something of Napoleon's great dream of a single central museum as a monument to the artistic genius of all mankind still hovers over the Louvre, but now it is founded on gratitude and not on conquest.

This very popularity of the Louvre in and outside France has raised some problems for its Directors. The jealous attention of the public made it impossible to relegate secondary material to the depot—one of the most effective ways in which to improve any collection—and public opinion rejected the idea of cleaning the pictures equally decisively. As a result, the Louvre became progressively more and more overcrowded with increasingly dirty pictures, and for a hundred years these two subjects, the darker side of the splendours of the Louvre, were discussed and re-gretted by critics and public alike—but with no noticeable result. It was not until the thirties of the present century that an energetic attempt was made to tackle these longstanding ills and to arrange the treasures it contained in a more systematic way. A most promising beginning was made with the re-arrangement of the Italian Primitives in the Salle des Sept Mètres and the creation of new galleries for the French nineteenth-century pictures, but all this was interrupted by the outbreak of war, which necessitated the evacuation of all the contents to places of safety. The pictures returned after the Liberation, undamaged and without any losses, except that the *Immaculate Conception* by Murillo had been ex-changed with the Prado for some pictures by El Greco and Goya. In point of fact the pictures came back better than when they were sent away, for in many cases the temporary removal from the eyes of a well-meaning but over-anxious public had provided the opportunity for a long overdue cleaning. The task of re-organization had been made easier by the evacuation and it was at once taken up again, so that some of the departments have already assumed their new form. The Musée de l'Impressionisme unites all the Impressionist pictures in the Jeu de Paume, whereas they had formerly been scattered over the most varied departments. The Grande Galerie was transformed in accordance with the ideas of the painter Hubert Robert, losing its previous warehouse look, and other transformations are complete or under way. The undiminished power of attraction of the Louvre is testified to by such important dona-tions as the fine collection of Dr Gachet, Van Gogh's friend and doctor

IV. James Abbott McNeill Whistler: *Arrangement in Gray and Black: Portrait of the Artist's Mother.*
Paris, Louvre

(Plate 85). In spite of all her present difficulties, France is determined to preserve, with spirit, taste and originality, that special place occupied by the national museum, where, more than anywhere else, the heritage of the past can be felt as the foundation and stimulus of perpetual creative power.

The Louvre

NOTES ON THE ILLUSTRATIONS

BOUCHER, François (1703–1770)

Diana after her Bath   Plate 73
Canvas, 22½ × 29½ in. (No. 30).

Signed and dated 1742.
An elegantly erotic scene of two charming nudes, Diana and her companion, set against a barely indicated landscape foil.

BROUWER, Adriaen (1605–1638)

The Smoker   Plate 69a
Panel, 16⅛ × 12⅝ in. (No. 1916).
Also called 'Smell'; possibly part of a series of the five senses. Although small in format it is not painted with miniature precision, but broadly in a sketchlike manner.

CÉZANNE, Paul (1839–1906)

The Card-Players   Plate 86
Canvas, 18½ × 22 in. (No. 38)

Painted about 1885–90. A splendid rendering of the composition, which Cézanne often repeated in his attempt to create a monumental composition from simple elements.

CHARDIN, Jean-Baptiste-Siméon
(1699–1779)
Saying Grace   Plate 75
Canvas, 19¼ × 15⅜ in. (No. 92)

Louis XV collection. The introduction of the bourgeois milieu into painting is an innovation corresponding to social changes which were taking place. Chardin bestows a colouristic refinement on this type of painting—this subject for instance he painted repeatedly—equal to that displayed in his still lifes.

COURBET, Gustave (1819–1877)

The Funeral at Ornans   Plate 78
Canvas, 124 × 250 in. (No. 143)

Painted in 1849. Presented by Mlle. Juliette Courbet in 1882.
One of the paintings in which Courbet wanted to display his social beliefs, and his conception of the naturalistic rendering of nature, on the grandest possible scale. The participants in the ceremony, given almost portraitlike character, are arranged in a frieze, suggesting the influence of popular graphic art, already noted by M. Schapiro. It is difficult to understand today the indignant rejection of this picture.

DAVID, Louis (1748–1825)

The Three Ladies of Ghent   Plate 81
Canvas, 52 × 41⅜ in. (No. 200)

Painted after 1816, when David moved to Belgium.
In this late period David treats scenes of bourgeois life with the same concentrated force which earlier in his life he had expended on classical themes.

DEGAS, Edgar (1834–1917)

Ballet Dancer on the Stage   Plate 87
Pastel, 22⅞ × 16¼ in. (No. 161)

Acquired by the Luxembourg through the Caillebotte donation.
Painted about 1877. Typical ballerina in full stagelight. Other ballerinas and a gentleman in frockcoat are lightly sketched in the wings.

DELACROIX, Eugène (1798–1863)

The Massacre at Scios   Plate 80
Canvas, 166⅛ × 138⅝ in. (No. 208)

Exhibited in the Salon of 1824. Collection Charles X of Luxembourg.
The contemporary events of the Greek war of liberation deeply moved the imagination of Romantics everywhere. Delacroix isolates one episode and translates its pathos into an exuberant experience in terms of colour.

DYCK, Anthony van (1599–1641)

Portrait of Charles I of England   Plate 68
Canvas, 107⅛ × 83½ in. (No. 1967)

Inscribed: CAROLUS I REX A VAN DYCK.
In Van Dyck's account of 1638–9 it is called
'Le roi alla chasse' and valued at £200, which
the king reduced to £100. In various French
collections; in 1771 it was purchased by
Madame du Barry, from whom Louis XVI
bought it in 1775 for 24.000 livres.
The proud bearing of the king dominates the
picture and completely subordinates his two
companions. The horse is inspired by Titian;
Van Dyck had drawn it in his Italian sketch-
book.

EYCK, Jan van (died 1441)

*The Virgin and Child Adored by the Chancellor
Rolin*   Plate 58
Panel, 26 × 24⅜ in. (No. 1986)

In 1800 it was brought into the Louvre by A.
Lenoir, from the Collegiate Church of Notre
Dame d'Autun.
The donor is Nicholas Rolin, Chancellor of
Burgundy, who founded the church mentioned
above. The double nature of his character—
violent in everyday life, but humble before the
Mother of God—is brilliantly expressed. The
foreground scene is set in front of a panoramic
landscape.

FOUQUET, Jean (1420–1481)

Portrait of King Charles VII   Plate 56
Panel, 33⅞ × 28¾ in. (No. 289)

Probably identical with the picture which used
to hang in the Sainte Chapelle at Bourges, till
it came to the Louvre in 1757. It was withdrawn from the Louvre during the revolution
but bought back in 1838.
The King, a lifesize, half-length figure, looks
out of a niche framed by curtains. The purely
northern conception of the portrait is the
reason for dating it before Fouquet's journey
to Italy in 1445.

FRAGONARD, Jean-Honoré (1732–1806)

The Music Lesson   Plate 74
Canvas, 42½ × 47¼ in. (No. 291)

Actually not a music lesson, but the prelude to
an amorous scene at the piano.

GÉRICAULT, Théodore (1791–1824)

The Raft of Medusa   Plate 79
Canvas, 193¼ × 282 in. (No. 338)

Exhibited in the Salon of 1819, it was bought
from the estate of the artist for King Charles X
in 1824.
Géricault, inspired by the deep public sym-
pathy for the tragic shipwreck of 1816, created
this composition of Michelangelesque grandeur.
All gestures and glances of the shipwrecked are
directed towards the upper right of the picture
where one of them is pointing to a sailing ship
on the horizon, the source of hope for them all.

GIORGIONE (1477(?)—1510)

Concert champêtre   Plate 62
Canvas, 43¼ × 54⅜ in. (No. 1136)

In 1627 it came from Mantua into the Collection of Charles I. At the 1649 sale of Charles's
collection it was bought by Jabach and given
by him to Louis XIV in 1671.
Although in old inventories always called
Giorgione, critics have attributed it variously
to Titian and Domenico Campagnola. In its
poetic mood and its atmospheric chiaroscuro it
is entirely in the spirit of the artist who lit the
path for his whole generation.

GOGH, Vincent van (1853–1890)

Portrait of Doctor Gachet   Plate 85
Canvas, 26¾ × 22½ in.

Donated by Gachet's heirs.
Painted in 1890, shortly before Van Gogh's
death, who was at this time under the medical
care of Dr Gachet. In this portrait he fixes
permanently the overpowering impression the
sitter made on him, both as physician and man.
Gachet holds a twig of digitalis in his hand.

HALS, Frans (1580–1666)

The Gipsy Girl   Plate 69B
Panel, 23 × 20½ in. (No. 2384)

Like the Berlin picture of Malle Babbe (Plate
162) it is a favourite with the public because of
its fresh naturalism.

HOLBEIN, Hans, The Younger (1497–1543)

Portrait of Erasmus of Rotterdam   Plate 66
Panel, 16½ × 12⅝ in. (No. 2715)

This picture, which belonged to Charles I, came into the possession of Louis XIII in exchange for Leonardo's *St. John the Baptist*.
It is executed in greater detail than the corresponding study from life in the museum at Basle. This portrait is probably one of those about which Erasmus wrote in a letter of June 3, 1524: "recently I have again sent two portraits of myself to England, painted by no mean artist."

INGRES, Jean-Auguste-Dominique
(1780–1867)

The Turkish Bath   Plate 82
Canvas, diameter 42½ in. (No. 3107)

Signed and dated "1862 à l'age de 82 ans."
In 1859 made up to rectangular shape; reduced to its original form in 1863. Originally in the collection of Prince Napoléon and later in that of Prince de Broglie. A gift of the Société des Amis du Louvre.
This work, which captures the linear rhythm of the young female form, expresses the detached sensuality of the aged artist.

LEONARDO DA VINCI (1452–1519)

Portrait of Monna Lisa   Colour Plate XII
Panel, 30¼ × 20⅞ in. (No. 1601)

Mentioned by Vasari as in the possession of the King of France. Lisa, the wife of Francesco di Giocondo, was painted by Leonardo about 1503–6. The enigmatic expression, especially the famous smile, which has inspired innumerable literary interpretations, has made this picture the most famous in the world.

The Virgin of the Rocks   Plate 57
Canvas, transferred from panel, 78⅜ × 48 in. (No. 1599)

Probably the painting commissioned from Leonardo on January 10, 1478, for the Chapel of St. Bernardo in the Palazzo Vecchio. It was, however, not delivered, but brought to the King of France in 1506. First at Fontainebleau (1645), then at Versailles, it has been in the Louvre since 1800.
The connection of this painting with the closely

related version in London, as well as the significance of the subject matter, have been much discussed, but no satisfactory solution has been found so far. The exciting rock landscape and the mysterious treatment of light, both it is true demanded by the subject, are yet unique in Florentine painting.

MALOUEL, Jean (died 1419)

The Martyrdom of St. Denis   Plate 59
Canvas, transferred from panel, 63¾ × 82⅝ in. (No. 995)

According to tradition it came originally from the Chartreuse of Champmol. Acquired by the Louvre under Napoleon III.
On the left the communion, on the right the beheading of the saint. In the centre Christ on the Cross. The originator of this precious *incunabula* of early French painting has not been established with certainty. Jean Malouel and Henri Bellechose, successive Burgundian Court painters, are possible candidates for the authorship of this panel, which according to a document was probably painted in 1416. Joint authorship has also been suggested.

MANET, Edouard (1832–1883)

Olympia   Plate 84
Canvas, 51⅛ × 74¾ in. (No. 613)

Signed and dated 1863.
Exhibited in 1865. Donated to the Luxembourg by a group of art lovers in 1890. In 1908 it was acquired by the Louvre.
The classic motif of the reclining nude is interpreted by Manet in such a modern idiom that the hostile reception of the picture by the majority of the contemporary public seems understandable. Today the painting is itself a classic.

MANTEGNA, Andrea (1431–1506)

The Parnassus   Plate 61
Canvas, 63 × 75⅝ in. (No. 1375)

Painted in 1497, it is the first of Mantegna's paintings for Isabella d'Este's Studio in Mantua. It came into the possession of Cardinal Mazarin before the Mantuan collection was sold to Charles I. A courtly allegory in mythological dress, with a composition reminiscent of theatre décor.

METSYS, Quentin (1466–1530)

The Banker and his Wife   Plate 65
Panel, 28 × 26¾ in. (No. 2029)

Signed and dated 1514.
This picture, of which a number of variants
exist, came into the Musée Napoléon in 1806.
An old genre motif is here raised to a new level
by the highly individual treatment of the
figures and imaginative use of detail in costume
and still life objects.

MONET, Claude (1840–1926)

The Cathedral of Rouen   Plate 88
Canvas, 42⅛ × 29 in. (No. 187)

Signed and dated 1894.
Acquired by the Louvre with the Camondo
Collection in 1914.
One of the four views of the Cathedral (all of
which are in the Louvre), which Monet painted
at different times of the day in order to record
the varying light effects. In this painting the
very stones crumble under the blazing sunlight.

POUSSIN, Nicolas (1594–1665)

The Deluge (Winter)   Plate 76
Canvas, 46½ × 63 in.

One of a series of *Four Seasons*, commissioned
by Cardinal Richelieu in 1660–64. All of them
were in the collection of Louis XIV and are
now in the Louvre.
In these pictures, the Biblical events are woven
into the mood of the landscape. In the Winter
scene, which represents the *Deluge* and is
dominated by grey-green tones, there appear
only a few persons, who have given up the
struggle for life.

RAPHAEL (1483–1520)

Portrait of Balthasar Castiglione   Plate 64
Canvas, 32¼ × 25⅝ in. (No. 1505)

Probably Raphael's second portrait of Castiglione, painted in 1519. From 1525–29 it was in
Spain; then in Mantua and in King Charles I
collection (?); van Uffelen sale, Amsterdam
1639; then in the collections of Alfonso Lopez,
Richelieu and Mazarin, whose heirs sold the
painting to Louis XIV in 1661.
The carefully thought-out composition is
typical of the classic High Renaissance
portrait.

REMBRANDT (1606–1669)

Self-Portrait at the Age of Fifty-Four
                Plate 71
Canvas, 43¾ × 33½ in. (No. 2)

Inscribed in a later hand: Rem F 1660.
In the collection of Louis XIV.
One of the artist's late self-portraits, painted in
the usual pose in which he turns to the right
(mirror-view) and omits his right hand.
Rembrandt's expression is one of embittered
contempt, yet without the laugh of the man
who can no longer be hurt, which characterizes
his very last self-portraits.

Bathsheba after the Bath   Plate 72
Canvas, 56 × 56 in. (No. 2549)

Signed and dated 1654.
Acquired by the Louvre with the La Caze
collection.
An old woman is drying Bathsheba's feet. Her
intimately portrayed body dominates the square
field. The essence of this picture lies in Bathsheba's complete unselfconsciousness and un-
awareness of the outside world.

RENOIR, Auguste (1841–1919)

Dance at the Moulin de la Galette   Plate 83
Canvas, 51⅝ × 69 in. (No. 230)

Signed: Renoir 76.
Acquired by the Luxembourg with the Gustave
Caillebotte collection in 1896; in the Louvre
in 1929.
Dates from Renoir's impressionist period; it
shows great directness and freshness in the
observation and rendering of the colourful,
vibrant milieu.

RUBENS, Peter Paul (1577–1640)

*King Henry IV Receiving the Portrait of Maria
de' Medici*   Plate 67
Canvas, 155 × 116 in.

Part of the cycle of the 'History of Maria de'
Medici', commissioned by the queen and
executed by Rubens and his workshop from
1622–1625 for the newly erected Luxembourg.
The cycle was transferred to the Louvre in 1815
in order to fill the gaps caused by the dissolution of the Musée Napoléon.
A superb example of baroque court allegory,
portraying the most trivial events with pompous
dignity.

The Flemish Kermesse   Plate 70
Panel, 58⅝ × 102¾ in. (No. 2115)

Bought in 1685 from the Marquis d'Hauterive
by Louis XIV, it was the earliest work by
Rubens to enter the Royal Collection.
This subject had been treated by other Flemish
painters in a down-to-earth manner; Rubens,
however, in this work of his mature period
depicts a scene overflowing with *joie de vivre* and
conveys excitement through the movement of
individual groups. This picture had a decisive
influence on the development of French
painting.

TITIAN (*c.* 1485–1576)

Portrait of King Francis I of France Plate 63
Canvas, 43 × 35 in. (No. 1588)

Very probably the picture presented to the
King by Pietro Aretino in 1538.
Although painted from a medal, perhaps the
one by Benvenuto Cellini, it is a spirited
characterization of the gallant king.

WATTEAU, Antoine (1684–1721)

The Embarkation for Cythera   Plate 77
Canvas, 50¾ × 75⅝ in. (No. 982)

Painted as his diploma work for the Academy
of Fine Arts in 1716–17. A second, somewhat
altered version was bought by King Frederic
the Great.
The most famous of Watteau's scenes of
galanterie in which a contemporary play is
raised to the sphere of a poetic vision. The
movement of the whole company towards the
ship on the left is shown as if observed by the
slow motion camera; some people are still
seated on the ground, others have half risen,
while the remainder are already walking
towards the ship.

The Actor Gilles   Colour Plate XIII
Canvas, 72½ × 58⅝ in. (No. 983)

Collections Vivant Denon 1826; Marquis de
Cyprierre 1849; acquired by the Louvre
through La Caze in 1867.
Dora Panofsky has recently given a satisfactory
explanation of the content of this painting and
its link with Parisian theatre life around 1716.
The conventional figure becomes in this painting a symbol of melancholy Comedy.

WHISTLER, James Abbott McNeil
(1834–1903)

Portrait of the Artist's Mother
                              Colour Plate IV
Canvas, 55½ × 63¾ in.

Signed with the butterfly.
Painted in 1871. Bought from the artist by the
French Government for the Luxembourg in
1891 for 4000 francs. Since 1926 in the Louvre.
The surface pattern of this painting in black
and white is inspired by Vermeer and Japanese
prints. The profile expresses the old woman's
fear of death with terrifying frankness.

SCHOOL OF AVIGNON (*c.* 1460)

The Pietà of Villeneuve-lès-Avignon
                                      Plate 60
Panel, 63¾ × 86 in. (No. 1001 B)

This magnificent composition, recently attributed to the Portuguese artist Nuño Gonçalvez,
is more likely to be of Provençal origin with
Iberian influence. Its literary sources are the
Meditations of the socalled pseudo-Bonaven-
tura. The deeply moving scene of the three
mourning figures surrounding the cruelly
distorted body of Christ, is experienced by the
praying donor as a vision.

THE PRADO IN MADRID

LIKE THE GALLERIES in Vienna and Florence, the Prado is the result of the activity of princely collectors, but the creation of the Spanish Hapsburgs is distinguished from the Medici collections on the one hand by reason of its much greater emphasis on the international, and on the other hand from the collections of the Austrian Hapsburgs by the greater importance given to the national School. The Spanish Hapsburgs prided themselves on ruling over an Empire on which the sun never set, and yet they still regarded themselves above all as kings of Spain; in addition, they had first Velazquez and then Goya as Court painters.

As a matter of fact, Court painters were appointed in Spain as early as the thirteenth century, but it was not a regular appointment until much later when collecting and the patronage of the arts had become a Royal sport, as elsewhere in Europe. Queen Isabella the Catholic begins the line of art patrons on the Spanish throne, for when she died in 1504 she left 460 pictures, many of which are still in the Royal Chapel in Granada Cathedral, where she herself was buried.

Isabella, because of her marriage to Ferdinand of Aragon and the expulsion of the Moors from Spain which was completed during her reign, can be called the founder—or at least the co-founder—of Spanish unity, and yet she had a distinct preference for Flemish painters. Some Flemings were attached to her entourage as her painters, while others, including Dirk Bouts, Rogier van der Weyden, Memling and David, are well represented in the collection she left. This interest in foreign art is typically Spanish and it endured throughout the next hundred years, the period when Spain reached its highest peak of political power and cultural leadership.

This international element may well have been in the blood of Isabella's grandson and successor, Charles V (Charles I in Spain). He was the son of a Spanish mother and a German father who was himself the son of the Emperor Maximilian I and Mary of Burgundy, and therefore the product of a mixture of cultures. Charles V was in every way a typical representative of that Renaissance which was instinctively but decisively rejected by Spain. It is unnecessary to go into the reasons why, of all the nations of

(55)

Europe, this was the one to struggle against the general tendency of the age: all writers on the history of Spanish culture are agreed on the fact itself. Charles's palace on the Alhambra makes the spectator aware how completely un-Spanish this Renaissance building is, both in conception and execution, and his general attitude to painting has as little relationship to Spanish ideas. His earliest protégés were Flemings, understandably enough, since he grew up at the Court of his aunt, the Regent Margaret of the Netherlands, at Brussels. Later on, the Emperor came to prefer the art of Titian above all others, and he acquired many of his pictures, aided by the anxiety his power caused the Italian princes. When Charles entered the peninsula a shudder ran through all the smaller courts in Italy and precious paintings, jealously guarded family treasures, came down off the walls. Even if they were not given to the Emperor himself, they were presented to those counsellors who had his ear, and an Imperial train ravaged the princely treasure houses like a swarm of locusts. The relationship between the Emperor and the artist was more than a matter of aesthetic preference, for Titian was official portrait painter to Charles V from 1532, or, in the pompous language of the day, the new Apelles to the new Alexander (Plate 103). Between the two there existed a kinship of mind which extended beyond a shared aesthetic taste. In the art of Titian Charles found that nobility which he wanted posterity to associate with his own character and an inwardness of feeling which could give form to his religious sentiments. When he retired to Yuste after his abdication, he took with him a number of the pictures Titian had painted for him—the *Gloria*, the *Mater Dolorosa*, the *Ecce homo*, and as a last farewell to his past life he took the portrait of his wife Isabella, long since dead. We know from contemporaries that the Emperor asked to see this picture as he lay on his deathbed—the portrait of a woman Titian had never seen. Perhaps because of this, the picture strikes us as unusually cold and impersonal and yet clearly it seemed to the Emperor to be the true image of his dead wife, and, after he had taken his farewell of her, the dying man's eyes rested on the deeply moving religious visions of his painter.

Titian's art harmonized with the grand manner of the Emperor Charles's life and with his own conception of his position, but his relationship with the painter depended on the recognition of his greatness rather than on a specifically artistic interest. This last is to be found much more clearly in Charles's son Philip II, whose patronage of the arts was more typically Spanish. His tendency to acquire large numbers was characteristic, for Philip II and his successors bought works of art on a scale far exceeding all earlier efforts. The reconquest of the peninsula, which was stretched over centuries, and its comparative isolation from the new centres of spiritual life, had caused a certain backwardness which was incompatible with the new position of Spain as a political and economic power in world affairs. The schism in the Church caused by the Reformation had made her feel that it was her destiny to become the protector of the true Faith; her armies and freebooters were victorious in many lands; discoveries and conquests had extended the bounds of her empire to an enormous extent and the American treasure ships brought back fabulous riches to the motherland. Works of art tend to flow to the centres of wealth and so Italian and Flemish painters and sculptors flocked to the country, and the incomparably rich collections of tapestries and arms and armour began to be formed. The situation in Spain in the sixteenth century has been rightly compared to that of the United States at the beginning of the twentieth century: a nation which up to that time had been engaged in other pursuits suddenly found itself a centre into which all the wealth of the earth was streaming, and it began to devote its energies to buying up works of art from abroad on the largest scale. The dynamic forces symbolized by the American skyscrapers can be found in the architecture of Spain, and Philip II's Escorial was reckoned as one of the wonders of the world.

It is unfair to Philip to regard him as no more than an instrument of such general tendencies, for he was a real lover of the arts whose wide range of interest was described many years ago by that great connoisseur of Spanish painting, Carl Justi. At first sight, his enthusiasm for the arts seems to contradict the usual conception of his austere, almost gloomy, personality; but we must not forget that it was the passions and disillusionments of a lifetime that transformed him into this terrifying figure. In his youth he had had his full share of sensuality and had taken a keen interest in creative activity; the Venetian Ambassador, in a careful character study of the king, wrote of him: "He has a good knowledge of painting and sculpture and from time to time he tries his hand at both arts." He had been brought up to admire Titian and he kept him on as Court painter—he also followed his father's example in being constantly in arrears with the payments due to Titian. The final account rendered in Titian's letter of December 22, 1574, lists a great number of pictures sent at various times to the Spanish court, and still not paid for; and even this account is incomplete since the painter, now a very old man, could not remember all the occasions on which pictures had been dispatched. Nevertheless, the relationship between Titian and the king was different from that which had obtained with the Emperor, for Philip admired him less as a painter of religious themes than for the erotic mythologies, which his imagination never wearied of varying. Philip owned the religious pictures which Charles had taken with him in his retreat to Yuste, as well as others which Titian had sent direct to him, yet these were clearly less to the king's taste. Titian's only contribution to the decoration of the Escorial was his *Martyrdom of St. Laurence*, a variant of an earlier composition, and his offer in 1567 to paint a whole series of scenes from the life of the Saint never seems to have been given serious consideration. Even as portrait painter to the king Titian no longer had the monopoly. Philip was not the restless traveller that his father had been, and Titian was now too old to go to Spain and refresh his vision of the king, whom he had painted as prince in 1550 (Plate 104), so the official duties of portrait painting went first to Antony Mor and then to Alonso Sanchez Coello. The religious requirements of the king were better served by the Italian and Spanish Mannerists who covered the endless walls of the Escorial with their anaemic frescoes, and, in strange contrast to them, by the pictures of the old Dutch master Hieronymus Bosch, for whose fantastic visions Philip had a particular predilection (Plate 97). This paradox, deeply rooted in the spiritual climate of the Mannerist period, is close to the division of interests in Rudolf II, whose admiration for Pieter Bruegel—incidentally, a follower of Bosch—was not incompatible with the Mannerist routine of his own Court painters.

The pictures which Philip inherited from his father and from his aunt, Mary of Hungary, who left him a number of Flemish pictures, including Rogier van der Weyden's *Deposition* (Plate 99), as well as some Titians, were all hung in the Escorial together with the pictures Philip had acquired for himself. These included Hieronymus Bosch's *Adoration of the Kings* and Bernard van Orley's *Louvain Madonna*, the first of which the king had obtained by confiscation, the second as a gift of the city.

Philip III was not interested in art. When Rubens came to Madrid in 1603 on a political mission from the Mantuan Court he brought horses and armour as presents for the king, while the chief Minister, the Duke of Lerma, gladly took pictures as well as having his portrait painted by the visitor. Otherwise the Spanish court had all its needs in this direction met by local artists such as Pantoja or Gonzales. In fact, the most important artistic event of the reign was the great fire of 1608, which destroyed many of the treasures of the royal palace of the Pardo.

His son and successor, Philip IV, was the greatest patron and collector of all the Spanish kings. His name is linked with no important military or political triumphs but it will always be connected with that of his Court painter: "The condescension with which he was treated by so great a monarch is hardly to be believed," wrote the Spanish art historian Pacheco of his son-in-law Velazquez. "He had a studio in the Gallery and the king had a key and a seat kept for him in it, so that he could come almost every day and watch him at work." The relationship between patron and painter is almost unique in the history of art, for Velazquez painted for the king for close on forty years and for practically no one else —which means that he had no need to consider the tastes of anyone but his patron, whom he himself had educated in the arts. In a sense it could be said that Velazquez was the only painter who was completely free to follow his own desires, and on top of this he was Keeper of the King's Pictures, which included his own works, so that he could retouch any of his own pictures whenever his artistic development led him to think it desirable.

His whole life and work was devoted to his royal patron, whom he eternalized in splendid pictures (Plate 95) together with his family and Court, including the half-witted or totally moronic dwarfs (Plate 94). For the king, too, he painted his large compositions—the mythologies, the histories (Colour Plate XIV), the scenes from the life of the Court—each of them 'a School of painting', as the later Court painter Anton Raphael Mengs said of *Las Meninas* (Plate 96). Velazquez also helped the king to add to his Gallery. His second trip to Italy, in 1649, was undertaken to buy pictures there and perhaps the finest things he brought back with him were the religious pictures by Tintoretto. At about this time, too, came the purchases from the collection of Charles I of England, at the sale of which, conducted under the Commonwealth, the Spanish agent was one of the most active buyers, securing masterpieces like Raphael's *Madonna della Perla* and Mantegna's *Death of the Virgin*.

Rubens was the other star of the first magnitude in Philip's firmament. Philip had already acquired his *Adoration of the Magi*, when Rubens returned to Madrid in 1628 and remained there for several months, during which time he painted a number of pictures, including several copies after Titian (Plate 107), and he continued to work for the Spanish Court after his return to his own country: in the year 1638 alone, one hundred and twelve of his pictures were sent to Spain for the decoration of the palaces of the Torre de la Parada and Buen Retiro. Only a few fragments remain in the Prado of the mythological cycle he painted for the Torre de la Parada, the great majority having been lost during the War of the Spanish Succession. At the sale held after Rubens's death Philip bought thirty-two pictures, seventeen of them original works by Rubens and the rest copies after Titian. In 1648 Rubens's cartoons for the

Triumph of Faith followed the other works to Spain, but they were lost during the Napoleonic Wars although some of the sketches survive in the Prado. Many smaller tributaries swell these two main streams, and many pictures were acquired by Ambassadors or given by people who were anxious to gain the king's favour, the most splendid of such acquisitions being the *Bacchanal* (Plate 105) painted by Titian for the Court of Ferrara, which was presented by the Spanish Viceroy in Naples, Monterey, in 1638. All things considered, Philip was not only the greatest collector among the Spanish monarchs but also the one in whose reign the native School won an equal place among the others. The position of Velazquez remained uncontested, but Philip also patronized Ribera, who, though he lived by choice in Naples, sent a good deal of his work to Spain (Plate 91).

This nationalism in the royal patronage lasted for a while after Philip, for his successor, Charles II, had Careño and Claudio Coello as his Court painters; but from the end of the seventeenth century onwards foreigners stood higher in the royal favour, the first being Luca Giordano and then, after the Bourbon Philip V, grandson of Louis XIV, had succeeded to the Spanish throne, various French artists were favoured. The only one of the older Spanish artists to benefit from Philip V's reign was Murillo, who was rediscovered and whose fame grew from a local reputation to a national one. The king bought no fewer than twenty-nine of his pictures, the opportunity to do so being afforded by the long sojourn of the Court in Seville, after the fire in the royal palace in Madrid which destroyed a good many of the objects in the royal collections.

Under Charles III, the exponent of 'Enlightened Absolutism' in Spain, the newly founded Academy of the Fine Arts flourished and at the same time the building which now houses the Prado was begun as a Museum of Natural History. The leading painter of the day was Anton Raphael Mengs, whose influence was beneficial as far as the collections were concerned, for it was he who, in 1768, induced the king to buy twenty-nine pictures from the estate of the Marques de la Enseñada—and these pictures included Bruegel's *Triumph of Death*, Velazquez's *Olivarez on Horseback* and Rembrandt's *Portrait of Saskia*. The last of the foreigners to dominate the arts in Spain was Giovanni Battista Tiepolo, some of whose brilliant creations for the Court are in the Prado. He was followed by Francisco de Goya y Lucientes, the last of the Spanish old masters and the first of the moderns.

Goya was appointed Court painter in 1786 and he survived all the changes and upsets of the stormy times which followed. He served

Charles III and Charles IV, who abdicated in favour of his son Ferdinand in 1808, he was equally esteemed by the French conquerors and by the British liberators, and he lived to see Ferdinand VII not only win back the throne of his fathers but also prove himself so unworthy of it that the aged artist preferred to leave his country and die in exile in Bordeaux. The Prado was opened as a public Gallery in 1828, the year in which Goya died, and many of his finest works are now among its proudest possessions (Plates 110–112): they include many of his tapestry cartoons, the celebrated portraits of Charles IV and his family, two compositions commemorating the rising of the people against the French in 1808 (Colour Plate XV), and the wall-paintings he made for his own house in the suburbs of Madrid, to list only a few.

To Joseph Bonaparte, the brother of Napoleon and a child of the French Revolution, it went without saying that the art treasures of the nation should be gathered together in one place and made available to the public, and his decree of December 20, 1809, provided for the creation of a Museum in Madrid, to contain works of all Schools, and to which the various public buildings and also the royal palaces were to contribute works of art. In the following year the plan was widened to include works from the convents suppressed in 1809 or confiscated from private owners, and the palace of Buena Vista was chosen as the seat of the new Museum, but it never entered its projected home as the finances were in too dubious a condition to allow of it. Some of the pictures already selected for the Museum were returned to the convents, others were sold or presented to French Generals, and still others were destined to be sent to Paris to represent the Spanish School in the Musée Napoléon. The selection of these representative pictures gave rise to a good deal of trouble since Vivant-Denon, the driving force behind this idea, considered only six of the pictures offered good enough for the Louvre, and when, later on, he came in person to Madrid and selected a group of 250 pictures, it was too late. It was 1813, and the fall of Napoleon saved the pictures for Spain.

After his restoration Ferdinand VII took over his predecessor's idea and instructed the Academy to form a picture gallery in the Buena Vista palace for the instruction of both masters and pupils, the delight of visitors and the fame of Spain, and in order to accomplish this the Gallery was provided with pictures from the royal palaces. The Prado building, originally destined to be a Museum of Natural History, was found to be better adapted to the needs of the collection. Both the king and his second wife Maria Isabella took a lively interest in the projected Gallery, and in 1818 he decided to enrich it by further additions from the royal collection,

so that when the Museum opened in 1819 it consisted of three galleries
containing 311 pictures, 21 of them by living artists. To this kernel
there was added in 1827 a group of pictures from royal residences, which
had been deposited at the Academy since 1816, as well as a further group
of pictures from the 'reserved rooms' of the Academy.

The earlier history of the last-named group has its amusing side. In
1764 Charles III had ordered the destruction of all pictures of nudities in
the Palace of Madrid, and they were saved only by the intervention of
Mengs, who pointed out that a young painter was in less moral danger if
he copied a Venus by Titian than if he painted her from life. Charles IV
continued the campaign, but the nudities were again reprieved, this time
on condition that they were banished to the 'reserved rooms' in the
Academy, accessible only to the professors. Thus times change: the pictures painted for the delight of that fierce defender of the Church, Philip
II, were condemned by the 'enlightened' monarch of the eighteenth
century and by his successor, whose Court was reckoned a sink of vice!
Even in the Prado, these thirty-one suspect pictures, mostly by Titian and
Rubens, were kept in special rooms on the lower floor, presumably to be
seen only on payment of an extra tip, and, as Richard Ford noted in his
'Handbook for Travellers in Spain' of 1845, "while much upstairs was all
drapery, more below was all flesh, colour and sex. . . ."

The newly arranged Prado was finally opened in 1829 with a collection
of 815 pictures, of which 381 were Spanish, 335 Italian, 99 French and
German; in 1830 two rooms of Netherlandish pictures were added. In the
following years the collection was increased by pictures from Aranjuez
and San Ildefonso, including Rubens's series of the Apostles (Plate 108),
Jordaens's group portrait and several Poussins (Plate 109); and by new
purchases—Velazquez's *Crucifixion* and El Greco's *Trinity*—and above all
by repeated transfers from the Escorial. The most comprehensive addition
came from the Museo de la Trinidad, a depot which had been used by a
Commission appointed in 1836 as a store for pictures from secularized
convents: in 1865 the Prado received 603 pictures, mostly Spanish, but
few of these were exhibited.

In 1868 the Prado, up till then maintained by the king's privy purse,
became the property of the State and subject to a more systematic admin-
istration. In 1894 the modern pictures were removed and transferred to
a new Museum of Modern Art, while in 1912 a Commission was set up
the scope of which is defined in the words, "It is to be hoped that the
Prado, now a wonderful but irregular Gallery, will become a true Museum
organism".

Various steps were taken to raise the Museum to the desired level, and it continued to grow through comprehensive bequests, none more important than that of the great collection of Pablo Bosch (1915), as well as numerous single gifts. The rich material was re-arranged and its value to the student increased, but unfortunately the upheavals of the last few decades have interrupted these efforts. During the Civil War the Prado and its contents were seriously endangered, but were successfully protected by the Government; in 1936 the majority of the pictures were put in places of safety and then sent to Valencia, and as the war came ever nearer, still farther afield to Catalonia. In order to remove them from the danger zone altogether, the International Committee for the Preservation of Spanish Works of Art arranged for them to be taken to Geneva, where the most important of them were exhibited in 1939. At the end of that year they went back to Madrid and were re-installed in their original home, apparently none the worse for their travels. Since then the collection has become even richer with the acquisition of the Cambó collection (1940), which contained few pictures, but all outstandingly good ones such as Botticelli's *Story of Nastagio degli Onesti*, which Vasari saw in Florence in the house of the Tucci family; and in 1941 Murillo's *Immaculate Conception* (Plate 92), which had been bought from the Soult Collection for the Louvre in 1853, and was now presented to the Prado in exchange for some Spanish paintings. Among still later arrivals the Romanesque wall-paintings from Santa Cruz de Maderuelo (Segovia) should at least be mentioned since they enrich the Prado by a chapter up to then entirely missing.

The criticism cited above, made in the Decree appointing the Commission to enquire into the re-organization of the Prado, is scarcely justifiable nowadays when the Prado takes its place with the other great National Galleries of the world. Like them it has a personality of its own, distinguishing it from them. It unites two elements: one is the collection brought together by the princely patrons of the sixteenth and seventeenth centuries in accordance with prevailing ideas and comparable with the best of the other collections assembled on the same principles; and the other is the wealth of Spanish art of many centuries deriving from ecclesiastical and secular collections, also in its way incomparable. Thus the Prado has made a unity of two parts, the one strongly international and the other strongly national. The two belong together, for the preference shown in the fifteenth and sixteenth centuries for foreign art—Flemish in the first case, Italian in the second—is an essential trait of the Spanish civilization and the wealth of the local production is a by-product of the new leading role played by Spain in the seventeenth century, when parts of the Netherlands and of Italy were under Spanish domination and Rubens and the Baroque masters of Italy were only half foreigners.

It is natural enough that the foreign Schools should be excellently represented, since the Flemish Primitives had been assembled by the leading collectors of that time and the Venetian masterpieces had been painted for the new masters of the earth, as their flatterers called Charles V and Philip II. The Spanish material, on the other hand, came from hundreds of churches and convents and could, therefore, be whittled down so that only the very best was retained. On top of this the Spanish kings chose their Court painters carefully and made good use of them. Velazquez is the most striking example, but there were other painters whose work was almost exclusively taken up by the Court so that the Prado now has a virtual monopoly of their pictures. Among those painters whose value was not recognized officially in their own day, Murillo was later discovered by the Court, but El Greco and Zurbarán remained alien to the royal taste; and although the Prado has made good some of the deficiencies caused by this neglect it is still true that, in order to know these masters well, it is necessary to seek them in Seville, Toledo, and the convents of the Estremadura.

The pictures in the Prado have the same spiritual atmosphere, irrespective of the country of their origin. The most impressive of the Flemish Primitives are unfathomable mysteries like Jan van Eyck's *Fountain of Life* or the awe-inspiring visions of Hieronymus Bosch. Raphael in the Prado is not the painter of charming Florentine Madonnas, as he is in Vienna and Florence, but the creator of compositions in the grandest manner. Even Titian, the darling of all the art-loving Hapsburgs, seems quite different in the Prado from what he appears in Vienna, where he is equally splendidly represented. In Vienna are his early, brightly coloured Madonnas, the whole row of state portraits, the piece of compositional bravura which is the *Ecce homo* (Plate 15), and the lyrical *Nymph and Shepherd* (Plate 13): in Madrid he appears principally as the master of erotic passions and ecstatic faith, his voice has warmer tones and his art depth and devotion. In the same way Rubens and other masters seem more expressive in Madrid and it is little wonder, since they painted for Spanish patrons, or their pictures were chosen by such men, in accordance with that spirit which found its expression in all the great painters of the country from Greco to Goya, from the master of religious ecstasy to the spokesman of a humanity convulsed in its innermost self.

NOTES ON THE ILLUSTRATIONS

BOSCH, Jerome (*c.* 1450–1516)

The Temptation of St. Anthony   Plate 97
Panel, 27⅝ × 20⅛ in. (No. 2049)

Weird hybrid creatures taunt the saint, huddled under a straw roof, others are seen in the distant landscape. Their objective realism and the precise and delicate execution of the landscape heighten the fantastic character of this imaginative painting.

CASTILIAN SCHOOL (*c.* 1490)

The Virgin and Child with SS. Thomas and Dominic, adored by the King and Queen of Spain   Plate 89
Panel, 48¾ × 44⅛ in. (No. 1260)

Painted for the Capilla del Cuarto Real de Santo Tomas in Avila.
Portrayed are the monarchs Ferdinand and Isabella with their children and advisers. The mixture of Flemish and Spanish elements in this solemn composition is typical of the period in which it was painted.

DÜRER, Albrecht (1471–1528)

Self-Portrait   Plate 98
Panel, 20½ × 16⅛ in. (No. 2179)

Detailed inscription dated from 1498. Bought at Charles I sale; in the Alcazar since 1686.
Dürer has portrayed himself in this painting with obvious delight in his distinguished appearance. The turn to the right and the fixed glance out of the picture are typical of a self-portrait. The view on the right of a mountainous landscape and cloudy sky is rendered with miniaturelike precision.

GOYA, Francisco de (1746–1828)

An Episode of May 3, 1808: The Execution of Rebels in Madrid   Colour Plate XV
Canvas, 104¾ × 135⅞ in. (No. 749)

Painted after March 9, 1814, when the Spanish

Government granted Goya an additional payment of 1500 Reales to paint the most important episodes in the revolt against the French. The composition greatly influenced the later Impressionists (Manet: *The Execution of Emperor Maximilian*). The crowd, apparently haphazard, is in fact carefully organized by a balance of the main accents.

Nude Maja   Plate 110
Canvas, 38⅛ × 74¾ in. (No. 742)

Painted at the same time as its companion piece, the *Dressed Maja*, probably about 1797–98. Both paintings appeared first under the title 'Gipsies' in the catalogue of Goya's paintings of 1808. Acquired by the Prado in 1901 from the Academy of San Fernando. All proposed identifications of the sitter belong to the realm of fiction. It is the classic pose of the seductive female who through the individual treatment of her body and expression creates as modern an effect as Titian's *Venus of Urbino* (Plate 52) probably did in its time. Manet's *Olympia* (Plate 84) continues this tradition.

The Manikin   Plate 111
Canvas, 105 × 63 in. (No. 802)

One of the numerous designs for tapestry which Goya executed in the first years of his court service. He is here closer to the gay world of the Rococo than to the tragic seriousness of his later works.

Portrait of King Ferdinand VII   Plate 112
Canvas, 83½ × 57½ in. (No. 735)

Painted in 1814 on the occasion of the reinstatement of the Bourbon king.
Acuteness of observation and the abandoning of conventional idealization express the spirit of a time in which the old order was being replaced by a new spirituality. A king begins to become something of an adventurer.

EL GRECO (1541–1614)

The Resurrection   Plate 93
Canvas, 108 × 50 in. (No. 825) Signed.

El Greco has fused Byzantine memories with mannerist tendencies of his period and created a magnificent vision in which all realistic elements of the event disappear completely.

Portrait of Julian Romero with his Patron Saint Louis   Plate 113
Canvas, 81½ × 50 in. (No. 2445)

Apparently it remained in the family till 1890. Bequeathed by Don Luis de Errazu in 1926.
The long inscription which identifies the sitter as Julian Romero is a later addition. The catalogue of the Prado casts doubt on the identification of the sitter with Romero, who died in 1578, especially since the painting is usually dated 1584–94.

MURILLO, Bartolomé Esteban (1618–1682)

The Immaculate Conception   Plate 92
Canvas, 107⅞ × 74¾ in. (No. 2809)

Painted for the hospital of the brotherhood of the Venerable Sacerdotes in Seville. It was removed from Seville by Marshal Soult in 1813 and became the sensation of the Soult collection sale in 1852, where the picture fetched 586.000 francs. It come to the Prado in 1941 by an exchange with the Louvre.
Of the numerous paintings of this subject by Murillo this is probably the most popular. The artist was able to create a symbol which appealed to the simple faith of the people, portraying the sweetness of the heavenly Virgin and the charm of the infant angels.

POUSSIN, Nicolas (1594–1665)

The Parnassus   Plate 109
Canvas, 57⅛ × 77⅝ in. (No. 2313)

Apollo and the Muses are in the centre; poets in idealized costume and without individual features at both sides. The impression the artist wanted to create is one of a festive gathering with little definite action.

RAPHAEL (1483–1520)

The Madonna with the Fish   Plate 101
Canvas, 84⅝ × 62¼ in. (No. 297)

In 1524 the painting was in the chapel of Giovanni Battista del Duco in San Domenico in Naples. In 1638 it was removed from there; brought to Madrid in 1644 and in 1645 it came to the Escorial. In 1813 it was carried off to Paris, where it was transferred from panel to canvas. It was returned in 1822 and brought from the Escorial to the Prado in 1837.
Tobias, led by the Archangel Raphael, carries in his hand a fish, from which the painting derives its name. On the right is St. Jerome. The motif of the Madonna enthroned, which in the earlier *Madonna da Foligno* had been elevated to a monumental composition, is here treated more intimately. This effect is achieved by excluding the landscape and using the half-drawn curtain to link the group with the onlooker.

RIBERA, José de (also called Lo Spagnoletto) (1591–1652)

Jacob's Dream   Plate 91
Canvas, 70½ × 91¾ in. (No. 1117)

Signed: Jusepe de Ribera español f. 1639.
In accordance with the earthbound realism of his Spanish temperament Ribera foregoes all idealization of the biblical story and depicts the patriarch as a peasant exhausted from a heavy day's work.

ROGIER VAN DER WEYDEN (c. 1400–1464)

The Descent from the Cross   Plate 99
Panel, 86⅝ × 103⅛ in. (No. 2825)

Painted for Louvain; it came to Spain through Mary of Hungary. It has recently been transferred to the Prado.
Lifesize figures, arranged as a relief in front of a gold ground, fill the composition. Bright local colours increase the expressiveness of the painting.

RUBENS, Peter Paul (1577–1640)

The Garden of Love   Plate 106
Canvas, 78 × 11⅜ in. (No. 1690)

Bought from Rubens's estate.
The various couples probably represent the artist's brothers-in-law and sisters-in-law of the family Fourment. Richness of architecture and costume combine to intensify the atmosphere of *joie de vivre*.

Adam and Eve Plate 107

Canvas, 101⅛ × 72½ in. (No. 1692)

A copy of the painting by Titian (No. 429) in the Prado. Painted during Rubens's second stay in Spain, in 1628–9. The copy is treated with a greater freedom than its classic prototype, due both to Rubens's temperament and the fact that it was created a century later than the original.

The Apostle Paul Plate 108

Panel, 42½ × 33⅛ in. (No. 1657)

Belongs to a series which Rubens painted for the Duke of Lerma in 1603. Whereas the other apostles are portrayed standing, Paul is shown seated in a powerful attitude.

TITIAN (*c.* 1485–1576)

The Deposition Plate 100

Canvas, 53⅞ × 69⅝ in. (No. 440)

Signed Titianus Vecellius Aeques Caes.
The painting, sent to King Philip in 1559, came to the Escorial in 1574 and in 1837 it passed to the Museum. The fundamental difference between this and the artist's early version of the same subject in the Louvre characterize Titian's late style and the renewed religious fervour of the second half of the century. The physical functions of lifting, carrying and lowering have become immaterial compared with the power of the emotions conveyed. The scene takes place as if behind a glass screen, excluding any sound.

Portrait of Emperor Charles V on Horseback
Plate 103

Canvas, 130¾ × 109⅞ in. (No. 410)

This painting came to Spain with the collection of Queen Mary of Hungary (a sister of Emperor Charles V). It hung in several royal palaces and suffered damage during the fire of the Alcazar in 1734.
It represents Charles V at the Battle of Muehlberg and was painted in Augsburg in 1548. The Emperor is shown at the moment of his triumph over Protestant Germany—a history painting in the true sense of the word. All compositional devices serve to convey the impression of the lonely victor as an instrument of higher forces.

Portrait of King Philip II in Armour
Plate 104

Canvas, 76 × 43¾ in. (No. 411)

Probably painted in Augsburg in 1550; sent to Mary of Hungary and probably came to Spain with the collection of her paintings.
In contrast to the equestrian portrait of his father (Plate 103), this picture aims at the objective portrayal of a personality of which the artist did not have so deep and sympathetic an understanding as he did of Charles V, to whom Titian felt somehow inwardly related.

The Worship of Venus Plate 105

Canvas, 67¾ × 68⅞ in. (No. 419)

Signed Di Ticianus f.
Painted for Alfonso d'Este of Ferrara in 1516–18; it was brought to Rome in 1598 by Cardinal-Legate Aldobrandini and remained in the Palazzo Ludovisi till 1638. In that year it was presented to Philip IV by Viceroy Count Monterey and hung in the Alcazar.
The composition is taken from the description of a painting by the ancient author Philostratus, in which playing Cupids have the main part. The bright colours of wings and apples create a summery gaiety, characteristic of Titian's Ferrarese period.

VELAZQUEZ, Diego (1599–1660)

The Surrender of Breda ('*Las Lanzas*')
Colour Plate XIV

Canvas, 120⅞ × 108⅝ in. (No. 1172)

Painted in 1634 for the Salon De Reinos del Buen Retiro and from there brought to the New Palais in Madrid. The surrender of Breda by Justus von Nassau to the Spanish Commander, Marquis de Spinola, took place on June 5, 1625.
The grandeur of the composition, with loose grouping of the vanquished and the tight massing of the Spaniards, characterized as victors by the stiff forest of lances, and the dignity in the spiritual characterization of the Commanders, make this painting one of the greatest history paintings of all times.

The Dwarf Calabacillas (*known as Bobo de Coria*) Plate 94

Canvas, 41¾ × 32⅝ in. (No. 1205)

This painting was in various royal palaces before it came to the Prado. Don Juan de

Calabacillas was in the service of Philip IV from 1632 until his death in 1639. Velazquez portrayed a number of these court dwarfs and court fools.

Portrait of Philip IV of Spain   Plate 95
Canvas, 75¼ × 49⅝ in. (No. 1184)

Painted about 1634–6 for the Torre de la Parada, and came from there to the New Palais in Madrid.
The King in hunting costume, with his dog beside him, is standing in a spacious landscape. This motif, somewhat reminiscent of Titian's portrait of Charles V of 1532 (Prado) is subordinated to the picturesque intentions of the artist. The royal figure is part of the muted harmony of landscape and costume.

The Maids of Honour ('Las Meninas')
Plate 96
Canvas, 125¼ × 108⅝ in. (No. 1174)

The painting, executed in 1656, was originally called 'The Family' and derives its present name from the two maids of honour attending the little Princess Margarita standing in the centre. Velazquez is busy painting her when the royal parents, visible in the mirror in the background, enter the room. The mixture of reality and fantasy, the complex composition, and the grotesque court entourage surrounding the little girl, alienate at first and require much devoted study.

VERONESE, Paolo (1528–1588)

The Finding of Moses   Plate 102
Canvas, 19⅝ × 16⅞ in. (No. 502)

The group of richly dressed young women, whose interest centres on the child found in so strange a way, was often treated by Veronese.

ZURBARAN, Francisco de (1598–1664)
St. Peter Nolasco's Vision of the Heavenly Jerusalem   Plate 90
Canvas, 70½ × 88 in. (No. 1236)

Bent over his book, the Saint has fallen asleep. An angel points to the Heavenly Jerusalem appearing in the clouds. The two large figures in white emerge mysteriously from the surrounding darkness.

The Prado

THE RIJKSMUSEUM IN AMSTERDAM

AS THE FRENCH Revolution, rounded off by the Napoleonic period, introduced the era of the centralized national States, so one of its creations, the Louvre museum in Paris, became the starting point for similar institutions elsewhere. In the same way that the Revolution produced a national collection in the Louvre, so in other countries we see similar national museums come into existence, among them the Rijksmuseum in Amsterdam and the Galleries in Madrid and Berlin. The essential difference between that in Amsterdam and the others is that, from the very beginning, the Rijksmuseum concentrated more strongly on the art of its own country, and in this respect it is closer to the Uffizi than to any other of the great museums. This preference for Dutch art is carried so far that the Rijksmuseum even attaches less importance to the periods in which Dutch painting had not yet reached full maturity, or had passed its peak, and the maximum emphasis is placed on the one epoch which is generally regarded as the Golden Age of Dutch art. In the seventeenth century Holland achieved its independence as a nation and built up its colonial empire through a heroic struggle against powerful enemies; it grew rich by means of its expanding trade, gave the world the two ideals of religious tolerance and International Law, and, over and above this, produced a school of painting which is almost unique in the number of its talented masters and in their close connection with the life of the nation as a whole.

Great artists appear in groups rather than one at a time, as we may see in other schools of painting besides the Dutch; it is one of the mysteries of history that at one moment the genius of a nation expresses itself in one special field of activity, producing a rich crop of talent, while other periods remain relatively barren. The lifetimes of Hals and Rembrandt, Ruisdael and Vermeer, Jan Steen, Hobbema and many others, all fell within much the same period of time, just as there were similar outcrops of creative activity in other countries—the Early Renaissance in Florence, the Age of Elizabeth in England, the *siglo de oro* in Spain, the era of Louis XIV in France, the flowering of music in Vienna and of German literature about 1800. Many attempts have been made to explain these festivals in the calendar of humanity, and, so far as Holland is concerned,

Hippolyte Taine and his disciples devoted many brilliant pages to the search for the reasons why art flourished at that precise time and place; yet all their references to republican pride, to the attitude of mind of the burghers, to the economic prosperity and so on, can hardly explain why Rembrandt created timeless masterpieces at just that moment.

Such attempts at explanation lead us to the sociological aspect of artistic production, which Holland presents in an almost unique fashion. No other people has shown so extensive and so firmly rooted an interest in painting as one finds in this country. It is not to be wondered at that the great merchants of Amsterdam, who controlled world trade, should set up as patrons of the arts, able to attract the art market to their own city. What is much more noteworthy is that everybody was interested in pictures and seems to have invested in them. We learn of farmers, millers, small tradesmen, all speculating in pictures and accumulating them in sheds and attics; pedlars hawked pictures from door to door as in other countries they hawked household goods. Bakers, butchers and landlords took them from painters in lieu of payment, and painters could live on their art more easily here than elsewhere since their works were a form of currency.

That is one side of the astonishing ubiquity of painting in seventeenth-century Holland, but it had also an important part to play in the innumerable corporate activities of the townsmen, who organized themselves in Shooting Companies, governed the countless orphanages, hospitals and almshouses through committees, and elected supervisors of the guilds, welfare societies and teaching faculties. Wherever people came together in such activities for the public good, they seem to have felt the need to have themselves portrayed as a group. The group portrait—that is, a portrait of a number of people who are not related by blood but are jointly engaged in some common service—is the most striking form of Dutch painting in this period (Plate 127).

These characteristics of Dutch life make it easier to understand some of the particular qualities of their painting: the enormous production at all levels of quality; the existence of hundreds of painters, all able to make a living out of their work; the specialization in different branches of art—portrait painting, landscape, interiors, sea-pieces, still life and so on—arranged, as it were, on a commercial basis; the preference for a small scale and popular themes which would appeal to the average buyer. In addition there is the immediate and unselfconscious relationship to nature which sets Holland apart, in a century that, on the whole, is the century of the Baroque.

These remarks indicate the background of the Rijksmuseum's system of collection, the leading idea of which is to present the art of the nation in the form in which it is closest to national ideals; not merely Dutch painting of all periods (although, naturally, minor phases are included) but painting which is most specifically Dutch. It is worth stressing that this programme did not exist from the beginning but grew up in the course of the Museum's development.

In fact, the beginnings of the Museum may be traced back to the need to conserve the art treasures of the nation, which had been scattered by the storms of the Napoleonic era. When Louis Napoleon, the Emperor's brother and representative in Holland, moved his residence from Utrecht to Amsterdam in 1808, he ordered the creation of a great Royal Museum in the new Residence, and he arranged for it to be housed in the famous Stadhuis, which then served as the Royal Palace. This Museum was to include all forms of art, and the idea was a reflection of the gigantic agglomeration of works of art which the great Napoleon had undertaken to bring together in Paris, and at the same time it was a measure of sound trusteeship which provided a home for the many works of art that had been scattered by the political, social and economic upheavals of the time. The works assembled in the new Museum were in fact a very mixed company; to begin with, there were the collections from the Palaces of the House of Orange, collected in The Hague after the dynasty fell in 1795; then there were sixty-five pictures bought for 100,000 guilders at the van der Pot Sale in 1810, a group of seven pictures belonging to the City of Amsterdam, and, finally, a huge quantity of miscellaneous objects.

Other pictures were bought in the following year from the heirs of the Van Heteren Collection and at the Bicker Sale, and here, as in the earlier collections, the Dutch School was preponderant, as indeed was the case in almost all collections of the time outside Italy. Nor is it very surprising that these bits and pieces from private collections and former Royal Palaces were mostly of average quality, yet this mixed bag did contain some things which have always been regarded as first-rate. For example, the van der Pot Collection had van Goyen's *View of the Valkhof near Nymegen* (Plate 124), Govaert Flinck's *Isaac blessing Jacob* and Jan Hackaert's masterpiece *The Avenue of Ash Trees* (Plate 125); while from the Van Heteren Collection there came Adriaen Brouwer's *Village Merrymaking*, Jan Brueghel's *Latona threatened by the Peasants*, Jan Steen's *Feast of St. Nicholas* (Plate 136), and Rubens's *Carrying of the Cross*, a sketch for the altarpiece from the Abbey at Afflighem which is now in the Museum at Brussels. The additions from The Hague were still more important, as a few examples will show: *The Virgin with Four Female Saints*, by the anonymous master who has been christened 'The Virgo inter Virgines Master', taking his name from this picture; the portrait of Philip of Burgundy by Mabuse, Jan van Scorel's *The Magdalen in a Landscape* (Plate 118) and two characteristic pictures by Cornelisz. van Haarlem. Among the seventeenth-century works the one which has gained most popularity is not a Dutch but a Flemish picture—the double portrait of Prince William II and his child bride, Princess Mary Stuart, the daughter of Charles I (Plate 129). The Dutch pictures of the same period include Carel Fabritius's *Decollation of the Baptist*, Melchior Hondecoeter's *Magpie Philosopher*, Jan Steen's *Joyous Return* and *The Quack*, and Adriaen van de Venne's *Fisher of Souls*, an allegory on the negotiations with Spain during the twelve year armistice. This allegory was intended to be a memorial of an important episode in Holland's struggle for independence, and it hung for many years in the Palace of the Stadholder.

Another picture has an allegorical significance which is the main reason for its popularity, and yet this meaning is possibly a later interpretation, for Jan Asselyn's *Enraged Swan* (Plate 120) may originally have been meant to represent no more than a swan defending its brood against a dog swimming towards the nest. Later inscriptions have turned the dog into an Enemy of the State ('Viant van de Staat'), one of the eggs in the nest has become 'Holland', the swan the agent of the Council ('De Raadspensionaris'), and the whole an allegory on the watchfulness of Jan de Wit. It seems too dramatic a presentation for a simple scene of animal life and the ease with which a deeper meaning can be read into the picture shows at least how living a force patriotism was in seventeenth-century Holland. The splendid role played by this century can be seen more easily than anywhere else in the group of seven pictures which the City of Amsterdam made over to the new foundation and which have since formed the backbone of the collection.

The masterpiece in this group is Rembrandt's *Night Watch* (Colour Plate XVI), the company of Civic Guards under the command of Captain Frans Banning Cocq and Lieutenant Willem van Ruytenburg. This greatest of all the Dutch group portraits was preserved in the Hall of the Crossbowmen until 1712, when it was transferred to the Stadhuis. After it went to the Rijksmuseum it came to be regarded so much as a symbol, so much as a monument, that for many years there could be no question of cleaning it and the picture became more and more like the title which it has borne since *c.* 1800. By the time that one of the most recent Directors, Dr Schmidt-Degener, was appointed, this symbol had

V. Jacob Ruisdael: *The Mill near Wijk bij Duurstede.* Amsterdam, Rijksmuseum

become so dirty that he made it a condition of his acceptance of the office that he should be allowed to have the picture cleaned and restored to its original brightness of colour. In fact, the fateful moment did not arrive until 1945, after the German Occupation, when the picture, which had been hidden away for safety, had to be relined. The opportunity was then taken for a thorough cleaning, with the result that one critic summed up the change in the words "A *Night Watch* has been destroyed, but a Rembrandt has been rediscovered".

The other pictures transferred from the Stadhuis to the newly-founded Museum display the same vitality and self-awareness—for example, Bartholomeus van der Helst's *Banquet of the Civic Guard on June 18, 1648*, celebrating the Peace of Munster which recognized the independence of the Dutch Republic (Plate 121), or Govaert Flinck's picture of a similar subject. Three of the other pictures in this group have the same historical interest but the seventh is one in which the historical interest is entirely submerged by its incomparable artistic quality. The *Staalmeesters*, the governors of the Cloth Guild for the year 1661, were painted by Rembrandt in the following year (Plate 127) as one of the usual commemorative group portraits of bodies which changed from year to year, and this group is generally reckoned as one of Rembrandt's greatest masterpieces —which is the same as saying that it is one of the greatest pictures ever painted. This picture summarizes those things in which seventeenth-century Holland could take justifiable pride—its whole way of life and the part it played in great art.

The new establishment began promisingly enough in this way, but it came to an abrupt end in 1810 with the French annexation of Holland. The Museum continued to exist but had no money for expansion until, five years later, Holland became an independent kingdom which also included Belgium. In September 1815 it was officially named the Rijksmuseum and was moved into the so-called Trippenhuis, which had been built in 1660 for the wealthy Tripp family. The new King, William I, took a personal interest in the Museum and made several purchases for it, in which he did not restrict himself to pictures of purely Dutch origin, for he bought a Garofalo and two Gaspar Poussins as well as Frans Hals's *Jolly Toper* (Plate 131) in 1816, Jordaens's *Satyr* in 1827, and Gerbrandt van den Eeckhout's *Christ and the Adultress* in 1828. Other new acquisitions came from various bequests and from an exchange with the Mauritshuis in The Hague, and to this latter the Rijksmuseum owes Paulus Potter's *Bear Hunt* as well as several pictures by Rubens and van Dyck, who, as Flemings, then came within the province of a Dutch Museum.

The Revolution of 1830, which gave Belgium her independence, destroyed the programme mapped out for the Rijksmuseum and apparently suspended its activities, for it remained inactive for nearly half a century, during which time very little is heard of it. From time to time pictures were sold and the proceeds used to buy works by living artists, but these new acquisitions went to Haarlem, where a special Museum of Modern Art was set up. Two important collections added to the Museum in Amsterdam are worth mentioning: the Dupper Bequest of 1870 which was important because the kernel of this rich collection went back to the old Rombout Cabinet, and, of the sixty-four pictures which the nation acquired, several were first-rate—Terborch's *Portraits of a Man and Woman*, Aelbert Cuyp's *Mountain Landscape*, Jan van Goyen's *View of the Maas near Dordrecht*, Salomon Koninck's *Solomon's Idolatry*, Nicolaes Maes's *Old Woman Spinning*, Hobbema's *Watermill*, Jan Steen's '*Prinsjesdag*' and others. The other bequest followed in 1873 and consisted of pastels and oil paintings by the Genevan artist J. E. Liotard, the gift of a descendant of his. This was one of those bequests which museums everywhere can hardly avoid, however ill they fit into their programme, but at that time the Rijksmuseum can hardly be said to have had a programme.

It eventually achieved one, however, in 1875, through the efforts of an energetic and competent man, Jonkheer V. E. L. de Stuers, who was not a specialist but the civil servant responsible for art and science in the Ministry of the Interior. He saw that, if the Rijksmuseum was ever to win a place for itself in the intellectual life of the nation, a thorough-going reform was necessary to break out of the rut of routine into which it had settled, and in order to achieve this he began arranging for the Museum to have new quarters. The architect P. J. H. Cuypers erected a Gothic building between 1877 and 1885, which, in that eclectic period of architecture, ranked as a masterpiece, although by modern standards it does not seem to be particularly well adapted to its purpose: as so often happened in that period the interior was sacrificed to the exterior, and the principal efforts of the architect were lavished on the façade and on obtaining 'purity of style' at the expense of the exhibition galleries, means of communication, lighting and storage space. A later critic maliciously remarked that the only real use the building could be put to would be to remove all the partition walls and use the resulting enormous hall to shelter a monument to Cuypers. It is easy enough to be wise after the event but, in spite of all its faults, when the Museum was built it was an important event, for the removal of the Museum to a building specially designed for it—a building which contemporaries thought highly

monumental—gave it almost at once an important place in the cultural
life of the nation. Before the new building was even roofed the collection
began to expand considerably both from bequests and from purchases; the
van der Poll Bequest of 1880, for example, contained no fewer than five
hundred good pictures. Then followed the bequests of Mevrouw van
Winter and of Jonkheer van Swinderen, consisting mostly of family
portraits, but still more important than these was the foundation of the
Rembrandt Society as a result of the rebirth of the Museum. In the
seventy-odd years of its existence this Society has proved itself the de-
pendable and efficient friend of the Dutch National Collections in general,
and the Rijksmuseum has not been the least among its beneficiaries.

When the Museum was re-opened in 1885 it contained 888 pictures
previously in the Trippenhuis, the nineteenth-century pictures which up
to then had been kept separately at Haarlem, 115 pictures belonging to
the City of Amsterdam and other public bodies, 224 pictures from the van
der Hoop Collection which had been left to the City and provisionally
stored, and finally, 34 pictures from the Archaeological Society. Since
then the collection has grown continually and only a few examples can be
given here: Vermeer's *Young Woman reading a Letter* (Plate 138), Judith
Leyster's *Merry Drinker*, Lucas van Leyden's *Sermon* (Plate 116), and in
1904, Geertgen tot Sint Jans's *Adoration of the Magi* (Plate 115), one of the
few really outstanding Primitives in the Museum. In 1907, the Hoogen-
dijck Collection consisting of 86 pictures, mostly of the early German and
Dutch Schools and the remainder of seventeenth-century pictures, was
deposited on loan, and when a few years later the heirs took back their
property they left 36 pictures as a gift. One of the most important
acquisitions was the purchase of 40 pictures from the famous Six Collection, including Vermeer's *Maid pouring out Milk*, followed a dozen years
later by the presentation of his *Little Street in Delft* (Plate 137) from the
same source. Soon afterwards came the Drukker Collection, all too rich in
works of the Hague School, beginning a new chapter which may be
compared with the relationship between the National and the Tate
Galleries in London, for from this time on the modern pictures, housed in
a separate wing added to the Rijksmuseum, formed an independent body
which developed rapidly, leaving the mother-house to concentrate
steadily on filling up the gaps in the older masters. Among the additions
made in the last few years to the masterpieces of the older Schools special
mention must be made of three from the Hermitage in Leningrad—
Rembrandt's *Peter denying Christ* and Antonis Mor's portraits of Sir Thomas
Gresham (Plate 117) and his wife.

These and other late-comers, however important in themselves, have not altered the basic character of the collection. Even the German Occupation was no more than a temporary interruption; the building was evacuated and the pictures removed to safety, to return to their home after it had been renovated. The essential features of the Museum as we now see it today are those given definitive form by Schmidt-Degener's Directorship. Before his time the Museum had been grievously overcrowded for many years since all their possessions, even second-rate works and replicas, were on exhibition. This necessity of using every square foot of wall space made it impossible to arrange the pictures in an orderly way and when the new Director took office the Museum was no more than a confusing and unpleasing depot. He used to say jokingly that his principal service had been to provide ample storage rooms, in which hundreds of less important pictures could be put away and yet be accessible to specialists who were not satisfied with the hundreds of pictures on exhibition. This increase in the amount of wall space available allowed of a more systematic arrangement, with the important works separated from the less important ones. The way in which the *Night Watch*, always the symbol of the Rijksmuseum and a sort of national anthem in paint, was rehung so as to form the centre and climax of the Museum is, in my opinion, a masterpiece of museum technique and shows profound understanding. The picture has ceased to be a night scene, inviting a romantic interpretation, and has returned to its original meaning as a fragment from the daily life of Holland in the heroic age, supreme through its artistic mastery rather than by any adventitious literary means.

Two points in the Rijksmuseum's programme are worthy of further study. The first is the preference shown for the seventeenth century, as compared to the fragmentary representation of the earlier Schools. Some of the earlier pictures have been in the Museum for a long time—for example, those by Geertgen tot Sint Jans or the Master of the Virgo inter Virgines—while others have been acquired to fill up gaps, such as the *Seven Works of Charity*, by an anonymous artist, also called the Master of Alkmaar (Plate 114), which was bought in 1918, but the Late Gothic art of Holland can be studied elsewhere better than in the Rijksmuseum. Even Renaissance artists like Jan van Scorel and Cornelisz. van Oostsanen, Lucas van Leyden and Dirck Jacobsz., Pieter Aertsz., and Dirck Barendsz. are not completely represented. The seventeenth century, on the other hand, is given pride of place and its completeness is obviously a cause of great satisfaction. Here we find the great colourists, Rembrandt, Vermeer, Frans Hals, and surrounding them there are the representatives of all the special subdivisions into which Dutch painting split up—group portraits of Civic Guards, Hospital Governors, doctors taking part in anatomical demonstrations, portraits of individuals and families, landscapes and seascapes, interiors, genre scenes, still life and flowers; all the subjects, in fact, which could be in demand in a country in which pictures were an ordinary article of commerce.

The second point, which the rearrangement of the Rijksmuseum has brought out more clearly, is what might be called 'variety in unity'—that is, the manifold local variations in Dutch painting of the classic century. The Rijksmuseum has always been in Amsterdam and in fact many of the pictures there are the legal property of that wealthy city and are only on loan to the State Museum. Nevertheless, it has not succumbed to the danger of becoming nothing more than a Museum of the art of the city, as are those in Haarlem, Delft or Leyden, but has always contrived to retain the breadth of outlook of a national museum. The principal Dutch cities lie near together in the south of the country, closely linked by an orderly system of communications, forming a genuine unity of life and work. In spite of this close link-up and community of interests, they have retained their individual characteristics, those characteristics which they had already begun to develop before they became parts of the same State. Even the most casual visitor to Holland cannot fail to notice the clear distinctions in vocabulary and accent, customs and outlook, between Amsterdam and The Hague, Rotterdam and Utrecht, and how much friendly banter goes on between them. This parochialism and individualism did not prevent the growth of a healthy national feeling and the same federalism holds good for the arts. Every city developed its own School and in this fruitful seventeenth century they all competed with one another in richness and originality. A general view of all these Schools can be obtained in the Rijksmuseum. Naturally, the local Museums form an indispensable complement to this and nobody can really know the Haarlem or Leyden Schools unless he has studied in the Frans Hals Museum at Haarlem or Lakenhall at Leyden, but nowhere outside the Rijksmuseum do these fragments form themselves into so natural and grand a unity. In its exhibition galleries we can experience the art of Utrecht, Leyden, Amsterdam, Haarlem, The Hague, Dordrecht, Delft and Rotterdam, and when we have seen these Schools we have grasped the essence of a great national art.

Yet it would not be complete without some foreign contributions. The Dutch half of the Netherlands is so closely linked, ethnically, politically and culturally, with the southern Provinces which make up modern

Belgium that they must also have influenced each other in artistic matters. In spite of the originality and independence of Dutch painting in the seventeenth century—not to mention the earlier periods—it was nevertheless frequently inspired by the art of its southern neighbour, and above all by the School of Antwerp just across the border. Jacob Jordaens, Frans Snyders (see Plate 227), David Teniers and other Antwerp painters have always been regarded in Holland as being half compatriots, and it was only right and proper that examples of their work should find a place in the Dutch National Gallery.

Even Italian art could not be entirely unrepresented, for the picture of Dutch painting in the seventeenth century would be incomplete without some reference to the role of Holland as the centre of the international art trade and of the part played by Italian works of art in it. "Youth has too much to do, to waste time in travelling," Rembrandt observed in this connection, "Why seek Italian masterpieces in Italy, where they are scattered and inaccessible, when there is an abundance of them here at home!" Even though Rembrandt never went to Italy, Italy came to him; and that holds good for Dutch painters in general, quite apart from the fact that many Dutch painters did go to Italy to study. There, these travellers from the North evolved a special type of picture which has a whole room at the Rijksmuseum devoted to it. In a Museum of Dutch painting the art of the Italians themselves can be no more than a modest accompaniment. From its foundation the Rijksmuseum has possessed a few examples, and from time to time a few more have trickled in, until the Rembrandt Society started to make some systematic purchases, partly from the Grand Ducal collection of Oldenbourg at its dispersal after the First World War. These purchases included pictures by Fra Angelico, Filippino Lippi, Lorenzo Lotto, G. B. Moroni, Tintoretto and Tiepolo, but scarcely any of them are of the first importance, certainly not by comparison with the masterpieces of Dutch painting to be found in the Rijksmuseum. As a result, they do not compete for the visitor's attention, but their modest and unassuming presence adds a few significant touches to the great picture of the art of Holland.

NOTES ON THE ILLUSTRATIONS

AERTSZ., Pieter (1509–1575)

The Egg Dance   Plate 122
Panel, 33¾ × 50 in. (No. 5). Dated 1557.

Purchased in 1839 from the Schepeler (von
Scheppler) Collection, Aix-la-Chapelle.
The aims of a mannerist artist are here ex-
pressed through a *genre* scene.

ASSELYN, Jan (1610–1652)

The Enraged Swan   Plate 120
Canvas, 58¼ × 69 in. (No. 382)

Signed with monogram.
Taken over as part of the National Museum at
the Hague in 1801. The symbolic character is
emphasized by the many inscriptions; or
perhaps imposed by them on the picture. It
represents the defence of Holland against her
enemies by Jan de Witt in an allegory drawn
from animal life.

BERCKHEYDE, Gerrit (1638–1698)

The Flower Market in Amsterdam   Plate 123
Canvas, 18 × 24½ in. (No. 483)

Signed.
Van der Hoop collection, Amsterdam. Be-
queathed to the City of Amsterdam in 1854.
On loan to the Museum since 1885.

DOU, Gerard (1613–1675)

Self-Portrait   Plate 141
Panel, 17½ × 15 in. (No. 791)

Signed. Dupper bequest, 1870.
There are more than a dozen self-portraits by
Dou in existence, dating from various periods
of his life, and reflecting various moods. In this
picture the emphasis lies on the informal: a
curtain is pulled aside, and the artist is seen
looking out of the window.

DYCK, Anthony van (1599–1641)

*Prince William II and his Young Wife,
Princess Mary Stuart*   Plate 129
Canvas, 73 × 57 in. (No. 857)

Judging by the dress and the ornaments of the
sitters, this picture was done in England in
1641, perhaps with additions by another hand.
In the Huis ten Bosch in 1637, transferred here
with the National Museum at the Hague in
1808.

GEERTGEN tot Sint Jans (c. 1465–1495)

The Adoration of the Magi   Plate 115
Panel, 36¾ × 28½ in. (No. 950A1)

Purchased in 1904.
The large figures of the magi in the foreground
correspond to the small figures in the background, leading the cavalcades. The reveren-
tial attitudes of these figures show their intense
awe. The ruined stable is symbolic.

GOYEN, Jan van (1596–1656)

The Valkhof at Nijmegen   Plate 124
Canvas, 37½ × 52¾ in. (No. 991)

Signed and dated 1641.
The dark boat in the left foreground is used as
a compositional offset to the broad shape of the
castle walls. On the left, in the background is a
typical, cloudy seascape.

HACKAERT, Jan (1628–1699)

The Ash-Tree Avenue   Plate 125
Canvas, 24½ × 21½ in. (No. 1021)

Acquired as part of the van der Pot Collection.
Hackaert's masterpiece; as in his other pictures,
certain details were probably painted by
Adriaen van de Velde.

HALS, Frans (1580–1666)

Portrait of Man and Wife   Plate 130
Canvas, 56¼ × 66¾ in. (No. 1084)

In the Museum since 1852.
Thought to be a portrait of the artist with his wife. The casual intimacy of the figures conveys expressly their enjoyment of their natural surroundings, and is reminiscent of Rembrandt's self-portrait with Saskia on his lap.

The Jolly Toper   Plate 131
Canvas, 32½ × 26¾ in. (No. 1091)

Acquired from the Baroness van Leyden's Collection in 1816.
The reveller, half-drunk, appears to be greeting the spectator.

HELST, Bartholomeus van der (1613–1670)

Banquet of the Civic Guard   Plate 121
Canvas, 93 × 219 in. (No. 1135)

Fully signed and dated 1648.
Originally in the St. Joris-, or Voetboog-doelen, later in the large court-martial room of the Old Town Hall. On loan to the Museum since 1808.
A supreme example of this kind of collective portrait, which was much admired; every person represented contributed to the cost of the painting. In this picture a company of musketeers is shown at a banquet provided by the city to celebrate the conclusion of the Treaty of Westphalia on June 18, 1648. As opposed to Rembrandt, whom he succeeded in popular esteem as the favourite painter of this type of picture, van der Helst was concerned to depict every sitter distinctly and to the best advantage rather than group the figures in an effective composition.

HOOCH, Pieter de (1629–1683)

The Small Country House   Plate 139
Canvas, 24¾ × 19 in. (No. 1251)

A. van der Hoop Collection; bequeathed to the City of Amsterdam; on loan to the Museum since 1885.
Domesticity, the sentiment most favoured by de Hooch in his interiors, sets the tone of this open-air scene. From the courtyard a further view into a garden is offered through a gate. This stratification of space is characteristic of the master.

KALF, Willem (1619–1693)

Still Life   Plate 119
Canvas, 29 × 25 in. (No. 1320)

Purchased in 1821 from the A. J. Brandt Collection.
This still life gives a good impression of the wealth of the Dutch middle classes.

LUCAS VAN LEYDEN (1494–1533)

The Sermon   Plate 116
Panel, 53½ × 39¼ in. (No. 1452)

Signed with a monogram.
In the nineteenth century recorded in various Russian collections; acquired by purchase in 1897.
The sermon is preached in a Renaissance church—the style was at that time still a novelty in the Netherlands. *Genre* themes—the crouching, sleeping women, for instance—were generally favoured in the north. On the right is a view into a forecourt, where alms are being distributed.

MASTER OF ALKMAAR, also known as the Master of the Seven Works of Charity

Feeding the Hungry   Plate 114
Panel, 40¾ × 22½ in. (No. 1538 B1)

One of a series of seven pictures showing the works of mercy, which were purchased in 1918 from the great church of St. Lawrence in Alkmaar, their original setting. The artist has been plausibly identified with a certain Cornelis Buys, whose name is recorded through the first quarter of the sixteenth century. The scene is conceived very much as a *genre* composition, and set in a typical Dutch urban landscape. This picture is, in effect, a predecessor of the later Dutch realism.

MOR, Antonis (1512–1576)

Sir Thomas Gresham   Plate 117
Panel, 36½ × 30¾ in. (No. 1673 B1)

Obtained by the Empress Catherine of Russia as part of the Sir Robert Walpole Collection in 1779, and purchased from the Hermitage.

Sir Thomas Gresham was the financial agent of the English Crown in the Netherlands, and founder of the Stock Exchange.

The identity of the sitter cannot be stated with absolute certainty. In any case the portrait may be taken as a typical representation of a great merchant and financier of the time when England was becoming established as a great power.

OSTADE, Adriaen van (1610–1684)

Travellers Resting   Plate 135
Panel, 15 × 12½ in. (No. 1818)

Signed and dated 1671.
Acquired in 1809 from the van Heteren Collection.
Painted during the artist's last period.

REMBRANDT (1606–1669)

The Night Watch   Colour Plate XVI
Canvas, 144 × 175 in. (No. 2016)

Signed: Rembrandt f. 1642.
Originally in the Banqueting hall of the Cloveniers-Doelen, since 1715 in the small court-martial room of the Old Town Hall, 1815 in the Trippenhuis. On loan from the City of Amsterdam since 1808.
This is the *chef d'œuvre* of Rembrandt's first great period, and the most impressive of all Dutch military group portraits. The company of musketeers is shown on the march led by its Captain, Frans Banning Cocq, and Lieutenant Willem van Ruytenburg. The other participants, all of whose names are recorded, each contributed 100 guilders; many of them considered it disparaging to be placed in less prominent positions in the composition. During centuries of neglect the picture had grown very dark; but on its return from its war-time shelter it was restored to its original magnificent colouring.

The so-called 'Jewish Bride'   Plate 126
Canvas, 45½ × 67 in. (No. 2019)

Signed: Rembrandt f.
A. van der Hoop bequest to the City of Amsterdam in 1854. On loan to the Museum since 1885.
The couple represented have been variously identified: as biblical figures (Isaac and Rebecca), as historical personages, or as Rem-

brandt's contemporaries (Don Miguel de Barrios and his wife Abigail de Pina) and as Rembrandt's son Titus with his wife. The wonderful colouring of this picture, which belongs to Rembrandt's latest period, and the overwhelming impression of the bond between the two figures which it conveys, make the question of identification seem relatively unimportant.

The Staalmeesters   Plate 127
Canvas, 77 × 112 in. (No. 2017)

Signed: Rembrandt f. 1661.
Originally in the Staalhof (Cloth Hall) in Amsterdam. Transferred to the Town Hall in 1778. On loan from the City of Amsterdam since 1808.
The five syndics of the cloth-merchants' guild, accompanied by an official, are grouped informally round a table. They appear to have interrupted some administrative activity in order to interview a person who is facing them. This late work of Rembrandt's is most important both for its composition and its colouring.

RUISDAEL, Jacob van (1629–1682)

The Mill near Wijk   Colour Plate V
Canvas, 33½ × 41 in. (No. 2074)

A. van der Hoop bequest to the City of Amsterdam in 1854. On loan to the Museum since 1885.
This is a free interpretation of the actual scene. The mill is still standing, but no longer occupies the dominating position which it has in the picture. The dramatic contrast between the dominant building and the unimpeded view over the plain is an artistic effect typical of the Dutch landscape.

The Castle of Bentheim   Plate 134
Canvas, 28 × 21 in. (No. 2080)

The history of the picture may be traced back to 1805. It was acquired for the Museum in 1810.

SCOREL, Jan van (1495–1562)

St. Mary Magdalene   Plate 118
Panel, 49 × 53¾ in. (No. 2189)

Originally in the St. Jan military headquarters in Haarlem, later in the town hall of the same town. Taken over in 1804 with the other paintings belonging to the Batavian Republic, and transferred here from the National Museum at the Hague in 1808.

The religious theme is wholly secularized. The attractive, richly dressed woman is set in a fantastic mountainous landscape.

SEGHERS, Hercules (1590–1638)

River Valley   Plate 132
Panel, $12\frac{1}{2} \times 22$ in. (No. 2198 B1).

Signed.
Acquired in 1931 through a bequest of Dr. Hofstede de Groot. The attribution is due to the previous owner, who identified the locality as the upper Rhine Valley.

STEEN, Jan (1626–1679)

The Feast of St. Nicholas   Plate 136
Canvas, $33 \times 28\frac{1}{2}$ in. (No. 2237).

Signed.
Purchased from the van Heteren collection in 1809.
The *genre* element in the activities of those participating in this family festival, and all the incidentals are described with verve.

TERBORCH, Gerard (1617–1681)

Portrait of Helena van der Schalcke Plate 128
Panel, $14 \times 11\frac{3}{4}$ in. (No. 573)

Acquired in 1898 together with the portraits of her parents.
The child looks at the spectator seriously and attentively; not one of Rubens's or van Dyck's sweetly smiling creatures, but a serious Dutch child already loaded with Protestant responsibility.

VELDE, The Younger, Willem van de (1633–1707)

The Ij before Amsterdam   Plate 133
Canvas, $72\frac{1}{2} \times 127$ in. (No. 2469)

Signed and dated 1686.
Ships forming round the 'Golden Leeuw', the flagship of Cornelis Tromp. The underlying theme of the picture is the widening estuary.

VERMEER, Jan (1632–1675)

The Little Street   Plate 137
Canvas, $21\frac{1}{4} \times 17\frac{1}{2}$ in. (No. 2527 A2)

Signed.
First mentioned on the occasion of a sale in Amsterdam in 1696, presented by H. W. A. Deterding in 1921.
A view from Vermeer's house in the Great Market in Delft. The composition is, in essence, the same as of 'The Woman Reading a Letter'. The clear articulation of the planes is used here to emphasize the sleepy atmosphere of a small Dutch town.

Young Woman Reading a Letter   Plate 138
Canvas, $18\frac{1}{4} \times 15\frac{1}{2}$ in. (No. 2527)

A. van der Hoop bequest to the City of Amsterdam. On loan to the Museum since 1885. The compositional planes are strongly articulated and set behind framed elements. The letter is read silently; the reader's strong excitement is set in a completely calm environment.

WITTE, Emanuel de (1617–1692)

Interior of a Gothic Church   Plate 140
Canvas, $49\frac{1}{2} \times 42\frac{1}{4}$ in. (No. 2697)

A. van der Hoop bequest to the City of Amsterdam. On loan to the Museum since 1885. The vertical lines of the great stone columns determine the impression made by this interior bathed in sunlight.

BERLIN : THE PICTURE GALLERY

NO OTHER great National Gallery has so eventful a history as
the Gallery in Berlin. I do not mean the Gallery which bears
the name Nationalgalerie, for this has the restricted function of
providing a home for German nineteenth and twentieth century art, and
for some examples of modern foreign art, but the collection in the Kaiser
Friedrich Museum, which was separated from the Deutsches Museum in
1930, although the administrative control still remains the same. From
the basis of a Royal Cabinet of art, these two elements combined to form
a whole which the State has made into a deliberate and large-scale means
of education, although it did not begin with the splendour of the Hapsburg art treasures, nor did it command the inexhaustible means of the
British nation, which, besides controlling a large part of the globe during
the nineteenth century, also controlled the better part of the art market.
The Berlin Gallery compensated for these two deficiencies by an admirable mixture of systematic work and an organization which knew what it
wanted and how to get it; for where Vienna inherited from the past
and London drew upon the riches of England, Berlin had the career
of a self-made man. The history of the Berlin collections is the history
of the rise of Germany in the nineteenth century and of her fall in the
twentieth.

The foundation of the Gallery goes back to the period immediately
following the Napoleonic Wars, when Prussia, much enlarged by the
peace treaties, took over the leading role among the States in a German
Empire which had been dominated by Austria until 1806. Prussia—or,
rather, a few of her leading statesmen—had the vision to see what the
future could hold for her, and was ready to undertake anything to
demonstrate her fitness for the task. The foundation of a Gallery which
could enter into rivalry with famous collections already existing elsewhere
was part of a policy which had found still more striking expression in the
refounding of the University of Berlin a few years earlier. At that moment,
soon after the Battle of Jena, when Napoleon had smashed the Prussian
war machine, King Friedrich Wilhelm was made aware of the principle
that what the State had lost in physical power must be made good in the
sphere of the spirit. The idea—and the mind from which the idea sprang

—was Wilhelm von Humboldt's, who taught two generations of Germans the duties and responsibilities of true intellectual leadership.

It is interesting to observe the methodical spirit which was to make the Gallery so great dominant there from the very beginning. Part of the material from which the collections grew was acquired purely accident-ally, although Joachim von Sandrart, the best seventeenth-century judge in such matters, said that the Cabinet in Berlin was the best in Germany. The pictures he mentioned were of the kind that comes into a dynastic collection in the normal course of things, but after the Cabinet had been scattered by the Thirty Years War the Great Elector, Friedrich Wilhelm, attempted to assemble a proper picture gallery.

The first systematic collector was Friedrich II—Frederick the Great—who gave full rein to his taste for contemporary or near-contemporary French art while he was Crown Prince and in the early years of his reign. It is, in fact, noteworthy that the King who so often defeated the French in battle, and who came to stand as the symbol of Prussia and of Germany in the nationalistic tendencies of the last few decades, was an enthusiastic admirer of the philosophy, literature and art of France. Diderot, Voltaire and Lammenais were favoured guests at his table, and his favourite artists were Watteau, Lancret, Pater, and Boucher. These preferences were not only contrary to the German taste of the time but even to French, for Watteau was then completely forgotten by his countrymen and the King of Prussia had no difficulty in obtaining for his residences a choice collection of pictures by the master and his followers which is in no way inferior to the collection in the Louvre. Only a few of these pictures later found their way into the Berlin Gallery—for example, Watteau's *Fête in a Park* and the two companion pieces of the *Italian* and the *French Com-edians* (Plate 167). Most of Frederick's pictures remained in his favourite palaces at Potsdam and Sanssouci where they have outlasted the Hohen-zollerns, but, of the few which were sold after the fall of the dynasty, one —Nicolas Lancret's *La Camargo dancing in a Park*—now adorns the National Gallery of Art in Washington.

Frederick the Great's early exclusive preference for the French eight-eenth century gave way in the course of time to an interest in Flemish and Italian masters of the classic period. Names like Rubens and Van Dyck, Tintoretto, Veronese and Guido Reni, began to predominate in the Gallery at Sanssouci, but the most outstanding work there was Correggio's *Leda and the Swan* (Plate 151), originally commissioned for Charles V.

When he became King, Frederick did not allow his activity as a collector to weigh heavily on his subjects. His agent Gotzkowski, who also worked for Catherine of Russia, received a letter from him in 1756 in which the King wrote: "The King of Poland may, if he wishes, pay thirty thousand ducats for a picture"—a reference to the purchase of Raphael's *Sistine Madonna* in the previous year—"and then imposes taxes of a million thalers in Saxony. That is not my way. I will buy anything that I can get at a reasonable price, and the King of Poland may have anything that is too dear. I cannot print paper money and will not tax my people severely".

The King of Poland and Saxony, with whom Frederick would not compete, was Augustus III, one of the greatest collectors of the time, and indeed when Berlin entered the collecting field there were already two very important Galleries in Germany. Both the one in Dresden and the one in Munich were typical Royal Collections, founded in the sixteenth century as Cabinets for an art-loving member of the dynasty and extended by the normal processes in such families, and finally, in the eighteenth century, brought to unheard-of heights by the activities of a passionate and successful collector.

These Galleries already possessed a surplus of masterpieces at the beginning of the nineteenth century, when the Berlin Collection consisted of about 300 pictures scattered over the Royal residences in Prussia. Some of these pictures, but not many of them, were to be reckoned among the treasures of the collection even at a later date, examples being the *Perseus and Andromeda* and the *St. Cecilia* by Rubens, Rembrandt's *Saskia* of 1643, and Poussin's *The Infant Jupiter nourished by the goat Amalthea*.

The gallery, which was officially founded in 1823 with this nucleus, was raised from the status of a more or less haphazard collection to that of a proper gallery by the acquisition of two important collections. The first of these, formed in the seventeenth century by the Marchese Vincenzo Giustiniani, was particularly rich in masterpieces of that period and contained the finest collection of Caravaggio's works anywhere (Plate 159). Apart from works of the Roman and Bolognese Baroque, the Gallery also received from this source a few good examples of other schools, such as Domenico Ghirlandaio's *Judith* of 1489 and three portraits by Lorenzo Lotto (Plate 155). Among the Dutch pictures was Gerard Terborch's misleadingly named *Fatherly Admonition*, which, in fact, represents a very unpaternal approach to the young woman by the seated cavalier.

The second acquisition, which became one of the main supports of the new Gallery, was the collection bought from the English banker, Edward Solly, and accounted, at the beginning of the nineteenth century, as one of the richest and best selected collections in the whole world. It enriched

Berlin with a great number of masterpieces of the Italian School from the Trecento onwards, and a small selection gives an idea of the importance of this addition: Filippo Lippi, *The Madonna adoring the Child;* Filippino Lippi, the *Crucifixion with the Virgin and St. Francis;* Andrea Mantegna, *The Presentation in the Temple;* Cosimo Tura, *Madonna and Child enthroned with four Saints;* Titian's *Self-portrait* from the Barbarigo Collection (Plate 157); and Raphael's Madonna which has been known ever since as the *Solly Madonna.* The most important works of the Northern Schools were the two wings of an altarpiece of about 1440, painted on both sides, by the Master of the Darmstadt Passion; Hans Holbein the Younger's portrait of the merchant, Georg Gisze, of 1532 (Plate 154), and the enchanting portrait of a girl by Petrus Cristus (Plate 146). Other still more important early Netherlandish works were the three parts from the wings of Van Eyck's Ghent Altarpiece and the two wings from Dirk Bouts's Sacrament Altar, which, after their double change of ownership following the two world wars, are now once again back in the places for which they were commissioned in Ghent and Louvain. In 1823 the Berlin Gallery thus consisted of three elements: 378 pictures from the Royal Collection, 73 from Giustiniani and 670 from Solly. All these were exhibited in the so-called Altes Museum, commissioned from the great architect Carl Schinkel in 1823, and opened to the public in 1830. The new Gallery could pride itself on being housed in one of the finest museum buildings ever erected.

It was part of the systematic programme of the Gallery to strive to create a setting worthy of its treasures. Corresponding to the Romantic ideas of its founder, King Wilhelm III, it sought to impart in a grand manner a knowledge of, and a reverence for, the arts. That it was able to do this in spite of the relative poverty of the State which it served, was due to the extraordinary talents of its first Directors and advisers. One of these was Karl Friedrich, a pioneer in the new subject of art-history; the other was Gustav Friedrich Waagen, the first Director of the Gallery and a man of international authority as a connoisseur. These two share between them the honour of having built up the Gallery in the years following its foundation. Existing gaps were filled with important acquisitions, and Raphael's *Solly Madonna* was followed in 1827 by his *Colonna Madonna,* in 1829 by a third *Madonna with SS. Francis and Jerome,* and in 1842 by the *Diotalevi Madonna* which is nowadays regarded as more probably the work of Raphael's teacher, Pietro Perugino, or of his fellow-pupil Eusebio di San Giorgio. A little later, in 1854, the *Madonna del Duca Terranuova* was added to these. In a similar fashion, the only Titian

—the *Self-portrait*—was joined in 1832 by the *Girl with the Fruit-dish*. On a single journey to Italy in 1841–42, Waagen bought three important Tintorettos, including the *Madonna with SS. Mark and Luke* and *Luna with the Horae*, the latter being a ceiling picture from the Fondaco dei Tedeschi in Venice. The same journey produced the celebrated Veronese ceiling pictures from the same place, as well as several portraits by Moretto and Moroni. To the works by Van Eyck, Bouts and Petrus Cristus, Waagen was able to add two altarpieces by Rogier van der Weyden—the *St. John Altar* from the Convent of Miraflores near Burgos in Spain, and the so-called *Bladelin Altar* of about 1450 (Plate 147) painted for the church at Middelburg in Brabant. The basis of a Spanish section was formed with Murillo's *St. Antony with the Christ Child* and Zurbaran's *St. Bonaventura pointing to the Crucifix*. The former was bought in 1835 from the collection of Mathieu Favier, who had been in the entourage of Marshal Soult in Spain, while the Zurbaran was bought in 1852 at the sale of the Soult Collection itself. At some of the other famous auctions of the time, such as the Pourtalès, Pommersfelden and Salamanca Sales, Berlin could not bid because its resources had been scattered over a number of purchases; above all, the years from 1852 to 1872 may be regarded as a dead period in the history of the Gallery. Only after the foundation of the German Empire in 1872 did it take such a bound forward that all its earlier history seems a mere prelude. In 1871 the Crown Prince, later to rule for a short time as the Emperor Frederick III, became the official patron of the art collections, and the advancement of the Gallery from a Royal to an Imperial institution required a broader outlook in every respect. The indemnity paid by the French after the Franco-Prussian War enriched the whole German economy, the meteoric rise of the Empire fed the national pride and a galaxy of brilliant men were there to carry out grandiose schemes. Berlin remained faithful to the tradition (which had begun so successfully with Waagen) that a great museum, like any other important institution, needs a great man at its head if it is to advance, and that the authority of experts should not rest on the fact that they are Directors or Keepers, but precisely the other way round—that Directors and Keepers should be appointed because they are authorities. Julius Meyer was the first great Director of the Imperial foundation, but his activities were put in the shade by those of his successor, Wilhelm von Bode, who may well be called the outstanding personality of the nineteenth century in the museum world. Bode did not become Director until 1890, although he had been on the staff of the museum since 1872, and many of the successes obtained before his directorate can probably be ascribed to him. He had the power of making the utmost use of any opportunity that offered, and he was able to convince the Government of the necessity of a lavish expenditure on the collection so that they could catch up with the lead which other nations already had. At the same time, and in the interests of the State Museums, he organized private collections which had received a powerful impetus from the economic prosperity of the Empire. He called into being the Kaiser Friedrich Museum Verein, a body analogous to the National Art-Collections Fund in England, on whose financial support he could rely at all times. He was also the personal friend and adviser of all German, and many foreign, collectors so that their collections formed, as it were, a reservoir which he could make use of when the opportunity arose, for every one was indebted to him and no one more than the art dealers whose business was very largely increased by his activities. It may be said that from about 1890 until the outbreak of the war in 1914, Bode was the uncontested king of the art market and for all practical purposes he had the first option on every object coming into the market. His well deserved authority rested equally on his talent for organization, on his outstanding connoisseurship and on his knowledge of his job. He mastered very differing fields, for he was the acknowledged authority on Oriental textiles, Italian ceramics and furniture, German and Italian sculpture, and the painting of almost every European School. It is clear that he was the man to fulfil the ideal of completeness and versatility which had been in the minds of the founders of the museum, and that he was the man to transform a more or less accidental art collection into what is generally recognized as a museum of universal scope.

A small selection of examples must suffice to show how systematically the Gallery was built up so that only the National Gallery in London is comparable to it in versatility. If the latter has a greater number of masterpieces than Berlin, Berlin has a better cross section. As a result of Bode's long period in office and his authoritative personality, the ineradicable stamp of his own virtues and weaknesses were impressed upon the collection. He rejected absolutely El Greco, or works which, as he put it, were before the invention of art; on the other hand, he did try to keep an even balance in his Gallery. Unlike, for example, the Louvre, it grew less by the incorporation of whole collections than by the acquisition of single works; it is true that at the beginning of the new era in 1874, the valuable collection of Bartholommäus Suermondt in Aachen was bought, and later the collections of James Simon and Adolf Thieme were bequeathed, yet nevertheless the main source of supply for the gallery consisted of gifts from collectors and dealers, works presented by the Kaiser Friedrich Museum Verein, and purchases in every end and corner of the art market.

The pictures in the Gallery are pretty generally known, perhaps better known than other works of the same quality by the same painters elsewhere, and the reason for this is that the Directors, Keepers and Assistant Keepers in Berlin were chosen on account of their academic abilities, which meant that the works in their charge were studied minutely and frequently published. Over and above this, the Museum always took care to have good Catalogues and photographs available, and it published an excellent Bulletin and a learned annual publication —the 'Prussian Jahrbuch'—which naturally preferred to publish the material actually in the Museum. This circumstance engendered an academic air, which gave a slightly aloof feeling to the collection: the energy with which the gaps were filled meant that many of the pictures so bought seemed to be of more interest to the art historian than to the art lover, and they seemed to reflect the glow of the lamp in the scholar's study rather than the bright day-light of the artist's studio. The admirable system of the Gallery is, in short, simply an expression of the national tendency towards strict discipline.

These considerations in no way lessen the worth of the collection which, first in Schinkel's noble classical building and since 1904 in the new and ornate Kaiser Friedrich Museum, grew into an institution of international importance. The aim was to display all the arts, in accordance with that cosmopolitan spirit which German philosophy and poetry of the classic age had made (or had seemed to make) a permanent feature of the German outlook, but it is also understandable that the products of the national School should have a special emphasis laid upon them in the capital of the German Empire. In spite of his many other interests, Bode devoted special attention to the galleries containing the German School. A few of the principal acquisitions have already been mentioned, and they soon attracted a host of lesser works, so that by the outbreak of the First World War this German section had grown so big, and the Kaiser Friedrich Museum was already so overfilled with works of the other Schools, that a full-dress reorganization was planned, which, however, had to be postponed until after the War. In fact, the reorganization planned by Bode was not completed until 1930. The main feature was the division into two parts of the Kaiser Friedrich Museum, which continued to exhibit the non-German Schools, while in an adjacent building the Deutsches Museum was devoted to German art up to the end of the eighteenth century—that is, up to the point at which the old Nationalgalerie took over. The Deutsches Museum included the Primitives of all the Northern Schools, including the French and the Flemish, although this was due to the numerous inter-relationships between the Schools of the different countries of Northern Europe in the late Gothic period, rather than to any attempt to incorporate Belgium and France into the Reich. It seemed instructive to show the notably international character of Late Gothic art in the North as an entity. This method ruling in the Deutsches Museum—of uniting an essentially national character with the internationalism of a specific period—gave rise to a somewhat complicated system and the same is true of the combination of sculpture and painting which was typical of the Kaiser Friedrich Museum from the beginning. Unlike the majority of the great Museums, it never separated the two arts, but exhibited them side by side in its galleries along with examples of the applied arts—furniture, textiles and ceramics—as historical interiors of the first rank. This may have been an expression of Bode's versatility which was in direct contrast to the tendency of specialists to separate things into clearly defined categories.

Bode, with his outstanding gifts as an organizer, never paid much attention to boundary disputes between the various departments since he was aiming at a grand Museum which should give a comprehensive representation of the arts of mankind, at all times and in all places. He did not live to see the completion of his plans for a group of prehistoric, ethnological and archaeological collections, subdivided by periods and types of art, yet even in their fragmentary state, his creation of the Museum Island in the heart of Berlin, where most of these institutions were housed, was an altogether extraordinary achievement. It was the fruit of the encyclopaedic tendencies of the nineteenth century, the result of German thoroughness in the best sense of the word, and a monument to the organizing genius of a great Museum director.

Unfortunately, his creation did not long survive its creator, for the Museum Island was so badly damaged in the Second World War that the fruits of more than a century of hard work were destroyed at one blow. The buildings have suffered so much from bombing or from fires, many of them having been entirely destroyed, that their restoration will take many years, and the collections themselves have suffered gravely from fire, looting and confiscation. As far as the Gallery was concerned, the pictures were evacuated at the outbreak of war, or during the course of it, and taken to what were hoped would be places of safety. So far as concerned the pictures taken to the salt mines near Grasleben, the measures proved

effective; American troops found the pictures there in 1945, and fortunately they included the most precious possessions of the Museum. A
selection from them—202 of the finest pictures, mostly small in size—
were taken to the United States for safety and were there exhibited and
admired in a number of cities; they were returned to Germany a long
time ago and are now partly restored to Berlin. On the other hand, the
taking of pictures and other Museum treasures to what was thought to
be the absolutely safe Flaktower at Friedrichshain, begun in 1942,
turned out to be a terrible disaster. It is true that they survived the war,
for, on May 5, 1945, after the end of hostilities, they were found by the
Museum staff, untouched and unharmed; but between then and May 10
they were destroyed by fire. Whether this was due to criminal negligence
on the part of the Russian Occupation troops or to malicious intent in
order to conceal thefts by civilians, or simply tragic ill-fortune, cannot
now be discovered even after a thorough investigation into all the
circumstances. It is unfortunately true that the Berlin Museum has lost
417 pictures,—341 from the main collection and 76 from the depot;
divided by Schools, the losses are: 158 Italian pictures (one quarter of the
whole inventory, and including 71 Solly and 10 Giustiniani pictures),
89 Dutch, 54 Flemish and 67 German pictures, and they included some
of the very greatest.

This horrifying list reads like the Catalogue of an important Museum.
Works by Rubens, Van Dyck, Jordaens, Tintoretto, Titian, Paolo Veronese, Caravaggio, Zurbaran and many others have gone for ever. In
particular, many of the larger pictures were taken to this ill-omened
tower at a time when it was no longer possible to transport them any
farther away. Perhaps the saddest loss of all was Luca Signorelli's *Pan*
(Plate 150).

Never in the course of history, not even in the fires in the Spanish Royal
Palaces, has there been so wholesale a destruction of art treasures.
Although their concentration in that particular place was the result of
generations of patient Museum work, they belonged to the whole civilized
world, and it is hard to see how, in the present circumstances, the survivors can be brought back to life again, but the previous history of the
Collection shows a tenacity of purpose that allows us to believe that somehow, sometime, it will happen.

NOTES ON THE ILLUSTRATIONS

ALTDORFER, Albrecht (1480–1538)

The Nativity   Plate 149
Panel, 14½ × 10¼ in. (No. 638E)

Altdorfer sets the scene in a completely ruined
building. Above it, in the clear, blue, night
sky a group of angels is dancing. The romantic
conception, with particular emphasis on the
buildings, is characteristic of the master.

BOUTS, Dirk (*c.* 1415–1475)

Christ in the House of Simon   Plate 148
Panel, 16½ × 24½ in. (No. 533A)

The event is recorded in the most simple and
serene style. Even Magdalene, whose figure is
so often, in Italian pictures, outstanding in her
beauty, seems wholly absorbed in her humble
gesture. On the right a praying donor.

CARAVAGGIO, Michelangelo (1573–1610)

Saint Matthew and the Angel   Plate 159
Canvas, 93 × 72½ in. (No. 365)

This picture, as well as other scenes from the
life of the Evangelist, was painted for the
church of S. Luigi dei Francesi in Rome.
Owing to the stark presentation, however, it
was replaced by a more agreeable composition,
also by Caravaggio. It was bought with the
Giustiniani collection in 1815.

CORREGGIO, Antonio (*c.* 1489–1534)

Leda and the Swan   Plate 151
Canvas, 62¾ × 76¾ in. (No. 218)

Probably painted as part of the decorations for
a room in the castle at Mantua (see also
Jupiter and Io in Vienna, Plate 18). Bought in
Spain in 1602 for Rudolf II, taken to Stock-
holm in 1648. Collection of Queen Christina;
since 1726 in the possession of Philippe
d'Orleans, whose son Louis cut the picture.
Restored by Charles Coypel, who provided
Leda with a new head. In 1755 it passed to

Frederic the Great and has been in the Museum
since 1830.
The incident of a girl bathing in a woodland
lake was entirely in harmony with the original
erotic setting of the painting. The incident is
here raised to a mythological level by the group
of Leda and the swan in the centre of the
composition. In spite of the serious disfigure-
ment, this remains one of Correggio's most
attractive pictures.

COSSA, Francesco (1435–1477)

Allegory of Autumn   Plate 156
Panel, 46½ × 28¾ in. (No. 115A)

Attributed to Cosimo Tura in the old Dominican friary in Ferrara, where it had once hung.
Bought from a Florentine dealer in 1894.
Probably one of a cycle of pictures representing
the months or the seasons. The *genre* figure of
a girl vine-harvester personifies the season.

CRANACH, Lucas, the Elder (1472–1553)

Rest on the Flight into Egypt   Plate 152
Panel, 28 × 20¾ in. (No. 564A)

Signed with a monogram and dated 1504.
Formerly in the Galleria Sciarra in Rome and
reached the Museum through the Konrad
Fiedler collection in 1904. This is Cranach's
earliest picture authenticated by a signature,
and shows the artist, in his free and enthusiastic
surrender to the mood of the landscape, to be
still very much attached to the Danube School,
and far removed from the cool linear manner
which characterized his art when he became
the court painter of Saxony. On the left, a
small angel is catching water from a rivulet,
suggesting the water miracle in the Infancy
Gospel.

CRISTUS, Petrus (active 1446–1467)

Portrait of a Girl   Plate 146
Panel, 11½ × 8½ in. (No. 532)

From the Solly Collection. The sitter has been
identified by Weale as the first wife of Edward

Grimester. The girlish charm and the almost mediaeval modesty are wonderfully expressed.

DÜRER, Albrecht (1471–1528)

Portrait of Hieronymus Holzschuher
　　　　　　　　　　　　　　Plate 153
Panel, 20 × 14¾ in. (No. 557E)

Inscribed with monogram, the date 1526 and the name of the sitter.
Acquired in 1884 from the Baronial family Holzschuher in Nuremberg. Hieronymus Holzschuher, a senator of Nuremberg and one of the champions of the reformation in that town, is shown in this picture as a personality composed of controlled energy and extreme vitality—a symbol of civic pride at the time of the Reformation.

ELSHEIMER, Adam (1578–1610)

Landscape with St. Mary Magdalene
　　　　　　　　　　　　　　Plate 165
Copper, 7¼ × 9½ in. (No. 1973)

Presented by Frieda Hintze in 1926. The emotional impact of the subject is weakened only by the scale of the figures. The mood of the landscape dominates both the artist and the spectator.

EYCK, Jan van (died 1441)

Madonna in the Church　　　　Plate 144
Panel, 13 × 5¾ in. (No. 525C)

Acquired in 1874 with the Suermondt collection. In this small picture, executed with all the delicacy of a miniature, every detail has its place in the symbolism of the composition.

FOUQUET, Jean (1420–1481)

Etienne Chevalier with St. Stephen　Plate 145
Panel, 37½ × 34¾ in. (No. 1617)

Bought from the Brentano family, to whom the famous illuminated Book of Hours of Etienne Chevalier, now at Chantilly, had also belonged previously.
One leaf of a diptych, which had remained in the church at Melun until the end of the eighteenth century; the other leaf, representing the Virgin and Child with angels, is now in the Antwerp Museum. This is the French version of the Italian life-size portrait.

HALS, Frans (1580–1666)

Malle Babbe　　　　　　　　Plate 162
Canvas, 29½ × 25¼ in. (No. 801C)

Acquired with the Suermondt Collection in 1874. This picture of Hals' has become particularly popular for its grotesque humour.

HOLBEIN, Hans, the Younger (1497–1543)

Portrait of Georg Gisze　　　　Plate 154
Panel, 37¾ × 33¾ in. (No. 586)

Dated 1532.
In the Galerie Orleans in 1727, and bought at the auction by Christian von Mecheln. After several years in Basle it passed to the Solly collection and from there to the Museum.
One of the earliest of Holbein's pictures painted during his second stay in England. The interest in the rendering of the third dimension and the concern with detail are characteristics far removed from Holbein's later English style.

LA TOUR, Georges de, or Dumesnil de
(c. 1600–1652)

St. Sebastian　　　　　　　　Plate 158
Canvas, 64½ × 52 in. (No. 2046)

The saint is being tended by St. Irene and her attendants; the theme gave de La Tour an opportunity to use strong contrasts of light and shade, a feature particularly dear to this Lotharingian painter, who has only been rescued from provincial obscurity in the last few years.

LOTTO, Lorenzo (c. 1480–1556)

Portrait of an Architect　　　　Plate 155
Canvas, 42½ × 34 in. (No. 153)

Signed: L. Lotto me fecit.
From the Giustiniani collection in Rome, where it was described as a portrait of Jacopo Sansovino, whose other portraits, however, it does not resemble. Recently the name of Sebastiano Serlio, an architect who was a friend of Lotto, has been associated with it. The beard is cut according to Venetian fashion. To show his sitter in the performance of an action—unlike the sitters of Titian's portraits—is characteristic of Lotto.

POLLAIUOLO, Antonio (1429–1498)

David with the Head of Goliath   Plate 143
Panel, 19 × 14 in. (No. 73A)

David's victory over the giant Goliath was
frequently painted by Florentine fifteenth-
century painters because of its topical symbolism. The figure of David with his legs
astride, painted with the fidelity of a portrait,
is characteristic of Florentine art in the
fifteenth century.

POLLAIUOLO, Piero (1443–1496)

Portrait of a Young Lady
                    Colour Plate XVII
Panel, 21 × 14½ in. (No. 1614)

Bought in 1897 from the collection of the Earl
of Ashburnham. This charming picture is one
of a group of portraits of fashionably dressed
and coiffured young women. This picture was
originally attributed to Piero della Francesca,
and later to Domenico Veneziano.

REMBRANDT (1606–1669)

Samson Threatening his Father-in-Law
                            Plate 163
Canvas, 63 × 52 in. (No. 802)

The scene is based on the incident described
in Judges, XV. There is, in this relatively
early picture, a definite inclination to the
anecdotal and an addiction to detail which are
absent from Rembrandt's later pictures.

The Vision of Daniel   Plate 164
Canvas, 39 × 47 in. (No. 828F)

Bought in Paris in 1883.
The young Daniel is listening to the Angel who
explains to him the vision of the he-goat by
the river (Daniel, VIII). The dream-like
quality of the vision has been fully expressed.

The Man with the Gold Helmet   Plate 166
Canvas, 29¼ × 21½ in. (No. 811A)

The sitter is often identified with Rembrandt's
brother Adriaen, but this is not very convincing.
The painter has dressed his model fantastically
to gain certain artistic effects.

ROGIER VAN DER WEYDEN
(c. 1400–1464)

The Adoration of the Child   Plate 147
Panel, 37 × 39½ in. (No. 535)

Central panel of the so-called Bladelin Altar.
This masterpiece of Rogier's, painted soon after
1450, was destined for the high altar of the
church at Middelburg, and is named after the
donor, who was also the founder of the town
and Treasurer of the Dukes of Burgundy.
The emotional impact is directed straight at
the spectator—a feature which Rogier introduced into Netherlandish painting.

SACCHI, Andrea (1599–1661)

*Portrait of a Man, presumed to be Alessandro
del Borro*   Plate 160
Canvas, 81¾ × 49 in. (No. 413A)

Purchased in 1873 from the Villa Passerini
near Cortona.
The identity of the sitter has been questioned;
and the attribution has varied from the original
one, to Velazquez, through various Italian
and Northern painters; its present attribution
to Sacchi is only a makeshift. At any rate it is
an excellent interpretation of the personality
of a southern Falstaff.

SIGNORELLI, Luca (1450?–1523)

Pan and his Court   Plate 150
Canvas, 30½ × 38 in. (No. 79A)

Signed.
This is probably the picture praised by Vasari
for the painting of the nude, and, according to
him, painted for Lorenzo de' Medici. Recorded
in the Palazzo Pitti in 1687, in 1865 in the
Palazzo Corsi, sold to Berlin in 1873. Its
destruction in the Flakturm in Berlin in 1945
is a particularly damaging loss.

STEEN, Jan (1626–1679)

Garden of an Inn   Plate 161
Canvas, 27¾ × 23½ in. (No. 795)

From the Royal Collection. A cheerful open-
air scene, which suits the popular character
of Dutch seventeenth-century art.

TITIAN (*c.* 1485–1576)

Self-Portrait   Plate 157
Canvas, 39 × 30½ in. (No. 163)

Bought by Cicognara in 1814 in the Casa Barbarigo in Venice, and sold to Solly soon afterwards. Acquired by the Museum with the Solly collection in 1821.

If this is the picture which Vasari had seen in Titian's house in 1566, then it must have been painted, as he states, in 1562, when the painter was nearly eighty years old.

A Girl with a Dish of Fruit
       Plate on Wrapper
Canvas, 41¼ × 32¾ in. (No. 166)

Bought in 1832 from the collection of the Abbé Celotti in Florence. Long believed to be a portrait of the painter's daughter Lavinia. Hadeln maintains however that this is an example of Titian's idealized half-portraits. The motif was repeatedly painted by Titian and his school.

VERMEER, Jan (1632–1675)

A Lady with Necklace   Colour Plate XVIII
Canvas, 22½ × 18½ in. (No. 912B)

Bought with the Suermondt collection in 1874. The lady is wearing an elegant morning dress and looks at herself in a rather distant mirror.

The fact that the contact with the mirror image is broken heightens the intimate character of the picture.

WATTEAU, Antoine (1684–1721)

The Italian Comedy   Plate 167
Canvas, 15 × 19 in. (No. 470)

The companion piece to *The French Comedy*, which also came from the Prussian Royal Collection and is now in the Berlin Museum. Both pictures were bought by Frederic the Great.

The two pictures depict national variants of a love scene. While the French picture shows a gallant episode, the representatives of the Italian 'Commedia dell'Arte' are shown in a more passionate relationship, and set in a romantic chiaroscuro.

WITZ, Konrad (*c.* 1398–1447)

Solomon and the Queen of Sheba   Plate 142
Panel, 33¼ × 31⅛ in. (No. 1701)

Part of the Heilspiegel altar, the larger part of which is now in the Museum at Basle. The treatment is bereft of the usual incidentals so much loved by painters—there is no throne, no suite, no gift, no landscape—and the scene is reduced to the barest essentials. The modelling of the bodies is strongly stressed.

THE NATIONAL GALLERY, LONDON

WHEN the National Gallery was founded in 1824, all the other institutions examined in this book (with the exception of that in Washington) were already in existence, as were also a number of other important museums. This late start is the more surprising in that England, ever since the seventeenth century, had been the classic example of an art-collecting country and, as a result of her great wealth and of the education given to the ruling classes, the country had acquired countless works of art. Everywhere in Europe—above all in Italy—the fabulously rich English tourist who bought and carried off masterpieces of painting and sculpture was a stock character, envied and made fun of, but the result was the accumulation of an incomparable wealth of masterpieces in the great English houses, a mine so rich that even today, after prolonged and serious losses, it still supplies the public collections of Great Britain.

Although the idea of a National Gallery was not new, it was the increase in public interest which led to the actual foundation. In 1777 John Wilkes raised the question of establishing such a Gallery during a debate in the House of Commons on the Annual Grant to the British Museum, since a favourable opportunity was offered by the impending sale of Sir Robert Walpole's celebrated Houghton collection. "A noble gallery ought to be built in the garden of the British Museum for the reception of this invaluable treasure," he said, but this appeal met with as little response as recommendations in a similar vein by Dr Johnson and Sir Joshua Reynolds. The Houghton pictures were bought by the Empress Catherine of Russia, but the idea of a National Gallery remained in the air, and in 1814 the Bourgeois Bequest to Dulwich College was the occasion of the opening of the public gallery there.

The phrase 'National Gallery' was first used by James Barry, but the idea of such a creation is the natural outcome of tendencies which, by the beginning of the nineteenth century, had grown in importance. The Napoleonic Wars had made all the nations of Europe conscious of their individuality, and Britain, more than any other country, could take a conscious pride in her gigantic struggle against the Emperor. Napoleon's short-lived attempt to unite in one central museum the masterpieces collected from all over Europe by his victorious armies must have exerted considerable influence: for example, Benjamin West, the President of the Royal Academy, had opposed the idea of a National Gallery, but was converted by his visit to Paris in 1811. West was not the only opponent: John Constable expressed the thoughts of the opposition in a letter of 1822: "Should there be a National Gallery (which is talked of) there will be an end of the art in poor old England, and she will become, in all that relates to painting, as much a nonentity as every other country that has one. The reason is plain; the manufacturers of pictures are then made the criterion of perfection, instead of nature." Constable did not take into account how deeply he and his contemporaries were indebted to the great landscape painters of the past.

The realization of the vague idea of an English National Gallery is bound up with the name of the patron and collector Sir George Beaumont, who offered his own important collection to the nation in 1823, on condition that the Government should provide suitable accommodation. A similar promise was made by the Rev. W. Holwell Carr, and these two offers encouraged Lord Liverpool's Ministry when the question of buying the Angerstein pictures was raised in the House of Commons in the following year.

John Julius Angerstein, born in Russia in 1735, had made a large fortune, which he used as a means of social advancement. His house, 100 Pall Mall, was open to all artists and connoisseurs and was a national showpiece. Obviously there were many English collections of far greater importance than Angerstein's, but their owners, mostly members of the higher aristocracy, had neither occasion nor desire to open them to the public or indeed to make their existence known. Angerstein, a self-made man with social ambitions, on the contrary, made his collection into a kind of public institution, and, as a result, the rumours of its imminent sale abroad aroused strong protests. The Government took action to avert the threatened cultural loss and voted £60,000 for the purchase, preservation and exhibition of the Angerstein pictures. The Treasury controlled them and the Gallery which grew out of them, and for the first few years they were exhibited in the house of their former owner. A committee of six gentlemen, increased in number from time to time, acted as Trustees and were responsible for the general direction of the Gallery, while the first Keeper appointed was Mr William Seguier.

Of the thirty-eight pictures from Angerstein's collection, about half are still among those important enough to be kept on permanent exhibition, while the remainder are no longer considered interesting to the public of today. This proportion is not too bad, especially when one remembers that a man of Angerstein's type may have had a certain weakness for sensational works, and something of this may be seen in the most important of the Italian pictures, Sebastiano del Piombo's *Raising of Lazarus*, which is still No. 1 in the Gallery Catalogue. At the beginning of the nineteenth century it was also given the primacy for aesthetic value, enjoying unbelievable popularity, and was placed—along with Raphael's *Transfiguration* (in the Vatican, Plate 220)—on the topmost peak of art. Another Italian picture which has kept its place in the Gallery, perhaps with more justification, is Titian's *Venus and Adonis*, another version of which King Philip II of Spain had obtained in England in 1553. Other Schools have stood the test of time perhaps even better—five Claudes, including the *St. Ursula*, and the *Queen of Sheba* (Plate 187), the *Rape of the Sabines* by Rubens, the *Woman taken in Adultery* (Plate 190) and the *Adoration of the Shepherds* by Rembrandt, *Lord Heathfield* by Reynolds (Plate 192) and seven Hogarths, including the *Marriage à la Mode* (Plate 168), were not a bad beginning for an English National Gallery.

The Gallery grew in the next few years, mainly through the fulfilment of the promises made by Sir George Beaumont and the Rev. W. Holwell Carr: from Beaumont there came, among other pictures, Rembrandt's *Jew Merchant* and the *Deposition*, Canaletto's *Stonemason's Yard* and Rubens's glorious *Château de Steen* (Plate 185). The Carr collection included Tintoretto's *St. George and the Dragon* (Plate 178) and Rembrandt's *Woman Bathing* (Plate 191), both works of the very highest rank. There were also a few equally fortunate acquisitions from other sources—such as Correggio's *Madonna with the Basket* (1825) and Titian's *Bacchus and Ariadne* (1826, Plate 181)—but on the whole the system of organization of the Gallery proved to be rather unsatisfactory in practice, for the Keeper had neither authority nor independence, and the Trustees had little time to spare for the Gallery, since they met only when Parliament was in session and their duties called them to London. Moreover, their connoisseurship left something to be desired and their tastes were onesided; even in their own day they seemed out of date—upholders of the conservative taste which Horace Walpole had summed up two generations earlier—"In short, in my opinion, all the qualities of a perfect painter never met but in Raphael, Guido and Annibal Carracci."

According to their lights they bought well enough, although the prices paid for some artists seem fantastically high by our standards. The onesidedness of their purchases soon aroused comment, and a Committee of the House of Commons recommended in 1836 that the Gallery should lay greater stress on the works of Raphael and his predecessors, but this early instance of Pre-Raphaelitism had no effect. Sir Robert Peel, one of the Trustees, justified his opposition to the early Italian masters with the words "I think we should not collect curiosities," and a few years later Lord Aberdeen expressed a similar opinion.

Under these circumstances it was no wonder that the Gallery was not particularly favoured by contemporary artists, even though a few of them had found their way into the collection. William IV had presented some pictures in 1836, including three portraits by Lawrence, and in the following year some of Constable's admirers presented his *Cornfield* (Plate 193), and yet the mistrust which Constable himself had expressed still persisted. It broke out afresh when it was decided that the Trafalgar Square building, claimed by the Royal Academy, was to serve also as the home of the National Gallery. Sir Martin Archer Shee, the President of the Royal Academy, expressed the point of view of the living artists when he said that he considered the Royal Academy a much more important institution to the Nation than the National Gallery. In his opinion, the R.A. was like a garden where the National Gallery was no more than a granary, and the living organism of the Royal Academy Schools had a salutary effect which could never be produced by the mere accumulations of the National Gallery. The controversy over the building went on until 1869, when the Royal Academy received suitable accommodation in Burlington House, leaving the National Gallery in undisputed possession of the building in Trafalgar Square, where, since 1838, it had been limited to five rooms. From the very beginning the space was insufficient for the rapidly growing collection and the unglazed pictures began to suffer from the London atmosphere. Repeated coats of varnish only made them darker until they reached that 'Gallery tone' which was regarded by contemporaries as the sign of a genuine Old Master. Sir George Beaumont expressed the sentiment of the age when he said that a good picture, like a good fiddle, should be brown.

In its new home the National Gallery continued its accustomed course. New purchases by the usual artists, Guido Reni, Murillo, Honthorst, and so on, were only occasionally interrupted by exceptional acquisitions which we now rank higher, such as Rubens's *Landscape: Sunset* in 1838, Raphael's *St. Catherine of Alexandria* in 1839 and, in 1842, Jan van Eyck's *Arnolfini* (Plate 170) for the ridiculously low price of £630.

Shortly afterwards, Seguier was succeeded as Keeper by Charles Lock Eastlake, who was then regarded as the leading authority on the history of art and the technique of painting, and within a few months the Trustees bought, on his recommendation, Giovanni Bellini's *Portrait of Doge Loredan* (Plate 177), followed shortly after by Rembrandt's *Rabbi*, but they rejected Michelangelo's *Madonna* (then ascribed to Domenico Ghirlandaio) in spite of the low price of 250 guineas. Thirty years later it was bought from Lord Taunton for £2,000. In 1845 the celebrated collection of Cardinal Fesch came up for sale and in the following year Lord Ashburnham's collection was offered as a whole to the Gallery, but nothing came of either opportunity; the most important work in the Fesch collection, Raphael's *Crucifixion*, passed to the Gallery three-quarters of a century later with the Mond Bequest.

Discontent with the management of the National Gallery vented itself in attacks on the methods of cleaning used. Eastlake had been empowered to clean the dirtiest, and, when they were re-hung, they stood out so sharply against the others that the adherents of 'Gallery tone' were outraged and declared them to have been practically ruined. At the same time the purchasing policy of the Trustees came under fire. The most important document in this first public outcry over the National Gallery was a letter to *The Times* from the young Ruskin, published in January 1847; in it he set forth all the faults which, in his view, had made the Gallery 'an European jest', and at the same time he laid down a programme for the future.

The moment for a thorough-going reform had not yet come, and Eastlake preferred to resign after his last purchase, Raphael's *Knight's Dream*. Palma's *Mystic Marriage of St. Catherine* and Titian's *Tribute Money* were bought at the Soult Sale in 1852: the Palma was not considered satisfactory and was taken over by Lord Lansdowne, but a tremendous storm broke over the *Tribute Money*. This 'scandalous purchase', as the critics called it, was used as a weapon against the Trustees in the campaign of the following year. Yet it should be said that this violently attacked picture, which spent most of its life at the National Gallery in the cellars, recently found a protector in Sir Kenneth Clark, during whose Directorship it was exhibited in a good position among the other Venetian pictures: which goes to show that all things are relative and the revolution of 1853, which raised the Primitives to the first place, need not necessarily have been the last word in the history of taste.

However, the Primitives certainly triumphed then, thanks largely to the intervention of the Prince Consort, whose attention had been drawn to the state of affairs at the National Gallery by the painter William Dyce. The House of Commons appointed a Select Committee, which, after a long and careful inquiry, produced a Report that must be regarded as the decisive turning-point in the history of the Gallery. On the question of the apparent damage to the pictures caused by unskilled cleaning it was established that those pictures whose barbarous destruction had been publicly lamented, were in sound condition. The second part of the report, dealing with the policy of the Trustees, is still more important: their outmoded conservatism had led to a long list of missed opportunities. They could, for instance, have had Titian's *Rape of Europa*, now the pride of the Isabella Stewart Gardner Museum in Boston, for £288, Mantegna's *Agony in the Garden* for about the same sum, and Cima's *Madonna with the Goldfinch* for as little as £62. On the whole, the Report was a justification of the grave doubts which had been raised against the existing system—or rather, lack of system. For the future, the Report recommended the abolition of the Keepership and the appointment of a properly qualified and responsible Director, the establishment of a regular annual purchase fund from the Treasury and the drawing up of a clear programme for the creation of a National Gallery worthy of its name and of the nation. One sentence in the Report expresses the intention of the proposed reforms: "What Chaucer and Spenser are to Shakespeare and Milton, Giotto and Masaccio are to the great masters of the Florentine School." In this, the Report was a triumph for the Pre-Raphaelite movement. Their ideas dominated the policy of the Gallery for the next decades, the more so since the first Director to be appointed was a supporter of theirs, for Sir Charles Eastlake returned in 1855 with increased authority and self-confidence to enrich the Gallery with a number of admirable purchases during the ten years of his Directorship. Examples of his acquisitions are Uccello's *Rout of San Romano* (Plate 174), Pollaiuolo's *St. Sebastian*, Piero della Francesca's *Baptism of Christ*, Piero di Cosimo's *Death of Procris*, Giovanni Bellini's *Agony in the Garden*, Titian's *Noli Me Tangere*, and John Crome's *Mousehold Heath*.

When Eastlake died in 1865 he was succeeded by Sir William Boxall, who was scarcely less successful as Director. During his period of office the Royal Academy moved to Burlington House, leaving the National Gallery free to expand. The most important acquisitions under Boxall were Carlo Crivelli's altarpiece from the Demidoff Collection, Terborch's *Peace of Munster*, Michelangelo's *Entombment* (Plate 176) and, two years later, his *Madonna*—the picture which the Trustees had rejected a generation earlier. 1871 was a great year, with the acquisition of the Peel Collection as a whole; there were twenty-seven pictures and thirty-seven drawings, and the more important pictures included Pieter de Hooch's *Interior* and Rubens's '*Chapeau de Paille*' (Plate 184). The

Government made a special grant of £75,000 for the purchase of this collection.

Frederick William Burton was Director for the next twenty years, and he began his career with the purchase of Botticelli's *Mars and Venus* (Plate 173) and Piero della Francesca's *Nativity* (Plate 175) from the collection of Alexander Barker, and Leonardo's *Virgin of the Rocks* from the Earl of Suffolk. In 1884 the Gallery negotiated for the purchase of twelve pictures from Blenheim Palace, including Raphael's *Ansidei Madonna*, Van Dyck's *Charles I* and seven large pictures by Rubens. The Duke of Marlborough began by asking £400,000 but eventually contented himself with £70,000 for the Raphael and £17,000 for the Van Dyck. The year 1890 was equally successful, with three outstanding works from Longford Castle—Holbein's *Ambassadors* (Plate 179), Moroni's *Italian Nobleman* and the *Admiral Pareja* once attributed to Velazquez and now ascribed to Mazo; the price was £55,000, to which Lord Rothschild, Sir Edward Guinness and Mr Charles Cotes subscribed £10,000 each.

In the same year Mr Henry Tate made his great offer of a separate Gallery for Modern British art, giving not only his own valuable collection but also providing the money for a separate building to hold his own and other nineteenth-century pictures. This was opened in 1897 as a part of the National Gallery, and it remained under the Trustees until 1917, when it became independent; since then the Tate Gallery has had its own Director and Governing body.

The National Gallery proper, which had had additional space since 1887, owned more than a thousand pictures by the end of the century. The admirable booklet by Sir Charles Holmes and C. H. Collins Baker, 'The Making of the National Gallery', 1924, which has provided most of the details in this chapter, may be quoted for a few more figures to illustrate the successful careers of the three great Directors of the second half of the nineteenth century. Eastlake acquired 139 pictures in the ten years of his Directorship, and time has shown about thirty of these to be of secondary importance; Boxall, in eight years, acquired 35 pictures, only two or three of which were inferior; and 180 pictures entered the Gallery during Burton's twenty years, about forty of these being later relegated to the secondary collection. Sir Charles Holmes makes the important point that Eastlake had practically no competition when buying Italian masterpieces, while the competition from Berlin during Burton's time forced up prices and made every important purchase more difficult and meritorious.

These new difficulties began to make themselves felt under the next

Director, Sir Edward Poynter. His début in 1894, with Mantegna's *Agony in the Garden*, Antonello da Messina's *St. Jerome* (Plate 171) and Pisanello's *St. Eustace*, all for £9,000, was highly promising; yet in the same year Rembrandt's *Anslo the Preacher and his Wife* went from the Ashburnham Collection straight to Berlin. It was to prevent further losses abroad of major works of art that the National Art-Collections Fund was founded in 1903, and the opportunity to prove its usefulness came almost at once, when in 1905 it became known that Velazquez's *Rokeby Venus* (Plate 188) was for sale. By every means in its power the Fund raised the necessary £45,000 and secured the *Venus* for the National Gallery; immediately afterwards the situation repeated itself, and the great Hals *Family Group* was acquired only by a special Treasury grant and by pledging future income. The next occasion arose with the Duke of Norfolk's intention to sell the Holbein *Duchess of Milan* (Plate 180), an occasion which found the Gallery and the Fund penniless, and all efforts to save the picture would have been in vain had not an anonymous lady come forward at the last moment with the £40,000 that still remained to be found.

This superb picture had been saved by a miracle, but the miracle was not repeated two years later, in 1911, when Rembrandt's *Mill* came on the market from the Marquess of Lansdowne's collection, to be bought for the then enormous sum of £95,000 for the Widener Collection at Elkins Park, Philadelphia. The loss of this very popular picture—which some modern scholars no longer regard as being by Rembrandt—was felt as a great blow, and the result was the setting up of a Committee under Lord Curzon, which made a long and careful inquiry into the whole question. The Report of the Committee was not published until 1914, but it contained several useful recommendations: the annual grant to the Gallery should be raised from £5,000 to £25,000; in extreme cases the Treasury should be approached for an extraordinary grant; if such measures were not acceptable, there should be a tax imposed on the sale of works of art at auction and the proceeds, together with the death duties paid on works of art, should be available for the National Collections. In addition, the owners of certain masterpieces should be approached and asked to give the nation the first option of purchase, in return for which the Government should make corresponding concessions. Some of these recommendations were to prove useful later on, but the outbreak of war in 1914 shelved the matter for the time being. The greater part of the pictures were taken to safety, the empty building transformed into Government offices, and the purchase grant suspended.

With the Armistice the National Gallery awoke to new life. Three notable bequests enriched the collection: the H. L. Florence Bequest, that of Sir Henry Layard, with its important early Venetians, and Sir Hugh Lane's, which brought the first modern foreign pictures to the National Gallery. The Tate Gallery at Millbank became a completely independent institution, with the task of collecting national and international art of the present day, partly by means of the fund given by Mr Samuel Courtauld which allowed of the purchase of Impressionist works in Paris, and partly because of the extensions paid for by Lord (then Sir Joseph) Duveen. The old National Gallery continued to grow within the framework laid down for it—the bequest of Dr Ludwig Mond brought Raphael's early *Crucifixion* and Titian's late *Madonna*, and a few gaps were systematically filled. In 1919 the King lent part of an altarpiece by Pesellino, to go with the parts already there, and El Greco's *Agony in the Garden* was purchased; this and Bruegel's *Adoration of the Kings*, bought in 1921, being splendid examples of masters previously unrepresented in the Gallery. These acquisitions were some compensation for the loss of other national treasures, such as Gainsborough's *Blue Boy*, which was felt as a severe loss when it was sold by the Duke of Westminster to Mr Huntington of San Marino, California. This was not only a case of a fine work of art going abroad, but at the same time—unlike Rembrandt's *Mill*—it was one of the most popular creations of the classic school of English portraiture. As a result of this sale the problem of the national treasures came once again before the public eye and, in 1921, objects sold to the national museums or to the National Art-Collections Fund were exempted from death duties, while in the following year the Chancellor of the Exchequer gave an official promise to assist in the retention for the nation of works of the very first rank.

Since then the threat to the British heritage of works of art has lost much of its former urgency, and the national collections have the first claim on all works of outstanding importance; yet nevertheless in the last few years some masterpieces have crossed the Atlantic even though none of them was of really crucial importance for England, and there have been cases of the reverse process—of European masterpieces recrossing the Atlantic and ending up in the National Gallery.

Further acquisitions in the last few decades maintained the same high level. In 1929 the precious Wilton Diptych (Plate 169) came from the Earl of Pembroke's collection, a work which has been claimed for various Schools but was most often given to the French School of the late fourteenth century, perhaps to André Beauneveu, the very latest idea being,

VI. AUGUSTE RENOIR: *The Umbrellas*. London, National Gallery

however, that it is a masterpiece of English painting. In the same year the Duke of Northumberland's Titian of the *Vendramin Family* was bought; in 1933 the *Mass of St. Giles* by the Flemish Master of St. Giles; in the following year Hogarth's *Graham Children*. Later still, in 1937, Mr Anthony de Rothschild presented Van Dyck's *Madonna and Child with the Abbé Scaglia as Donor*; we still see the owners of great pictures endowing the national treasure-house in Trafalgar Square. Perhaps even more significant is the number of works purchased from public moneys or with the help of the National Art-Collections Fund. Even the Second World War did not interrupt the progress of the Gallery, for in 1941 Rembrandt's *Margaretha Trip* of 1661, another version of a picture (Plate 189) already in the Gallery, was acquired from Lord Crawford and soon afterwards Sir Francis Cook presented Titian's 'Schiavona'. Other acquisitions of this period include a fine *Pentecost* from Giotto's workshop, Pannini's *Interior of St. Peter's*, Hogarth's *Staymaker*, and four panels of the *Life of St. John Baptist* bought from the Executors of J. Pierpont Morgan for £12,000. The latest accession of importance is Cézanne's *Old Woman with a Rosary* (Colour Plate XX), bought from a private French collection in 1953.

In 1939 the Gallery had to be hastily and completely evacuated, and several of the rooms were destroyed by bombs. The restoration of these rooms, necessarily slow, has made it impossible to show the whole collection for many years, and the selection has had to be limited to the greatest works. This long interruption made it possible to go very thoroughly into the whole question of cleaning the pictures, the question which had caused so many stormy discussions, and on this occasion too the treatment of many long neglected pictures roused some opposition but, on the whole, met with approval. A cleverly arranged and superbly documented special exhibition in 1947 showed that some of the results were nothing less than rediscoveries of lost aesthetic qualities. The lacerated feelings of some amateurs who found it difficult to reconcile their memories of the pictures, unified by 'Gallery tone', with the new colourfulness were gradually won over by the pleasure of seeing the pictures as their creators intended them to be seen. The history of the National Gallery provides plenty of examples of such a change of heart.

This improvement of the Gallery from inside is the more important since any increase in numbers from outside is bound to be a slow process, because it is now much more difficult than formerly to obtain great masterpieces and the National Gallery no longer enjoys the virtual monopoly that, for so many decades, allowed it to select the best. It must now compete with other institutions, principally in the United States, which are every bit as determined to get the best that the shrinking art-market offers; yet the National Gallery has so long a lead over all rivals that it is scarcely possible to imagine it ever being displaced from the position of greatest of the great galleries. In part at least, it owes this lead to the riches of the nation which has been collecting on the grand scale ever since the days of Charles I, Buckingham and Arundel, and has thus built up an enormous reserve. In addition to this, the Gallery has been a truly national possession from the beginning, watched over by the whole country, and again, it has enjoyed a succession of outstanding Directors, who, in their best years, enjoyed great freedom from bureaucratic control. The justifiable interest in British art, which found its own home in the Tate Gallery, never interfered with the development of the National Gallery, for it was always felt that a great nation should be broad-minded and generous enough not to overestimate its own productions, but should cherish all the great Schools of the past in their finest examples. With this in mind England created in her National Gallery a collection which includes everything that is worthy of the nation's admiration.

The National Gallery, London

NOTES ON THE ILLUSTRATIONS

ANTONELLO da Messina (1430–1479)

St. Jerome in his Study   Plate 171
Panel, 18 × 14¼ in. (No. 1418)

This Southern Italian artist was obviously in touch with Flemish painting. In the last years of his life he exercised a strong influence on Venetian art. The intimate scale of this interior —painted during the artist's early period— and the loving record made of every detail create an atmosphere which corresponds admirably to the concentration of the scholar-saint.

BELLINI, Giovanni (c. 1430–1516)

Doge Leonardo Loredan   Plate 177
Panel, 24¼ × 17¾ in. (No. 189)

One of Bellini's duties as court painter to the Venetian Republic was to provide portraits of the reigning Doge. This portrait, the best authenticated of the many attributed to Bellini, must have been painted shortly after the Doge's accession in 1501. The treatment of the bust and the splendour of the state robes heighten the effect of authority.

BOTTICELLI, Sandro (1444–1510)

Mars and Venus   Plate 173
Panel, 27¼ × 68¼ in. (No. 915)

The composition was inspired by an antique sarcophagus. The intellectual background of this painting owes much to the same neo-Platonic ideas which inspired the two mythological paintings in the Uffizi (Plate 45 and Colour Plate XI).

CANALETTO, Antonio (1697–1768)

The Piazza, Venice, seen through an Arch-way   Colour Plate XIX
Canvas, 18½ × 14½ in. (No. 2515)

The view is taken through one of the arches of the colonnade enclosing the Piazza, and looks towards San Marco and the Campanile. It is a late work of this master who created the Venetian 'Vedute' (Views)—a manner of painting which best suited the taste of the cultivated public at that time.

CÉZANNE, Paul (1839–1906)

Old Woman with Rosary   Colour Plate XX
Canvas, 33½ × 25½ in. (No. 6195)

Formerly in the collections of Joachim Gasquet, Aix, and Jacques Doucet, Paris.
A portrait of an old woman whom Cézanne had maintained. It conveys the tragedy of life in the last stages of dissolution. (Lionello Venturi.)

CLAUDE Lorraine (Gellée) (1600–1682)

Seaport: Embarkation of the Queen of Sheba   Plate 187

Canvas, 59 × 77½ in. (No. 14)

Fully signed and dated 1648.
Classical buildings frame the view of an open harbour. As is usual with Claude, the ideal landscape is more important than the action which is taking place in it—here the gathering of the Queen's train on the right.

CONSTABLE, John (1776–1837)

The Cornfield   Plate 193
Canvas, 56¼ × 48 in. (No. 130)

Signed and dated 1826.
Bought from Constable's estate by a group of his admirers in 1837 and presented to the Gallery.
One of the artist's most spontaneous pictures, and based on direct study of nature. The painting has recently been cleaned, and this has given it new life.

CRIVELLI, Carlo (1430/35–1495)

The Annunciation   Plate 172
Panel transferred to canvas, 81½ × 57¾ in. (No. 739)

Signed and dated 1486.
Painted for the convent of the Annunziata in Ascoli, where it remained until 1790. Transferred from there to the Brera, which exchanged

it for another picture in 1820. In the Edward Solly Sale, London 1847, then in the collection of Lord Taunton, who presented it to the Gallery in 1864.

This Annunciation is set in all the splendour imaginable; a remarkable feature is the fact that the angel is accompanied by St. Emidius, who is holding a model of the town of Ascoli in his hand.

EYCK, Jan van (died 1441)

Giovanni Arnolfini and his Wife (?) Plate 170
Panel, $32\frac{1}{4} \times 23\frac{1}{2}$ in. (No. 186)

Signed: Johannes de Eyck fuit hic 1434.
The traditional provenance of the picture is as follows: bought by Don Diego de Guevara in 1490; presented by him to Margaret of Austria before 1516. Later acquired by Mary of Hungary, and moved to Spain together with her other pictures. In the Palace in Madrid in 1789. Taken from there as plunder by a French general; found in Brussels after the Battle of Waterloo, and brought to England. In 1842 acquired by the National Gallery. This provenance has recently been questioned by Mr Maurice W. Brockwell, who argued, though not convincingly, that the two figures may be identified as Jan van Eyck and his wife. But whoever the two sitters may have been, the picture will always remain one of the most solemn symbols of the marriage bond. The mirror on the back of the wall which, with many other details, belongs to the symbolic apparatus of the picture, shows the couple facing the witnesses of the wedding.

FRENCH OR ENGLISH SCHOOL, c. 1395

The Wilton Diptych, Right half   Plate 169
Panel, $18 \times 11\frac{1}{2}$ in. (No. 4451)

On the left leaf there is a portrait of King Richard II (died 1400) with his patron saints, on the right the Virgin and Child surrounded by angels. The picture was in the collection of Charles I and since 1724 has been recorded in the possession of the Earls of Pembroke at Wilton House, where it remained until it was bought by the National Gallery in 1929.

This important work, painted at the close of the fourteenth century, has in the past been attributed, among others, to the School of Paris; in recent years, however it has been held to have been the work of an English painter, on good evidence. This origin would alone assure it a unique position.

GAINSBOROUGH, Thomas (1727–1788)

Mrs. Siddons   Colour Plate I
Canvas, $49\frac{3}{4} \times 39\frac{1}{4}$ in. (No. 683)

Painted in 1785 when the sitter was 30 years old. Bought in 1862 from Major Mair, the husband of Mrs Siddons' grand-daughter.
There are many portraits of this great actress, who was also acknowledged as one of the most remarkable beauties of her time. Here she is shown in an informal pose, as an elegant *grande dame*.

HOBBEMA, Meindert (1638–1709)

The Avenue, Middelharnis   Plate 186
Canvas, $40\frac{1}{2} \times 55\frac{1}{2}$ in. (No. 830)

The characteristic traits of Dutch landscape—extended plains, a wide sky, few verticals—are set down here with greater intensity than in the work of any of Hobbema's more romantic contemporaries.

HOGARTH, William (1697–1764)

'*Shortly after the Marriage*'   Plate 168
Canvas, 27×35 in. (No. 114)

The second picture of the series 'Marriage à la Mode', finished in 1744. Bought by Angerstein in 1797 and passed to the Gallery with his collection in 1824.
A characteristic presentation of the manners of the day; Hogarth gave the theme the moralizing slant demanded by the taste of his contemporaries. The mood of hangover after a party is stressed by the large number of symbolic details.

HOLBEIN, Hans, the Younger (1497–1543)

The French Ambassadors   Plate 179
Panel, $81\frac{1}{2} \times 82\frac{1}{2}$ in. (No. 1314)

Signed and dated 1533.
In the possession of the Polisy family until 1653, then in various French collections until 1790. In the possession of the Earls of Radnor since 1809, from whom it was bought with the aid of private contributions in 1890.
The picture shows Jean de Dinteville, Lord of Polisy, and George de Selve, Bishop of Lavaur. It is Holbein's masterpiece. He has taken particular care to record the details of the mathematical and musical instruments which are set on the table, between the two figures. In the foreground, a skull in forced perspective as a *memento mori*, a conceit very much in favour at that time.

Christina of Denmark, Duchess of Milan
Plate 180

Panel, 70½ × 32½ in. (No. 2475)

In the Royal collection since 1542; passed through the Arundel and Lumley collections to that of the Duke of Norfolk. Bought by the Gallery in 1909 through the National Art-Collections'-Fund with the aid of an anonymous gift of £40,000.

Holbein painted this picture after a drawing he had made during a three-hour sitting in Brussels in 1538, when the young widow was 15 years old. This life-size, official portrait has retained all the spontaneity of that rapid sketch.

MICHELANGELO Buonarroti (1475–1564)

The Entombment
Plate 176

Panel, 63½ × 59 in. (No. 790)

First attributed to Michelangelo by the Nazarene painters Cornelius and Overbeck. This attribution was accepted by many scholars—as far as the composition was concerned, at any rate. Most, however, rejected it. It has been attributed to Pontormo, and also to an unknown painter called the 'Master of the Manchester Madonna', who in this picture through the influence of Michelangelo surpasses his usual achievement in the pathos and grandeur of the composition.

PIERO DELLA FRANCESCA
(1416?–1492)

The Nativity
Plate 175

Panel, 49 × 48¼ in. (No. 908)

The picture would seem to have remained in Borgo San Sepolcro in the possession of the descendants of Piero's brother Marco. It is first recorded in 1825 in the possession of Giuseppe Marini-Franceschi. After being deposited for a short time at the Uffizi, it was bought by Alexander Barker in 1861, and purchased from his estate in 1874. The picture is unfinished.

The ritual composition of the group of angels encircled with light, the stiffly kneeling Madonna and the other figures emphasize the vertical element, while the horizontal is introduced by the roof of the hut behind them; this makes the picture, though much smaller in size, seem like an echo of Piero's great fresco cycle at Arezzo.

REMBRANDT (1606–1669)

Portrait of Margaretha Trip
Plate 189

Canvas, 50¾ × 38 in. (No. 1675)

In the Sir Wm. Middleton collection in 1842, where it was described as a portrait of the artist's mother. Bought from Lord de Saumarez in 1899.

A wonderful example of Rembrandt's later manner.

The Woman Taken in Adultery
Plate 190

Panel, 32½ × 25½ in. (No. 45)

Signed and dated 1644.
Painted for Jan Six, in whose family it remained until 1803; bought by Angerstein in 1807, and acquired with his collection in 1824.

The crowded composition culminates in a steeply rising construction. On its summit there is a richly decorated throne, round which a crowd is collecting. The incident round the figure of Christ is isolated in the left foreground, and picked out by concentrated lighting.

A Woman Bathing
Plate 191

Panel, 24 × 18¼ in. (No. 54)

Signed and dated 1654.
Hendrickje Stoffels is shown here in a casual pose, not disguised as a biblical figure like the Bathsheba in Paris (see Plate 72). This freedom in presentation is remarkable, even for Rembrandt. One of his finest colour compositions, this picture has been most successfully cleaned a short time ago.

RENOIR, Auguste (1841–1919)

The Umbrellas
Colour Plate VI

Canvas, 71 × 45¼ in. (No. 3268)

Signed.
Bought from the artist in 1892 by Durand-Ruel; in Sir Hugh Lane's collection and acquired through his bequest.

Belongs to Renoir's period of transition from his earlier, impressionist manner to the later style which was dominated by Ingres. The spontaneity and ease, however, characterize both periods equally.

REYNOLDS, Sir Joshua (1723–1792)

Lord Heathfield, Governor of Gibraltar
Plate 192

Canvas, 56 × 44¾ in. (No. 111)

Painted in 1787 and bought with the Angerstein collection in 1824.
The sitter, George Augustus Eliott, was created
Lord Heathfield in 1787. Owing to his fame
as defender of Gibraltar from 1779 to 1783,
Reynolds has represented him holding a large
key—the 'Key of the Mediterranean'—and
with a cannon in the background. A fine combination of middle-class virtue with panache.

RUBENS, Peter Paul (1577–1640)

The Triumph of Silenus   Plates 182–3
Canvas, 54 × 77½ in. (No. 853)

A typical Bacchanalia, such as the master and
his school repeatedly supplied them.

'Chapeau de Paille': Susanna Fourment
Plate 184

Panel, 30½ × 21 in. (No. 852)

Recorded in the inventory of Rubens's estate,
and later in the possession of Nicolas Lunden,
who married Rubens's daughter Isabella.
Bought in 1823 by Sir Robert Peel and passed
to the Gallery with his collection in 1871.
It is not known exactly how this painting, a
portrait of the sister of Rubens's second wife,
came by its popular name, as the lady is not
wearing a straw hat at all. This is one of the
lately cleaned pictures.

The Chateau de Steen   Plate 185
Panel, 53 × 93 in. (No. 66)

Painted in 1636. Presented to the Nation by Sir
George Beaumont in 1826.
On the left is the artist's Chateau Steen near
Malines; the small figures near it may be identified as Rubens with his wife and a nurse with a
child. The incidentals serve to suggest autumn
occupations and the fertile countryside.

TINTORETTO, Jacopo (1518–1594)

St. George and the Dragon   Plate 178
Canvas, 62 × 39 in. (No. 16)

The princess, who is kneeling facing the picture
plane, is the principal figure of the composition;
the fight with the dragon is taking place in the
middleground. The delicate colour, the relatively small scale of the figures and the dreamy
landscape are characteristic of the early period
of the painter.

TITIAN (c. 1485–1576)

Bacchus and Ariadne   Plate 181
Canvas, 69 × 75 in. (No. 35)

Painted about 1520 for Alfonso I of Ferrara.
Passed through the collection of the Cardinal-
Legate Aldobrandini to the Villa Aldobrandini
in Rome in 1598. Sold to England in 1806. In
the Gallery since 1826.
Edgar Wind has explained the theme of this
picture, the flight of Ariadne from Bacchus, by
reference to texts from Catullus and Ovid.
These classical texts have here been given a new
lease of life through this interpretation in the
spirit of the still young Renaissance.

UCCELLO, Paolo (1397–1475)

The Rout of San Romano   Plate 174
Panel, 72 × 125¾ in. (No. 583)

One of the four battle pieces which Vasari had
seen, and which were later hung in the Medici
Palace in Florence. The two other surviving
panels are in the Uffizi and in the Louvre.
The London picture is the best preserved of the
three, and perhaps is also most characteristic
of Uccello's technique of articulating volume
through the use of scientific—as opposed to
visual—perspective. The impression given is
that of a superreal world.

VELAZQUEZ, Diego (1599–1660)

The Rokeby Venus   Plate 188
Canvas, 48½ × 69 in. (No. 2057)

Belonged to Don Gaspar Mendez de Haro,
Conde Marques del Carpio in 1682, and was
part of his daughter's portion when she married
the Duke of Alba in 1688. In the Alba collection
until 1802. Imported to England before 1813,
and sold to J. B. S. Morritt of Rokeby Hall.
Bought in 1906 through the National Art-
Collections Fund.
The reinterpretation of this classical theme of
the resting Venus is unique in the *œuvre* of this
painter. The figure of the goddess is seen from
the back; she is looking at herself in a mirror
which is being held up to her by a putto.
Both these motifs may be derived from Venetian art of the sixteenth century.

THE NATIONAL GALLERY OF ART
IN WASHINGTON

THE NATIONAL GALLERY OF ART in Washington owes its
origin to the gift made by Mr Andrew Mellon to the American
people in a letter which he wrote to President F. D. Roosevelt on
December 16, 1936; his offer was accepted by Congress on March 24,
1937. The building erected by Mr Mellon to house his splendid collection
and the additions which would make it into a National Gallery was
opened on March 17, 1941. Both the enormous number of visitors and
the numerous gifts which have poured in since that date testify that the
new institution has been accepted by the public in the sense in which
the donor intended it, as the promise of a great national possession. Compared with its sister institutions in Europe the National Gallery of the
United States is a mere child with a history of only a few years, whereas
many of them can look back on centuries of existence, and for this
reason our examination must deal with the future as much as with the
past.

If the Washington National Gallery is only a child by comparison with
its European counterparts it is certainly a child born with a silver spoon
in its mouth. This applies not only to the richness of its beginnings, but
also to the fact that, as a latecomer, it is in a position to learn from the
experience of the older collections, and thus to reach its goal with fewer
side-trackings on the way than many of them have had. This goal was
described with admirable clarity in Mr Mellon's letter to the President:
"It is of the greatest importance," he stated, "that future acquisitions of
works of art, whether by gift or purchase, shall be limited to objects of
the highest standard of quality, so that the collection . . . shall not be
marred by the introduction of art that is not the best of its type." This
idea has been expressly formulated in the Constitution of the Gallery.
Mr Mellon himself added "I have tried to adhere to this standard in
the collection which I have made."

The collection formed on these principles by Mr Mellon, with one eye
to its future as the nucleus of a National Gallery, consisted of 126 paintings
and 26 pieces of sculpture. In accordance with the purpose of forming the

skeleton of a great National Collection, the pictures included outstanding examples of the major European Schools of the past—Italian,
Dutch, Flemish, Spanish, English, French, and German—and, as a sort
of appendix, a group of American portraits, chosen because they represented important personalities in the history of the American people.
Leaving aside this secondary material, corresponding more or less to the
National Portrait Gallery in London or to the material at Versailles, we
may safely assert that the Mellon pictures form one of the most carefully
selected collections ever brought together by a private person.

The expression 'private collection' has been deliberately avoided, for
until the moment when they all entered the National Gallery the pictures
had in fact never been shown as a unity. One group among them required
particular tact in the negotiations, possibly because of the unusual circumstances under which they had been acquired. These were the pictures
from the Hermitage, sold by the Soviet Government at a time when it
was not yet officially recognized by the U.S. Government; and at that
time Mr Mellon was a member of the American Government. This sale
enriched several museums with pictures far superior in quality to anything normally obtainable on the art market, but the list of the pictures
from the Hermitage which are now in the National Gallery shows that
Mr Mellon obtained the greatest treasures. This list is: Botticelli, *The
Adoration of the Magi* (Plate 203); Chardin, *The House of Cards*; Van
Dyck, *Susanna Fourment and her Daughter*; Jan van Eyck, *The Annuncia-
tion* (Plate 195); Frans Hals, *Portrait of a Young Man*; Pietro Perugino,
Crucifixion with Saints; Raphael, *The Alba Madonna* (Plate 202) and *St.
George and the Dragon*; Rembrandt, *Girl with a Broom*, *Woman holding a
Pink*, *Polish Nobleman*, *A Turk*, *Joseph accused by Potiphar's Wife*; Titian,
Venus with a Mirror (Plate 201) and Velazquez, *Pope Innocent X*.

The pictures from the Hermitage were not the only ones Mr Mellon
was able to secure as a result of the political and economic upheavals
following the First World War. He acquired Nicolas Lancret's *La
Camargo dancing in a Park* from the ex-Kaiser Wilhelm II, the descendant
of Frederick II of Prussia, who had bought the picture for his palace at
Sanssouci. Other deposed German Princes parted with such pictures as
Holbein's *Edward VI as a Child* (from the Royal House of Hanover),
which is usually regarded as the picture given to Henry VIII on New
Year's Day, 1539, Filippino Lippi's *Madonna adoring the Child* (from the
Grand Duke of Saxe-Meiningen), and Roger van der Weyden's charming
Portrait of a Lady (from the Duke of Anhalt-Dessau; Plate 196). There
is no doubt that the times aided Mr Mellon in the formation of his

VII. ANTHONY VAN DYCK: *Paola Adorno, Marchesa Brignole Sale, and her Son.*
Washington, National Gallery of Art (Widener Collection)

collection; but it is the merit of a great collector to make better use of his opportunities than his rivals.

Mr Mellon had a distinct preference for pictures with splendid pedigrees—he liked to buy out of 'good houses', and this may have been encouraged by Lord Duveen, his chief supplier, when he used to say jokingly, "If a painting has been a Rubens for the Dukes of Devonshire for hundreds of years, it is a good enough Rubens for my customers, in spite of anything some German art critic may object." In such a house—Lord Spencer's Althorp, to be precise—Mr Mellon (or Lord Duveen acting for him) found Gainsborough's *Georgiana, Duchess of Devonshire*, a much admired sitter, whom Gainsborough often painted; and in another good house, in this case that of the family for which it had been painted, he found Goya's *Marquesa de Pontejos*. Other examples of pictures with outstanding pedigrees are Raphael's *Niccolini-Cowper Madonna*, which had belonged to the Earls Cowper from 1780 until 1918; Rembrandt's *Self-Portrait* of 1659, from the Duke of Buccleuch in Scotland; Reynolds's *Lady Caroline Howard*, from Castle Howard, and the *Portrait of a Young Man*, which passed as a Velazquez for many years in the collection of the Counts Harrach in Vienna, but is now generally thought to be the masterpiece of Velazquez's son-in-law Juan Bautista del Mazo. El Greco's *St. Ildefonso* can boast of an exalted pedigree of a different kind, since it once belonged to two great French painters—first to Jean-François Millet and then to Degas.

Other acquisitions, scarcely less splendid in themselves, came from less well documented sources: two exceptionally fine Quattrocento portraits, the *Lady* (Plate 194) attributed to Pisanello (?), and the *Man*, now believed to be by Andrea del Castagno, as well as the Hals *Old Lady*, Rembrandt's *Lucretia* and the three Vermeers. If one looks back to the Angerstein Collection, the germ of the National Gallery in London, the purchase of which in 1824 began that Gallery on its glorious career, it is scarcely possible to doubt that the National Gallery in Washington has started out on its career under far more favourable auspices. Even apart from the much greater number of masterpieces of the first rank, the general level of quality of the Washington pictures is much higher. Only about half of the thirty-eight Angerstein pictures are still considered worthy of permanent exhibition, whereas it is easy to prophesy that a far higher percentage of the Mellon pictures, perhaps ninety per cent or even more, will still be worthy of exhibition in a great National Gallery in fifty or a hundred years time. Nearly all of them are of such quality that they are above the normal fluctuations of taste—that is to say, they possess that outstanding artistic worth predicated by Mr Mellon for any additions to be made to the Gallery.

However, a large collection of pictures cannot limit itself to great masterpieces for ever, and other Galleries know from experience that works of secondary importance come in ceaselessly, so that the giants of the forest are gradually surrounded with more or less thick undergrowth, and the older the collection the richer this secondary material becomes. It forms a reserve which can be put into the depot or lent to smaller Museums, but it is certainly not lacking in interest and importance. Such pictures may be used for study, as comparative material, and as the proper background and standard of measurement for the works of primary importance. The Washington gallery could no more remain on the heights achieved by Mr Mellon's gifts than could any other gallery in the world. From the beginning it had been his intention, as he expressed it in his letter, that his example should inspire his fellow-countrymen, attracting the gifts of anyone who, in the future, might wish to present works of the highest quality in the effort to build up a great National Gallery. His decision to build so large a house right away, big enough to contain all the additions for many years to come, was part and parcel of his desire to encourage such gifts. It is possible that in the process he underestimated the magnetic power of such a vacuum, which attracted other collections, and which makes it difficult to avoid a lowering of the general level of quality. Mr Mellon was farsighted enough to fear this as the greatest danger the National Gallery would have to face.

When the National Gallery was opened the Mellon pictures were already surrounded by a crowd of those lesser works which usually accumulate gradually in any great collection. Anticipating this natural development, the National Gallery began life with a combination of first and second rate works; but this must certainly not be taken to mean that the collection which, thanks to the generous benefaction of Mr Samuel H. Kress of New York, came to be added to the Mellon pictures was in any way secondrate or unworthy of a major museum. It is simply that the Kress Collection was assembled on different principles from those which governed the formation of the Mellon Collection. Mr Mellon had from the beginning, or at any rate from a definite moment, the idea of the creation of a National Gallery before his eyes, whereas Mr Kress was not so much concerned with that as with buying pictures which he found interesting. His original intention was to further American Museums in general by providing them with good material; and the differing aims of the two collections can best be seen by a comparison of figures, for while the Mellon Collection contained 126 pictures chosen from all the most important Schools, the Kress Collection, when it was first made over to the National Gallery, contained 375 pictures, all of them Italian. This alone shows that the principle of quantity had to some extent replaced that of quality.

This is not to say that the Kress Collection in the National Gallery, now considerably enlarged by later additional gifts, has not enriched the Gallery with a number of highly important works. At the head of any list of them must be mentioned the *Allendale Adoration* (Plate 204), named after its former owner, Viscount Allendale, which is regarded by the majority of critics as an early work by Giorgione, although neither Berenson nor the author of this book concur in this view. This would be followed by Duccio's *Calling of the Apostles Peter and Andrew*, once part of the *Maestà* in Siena Cathedral and of which the Mellon *Adoration* also once formed a part; by Giovanni Bellini's *Portrait of a Condottiere*, a picture which is still being argued over, both as to its painter and the sitter; by Sassetta's *Meeting of SS. Anthony and Paul* (Plate 198), part of an altarpiece the remaining portions of which are scattered over a number of collections; by two charming little pictures by Lotto—the *Maiden's Dream* from the Conway Collection and the *Allegory* which once served as the cover to the portrait of Bernardo Rossi in Naples; and, finally, by the *Christ at the Sea of Galilee* (Plate 205) ascribed to Jacopo Tintoretto but which may also be considered as a possible El Greco. A particularly important addition was the group of eighteenth-century pictures, since this second flowering of Italian painting was not represented in the Mellon Collection. In this category there are some fine Venetian views by Guardi (Plate 212), several small Tiepolos and, from a different School, Pannini's *Interior of the Pantheon in Rome*. Several dozen other pictures provided the National Gallery with rich material for comparative and critical studies.

At the time of its opening, the National Gallery had already received several single gifts in addition to the two main collections, and it soon justified the conviction expressed by Mr Mellon that the high standard set by his pictures would prove a magnet to other pictures; by the second year of its existence the Gallery had already had two major additions which were important although basically different in character, and both of them completely fulfilling the ideal laid down for the Gallery. A selection of pictures from the Chester Dale Collection in New York came on long loan and the Joseph Widener Collection, formerly at Lynnewood Hall, Elkins Park, Philadelphia, passed into the possession of the Gallery—but to the visitor the difference in legal ownership is of no moment.

The Chester Dale pictures are intended to demonstrate the main development of French painting from David to Cézanne—a School previously unrepresented in the Gallery, which now contains several masterpieces by the leading artists, such as the works by Corot, Manet's *Old Musician* of 1862, which once belonged to the Vienna Gallery, and Renoir's early *Odalisque*. Among the numerous portraits by Degas is one of the Duke and Duchess of Morbilli, painted in 1856, which is slightly earlier than the better-known version in the Museum of Fine Arts in Boston, and a comparison of the two versions is extremely instructive from an art-historical point of view, even though this kind of instruction is less a part of the programme of the National Gallery than the education of public taste by the exhibition of supreme masterpieces only. In this respect, practically no other acquisition can compare with the Widener Collection, which can be reckoned as one of the most carefully chosen private collections in the world, since its last owner inherited 302 pictures, mostly fashionable French ones, from his father and then, by weeding them out, reduced the collection to 47: in this way it provides a classic example of Mellon's principle of quality before quantity.

The most important part of the collection consists of the Dutch pictures, with Frans Hals's *Man*, two splendid Vermeers—the *Woman weighing Gold* (Plate 208) and the *Girl with a Flute*—several fine works by Pieter de Hooch, Cuyp, Ruisdael and Hobbema, and to crown them all no less than fourteen Rembrandts, including some of his finest works (Plate 207). Van Dyck is the best represented among the Flemings, and two of his sumptuous portraits of great ladies of the Genoese aristocracy, *Paola Adorno, Marchesa di Brignole Sale* (Colour Plate VII) and the *Marchesa Elena Grimaldi*, now hold their own alongside the *Marchesa Balbi* which had already entered the Gallery with the Mellon pictures.

Other high-lights of the Widener Collection include Murillo's *Girl and her Duenna*, one of the rare secular works by the painter of Madonnas; and a pair of religious works by El Greco, the *St Martin and the Beggar* and the *Virgin with Saint Agnes and Saint Thecla*, which have never been separated since Greco painted them in 1597/99 for the chapel of St. Joseph in Toledo. In spite of the *Small Cowper Madonna* of 1505 the Italian pictures would have been less important than their counterparts in the Mellon and Kress Collections had it not been for the presence of one of the most enchanting works of the whole School, the so-called *Feast of the Gods* which was signed by Giovanni Bellini in 1514 and was then modernized by Titian a few years later (Colour Plate XXI).

This assemblage of so imposing a beginning was followed by a large number of additions, such as the J. L. Rosenwald Collection of Graphic Art, one of the finest in its special field. In addition, there were such things as the Ralph and Mary Booth Gift and some single acquisitions like Van Dyck's *Duc de Guise* and El Greco's *Laocoön* (Plate 206), a unique excursion into classical mythology by the great Spanish mystic. Still more important is the lasting care bestowed on the Gallery by the Samuel H. Kress Foundation, for more pictures were added to the first gift of 375 Italian pictures—71 in October, 1944, and another hundred in January, 1946, some of them French. In 1951 the National Gallery held a loan exhibition of the most recent acquisitions of the Foundation, and many of the most important have meanwhile passed into the possession of the Gallery. Among the most splendid of the Italians there is the tondo of the *Adoration of the Kings,* begun by Fra Angelico and apparently finished by Fra Filippo Lippi, evidently the picture so fully described in the Inventory of Lorenzo the Magnificent, the group portrait of Cardinal Bandinello Sauli with his secretary and two geographers, by Sebastiano del Piombo, and Titian's portrait of Ranuccio Farnese, which, like the Fra Angelico, came from the famous Cook Collection in Richmond, Surrey. These pictures were now joined by North European works of comparable importance, such as the two panels of *Scenes from the Life of St. Remigius,* by the Master of St. Gilles (Plate 197), which are pendants to two panels in the National Gallery in London; Pieter Bruegel the Elder's *Landscape with the Martyrdom of St. Catherine;* two big compositions by Nicolas Poussin, one mythological and one religious, and Chardin's *Nurse,* formerly in the Liechtenstein Gallery in Vienna. Two pictures by Dürer were particularly important acquisitions since he is so poorly represented in America. These are the *Thyssen Madonna,* with *Lot and his Daughters* on the reverse, and the exciting *Portrait of a Clergyman,* signed and dated 1516 (Plate 199), from the Count Czernin Gallery in Vienna, which some Swiss scholars would like to identify as a portrait of the Reformer Ulrich Zwingli. The improvement in quality of the Kress additions to the National Gallery has allowed some of the earlier gifts to be transferred to the study collection, and it is all the more promising for the future of the National Gallery since the Foundation is destined to remain the most important and generous helper in its future expansion. There are already rumours of still grander acquisitions, not yet handed over to the public, one of which we obtained the special privilege of including in this book, the so-called *Little Crucifixion* by Matthias Grünewald (Plate 200).

However much we may admire the achievements of so short a period we must not forget that they are no more than a beginning, a beginning with a better foundation than any comparable institution has ever had in its early years, and a beginning which is so glorious that it also involves heavy responsibilities. It is very likely that the Gallery will grow by leaps and bounds and that Mr Mellon's hope of attracting further donors will be fulfilled to such an extent that his principal desire, that quality should not be sacrificed to quantity, may be in danger of being overlooked.

As a means of guarding against a lowering of the general level of quality several Museums, including the Metropolitan, have adopted the general rule of refusing on principle all collections offered to them as gifts if they are accompanied by the condition that they must be exhibited as a whole and in entirety. The National Gallery has already reached so high a level that no existing or future private collection could hope to equal, let alone surpass it. At best, such a collection could hope to fill up some gaps and round off the whole.

Possibly the day may come when the frontiers which now separate the collections of different origin in the National Gallery, even though these boundaries are modified by the accommodation of related material in adjoining rooms, may be done away with altogether. It is only human for the donor of a valuable collection to want the memory of his public-spirited action to be preserved for all time, and it can also be an interesting study to observe how the individualities of varying collectors are reflected in their collections. If all the great collections made a practice of adopting the origin or provenance of pictures as the basis of their hanging arrangements they would merely deprive themselves of the possibility of organic development of their museums. This is not to say that all pictures by one artist or of one School must always and everywhere be exhibited together. Many other arrangements may be permissible and desirable but in the last analysis the arrangement of a museum must be determined by aesthetic and historical considerations, and not with regard to persons who may once have had the privilege of bequeathing their treasures to their country. A truly national Gallery cannot rest satisfied with a group of more or less important private collections housed under one roof, for its aim is far higher than to provide a permanent homage to successful collectors.

This question would seem to be losing its urgency for future generations, since the era of enormous private collections seems to be over, or nearly so. Gigantic fortunes are hardly likely to be made again on the scale applied in the formation of the collections put together in the first decades of the present century. The duty of founding and maintaining public collections and similar institutions is passing from the multi-millionaire to other patrons. The history of comparable institutions in Europe shows parallel cases of collections founded by princely families being taken over by the State, and, where individuals were no longer rich enough to dominate the art market, we find societies—the National Art-Collections Fund, the Amis du Louvre, the Kaiser Friedrich Museum Verein, the Rembrandt Vereniging—formed to assist the public collections. Lovers of the arts who earlier might have been able to afford the luxury of building up and eventually bequeathing whole collections will in future have to content themselves with the presentation of individual works or with taking part in presentations made by societies of which they are members. When we add up what the Louvre, the Rijksmuseum, or the National Gallery in London owe to this kind of support we find treasures no less important than those acquired by the gift of whole collections. It is particularly true of France, the home of the true amateur, that there is hardly anyone who has not dreamed, or does not dream, of having the honour to offer the Louvre a picture belonging to him or to be able to help in the purchase of a new work of art.

The presupposition underlying such an attitude is that a National Gallery is in every sense of the word the property of the nation and that it is run by competent people within the framework of a fully considered long-term programme, by a staff which is responsible to the nation as a whole and not to special interests, and which can cope with the problems of purchase, rejection, critical arrangement, and all the details of research into the works in their charge. Without such a conscious sense of responsibility the National Gallery in Washington would find it hard to make a niche for itself in the life of the nation, just as a century ago the London National Gallery needed such a raising of its status in order to make itself a truly public institution instead of remaining the plaything of a few noblemen.

Several of the great European galleries went through such growing-pains before they became aware of their special obligations as National Galleries. In the Introduction it was shown that the idea of a National Gallery as distinct from other collections, sometimes nearly as rich, was a result of forces unleashed by the French Revolution. These ideas made the nations of Europe conscious, sometimes unfortunately all too conscious, of their individual characteristics. In the United States, where the assimilation of heterogeneous elements into a single nation began later and is still to some extent in progress, the conditions are somewhat different. An instructive example is afforded by a comparison of the rather grudging acceptance of the Smithsonian Institution, a hundred years ago, with the nation's acceptance of the National Gallery. At that time there was strong opposition, led by John S. Calhoun on constitutional grounds, against the acceptance of James Smithson's gift to the United States 'for the establishment of an institution to increase and diffuse knowledge among men' and only the heroic efforts of John Quincey Adams in the legislature saved for the nation the Institution which has since become so great. There was no such opposition to the acceptance of the National Gallery and the importance of the new body for the whole nation was recognized without any reservations in the debate in Congressional Committee on the technical aspects of the gift.

A National Gallery is not complete from the first day of its existence and the nation and the gallery have to grow together into a unity. Problems crop up which the older sister institutions have had to face and settle: what, for example, should be the position of the national School in relation to the whole? This problem has been settled by different Galleries in different ways, but the most general solution is to incorporate the really outstanding examples in the Gallery and to create a special Gallery for the average level of the National School. Mr Mellon had included a number of American pictures in his gift, most of which were of greater historical than artistic interest, but he also left the door open for American works of aesthetic merit and paintings by Sully, Inness, Ryder (Plate 215), Homer, Eakins (Plate 216) and Bellows, have in fact found their way into the Gallery. In this the example of the National Gallery in London has been followed, where the ruling principle is that such works should be accepted only when this distinction is merited on purely artistic grounds. American pictures will be sought after with increasing vigour as the nation becomes increasingly conscious of its ownership of the Gallery, for it is obvious that the art of our own country is important to us for many and deep reasons other than pure aesthetic reaction or historical interest. In order not to destroy the balance of the international side of the Gallery it will need a second centre for the display of those works which, right or wrong, touch the spectator most nearly, because they spring from his native soil and express its spirit.

Closely linked to this problem is the one of contemporary art. Nearly all the great Galleries at the outset of their careers divided their energies and their funds between the art of the past and that of the present, and everywhere the same thing happened—a sharper division between the two, in the interests of both and of the public as well. Sometimes the line of demarcation is drawn at a fixed point, such as the beginning or the middle of the nineteenth century, but a more organic solution seems to be that adopted by the Tate Gallery in London and the Luxembourg in Paris, whereby works by living artists, which seem at the time to be important, can be secured for the nation although they are not incorporated into the official collection of the nation's treasures until after the death of the artist and the expiry of a waiting period.

The motion introduced by Senator Walsh in 1937 and repeated in a slightly different form in the following year by Congressman Keller had something similar in mind when it proposed the completion of the National Gallery by the creation of a second national institution to be devoted to American and contemporary art.

The National Gallery adopts the same standpoint in practice, if not in its constitution, even though it has accepted works by living artists with the twentieth-century pictures in the Chester Dale loan, although they are not permanently there. It seems natural that here, as elsewhere, the National Gallery is feeling its way towards the definitive form which will express its special character: as was observed at the beginning of this chapter, it stands between past and future. As time goes on, its duty becomes clearer: to revive the artistic heritage of Europe on new soil, to fit it into the specific needs of American culture, and to recast a treasure house into a spiritual possession.

View of the National Gallery of Art. Pen and ink drawing by Rockwell Kent.

NOTES ON THE ILLUSTRATIONS

BELLINI, Giovanni (*c.* 1430–1516)

The Feast of the Gods   Colour Plate XXI
Canvas, 67 × 74 in. (No. 597)

Signed and dated 1514.
Painted for Alfonso d'Este of Ferrara. In 1598
it was taken to Rome by Cardinal Pietro
Aldobrandini, and from the Palazzo Aldobrandini it came into the possession of the
painter Camuccini in Rome, whose collection
was bought by the Duke of Northumberland
in 1856. From Alnwick Castle it passed to the
Widener Collection in 1920.
Vasari mentions that Titian worked on this
picture and his style can indeed be recognized
in the sweeping landscape on the left. This
'modernization' was probably carried out in
1525. The subject of this picture is the amorous
assault by Priapus on the sleeping nymph on
the right, which is foiled by the braying of the
donkey. Ovid's *Fasti* are the source for this
story.

BOTTICELLI, Sandro (1444–1510)

The Adoration of the Magi   Plate 203
Panel, 27¾ × 40⅝ in. (No. 22)

Since 1808 in the Hermitage, Leningrad;
from there it came into the Mellon Collection
in 1937.
Most scholars believe it to date from the artist's
Roman period, i.e. 1481-2. In general composition it is related to the version in the Uffizi
(see Plate 41) but it is more loosely composed
and placed in a wide landscape.

COROT, Camille (1796–1875)

Rocks in the Forest of Fontainebleau
                                    Plate 214
Canvas, 18 × 23 in. (Chester Dale Collection)

A nature study in which special attention is
given to the effect of light.

DÜRER, Albrecht (1471–1528)

Portrait of a Clergyman   Plate 199
Parchment on canvas, 16⅞ × 13 in. (No. 85)

Signed in monogram and dated 1516.
If the identification of the sitter with Johann
Dorsch, vicar of St. Johann, Nürnberg, is
correct, the painting may come from the
Praun cabinet in Nürnberg. Later in Count
Czernin's Collection in Vienna. Samuel H.
Kress Collection. (It has recently been sug-
gested that the sitter is Ulrich Zwingli.)
In spite of its simplicity, found in Dürer's late
portraits, its creates a deep impression.

DYCK, Anthony van (1599–1641)

*Paola Adorno, Marchesa Brignole Sale, and her
Son*   Colour Plate VII
Canvas, 74½ × 55 in. (No. 687)
Widener Coll.

EAKINS, Thomas (1844–1916)

The Biglen Brothers Racing   Plate 216
Canvas, 23⅝ × 35⅞ in.

Whitney Museum of American Art, New York;
presented to the National Gallery by Mr and
Mrs C. Vanderbilt Whitney in 1953.
Probably painted in 1873, shortly after Eakins'
return from his European apprenticeship. The
exaggerated anatomical detail and the frozen
movement of the boat characterize it as an
early work. The scene is the Schuylkil River in
the artist's native Philadelphia, where sculling
is a favourite sport.

EYCK, Jan van (died 1441)

The Annunciation   Plate 195
Transferred from panel to canvas, 36¾ ×
14½ in. (No. 39)
It came from the Hermitage into the Mellon
Collection. The Annunciation is taking place in
a high, late-mediaeval church, whose furnishings not only suggest decorative splendour but
also have a symbolic significance interpreted by

numerous inscriptions. In its gentle dignity and harmonious lighting, the painting, probably the wing of a lost altarpiece, is one of the artist's masterpieces.

GAUGUIN, Paul (1848–1903)

Self-Portrait   Plate 219
Panel, 31¼ × 20¼ in.

Signed and dated 1889.
Painted on a wooden cupboard door in Mlle. Marie Henry's inn in Le Poulde, Brittany. From the collection of Mrs. R. A. Workman, London, and Hodener, Paris, it came into the Chester Dale Collection.
The clear colour is reminiscent of stained glass or enamel with its dividing lines. Typical of the 'Art Nouveau' of the end of the nineteenth century.

GIORGIONE (1477?–1510)

The Adoration of the Shepherds   Plate 204
Panel, 35¾ × 43½ in. (No. 400)

It can first definitely be traced in the collection of Cardinal Fesch in Rome; when this was dispersed in 1841, the painting passed into the possession of Claudius Tarral. 1847 in the collection Wentworth Beaumont and then by descent to Lord Allendale, London. Samuel H. Kress Collection 1939. Most scholars, with the exception of Berenson and Tietze, believe this painting to be an early work by Giorgione, painted about 1500–1505. Its connection with the late style of Giovanni Bellini does not contradict this attribution.

GOYA, Francisco de (1746–1828)

Señora Sabasa Garcia   Plate 209
Canvas, 28 × 23 in. (No. 88)

From the James Simon Collection, Berlin; Mellon Collection. The youthful sitter is portrayed with striking simplicity and sympathetic understanding.

EL GRECO (1541–1614)

Laocoön   Plate 206
Canvas, 54⅛ × 68 in.

The early history of this painting is uncertain, but it passed through various collections in Spain and Germany into that of Prince Paul of Yugoslavia, Belgrade; Samuel H. Kress Collection 1945.

The only mythological painting in the work of the artist. In composition it is independent of the antique sculpture discovered in 1506. Nor was Virgil the immediate source. The two figures on the right have been interpreted as Apollo and Artemis.

GRÜNEWALD, Matthias (died c. 1530)

The Crucifixion   Plate 200
Panel, 24⅝ × 18⅛ in.

This picture, which appeared in the Rhineland in 1922 and came into the collection of F. Koenigs in Haarlem, is identical with the 'Small Crucifix' which Joachim von Sandrart saw and greatly praised in the collection of Duke Wilhelm the Pious of Bavaria.
Christ is far more emaciated than in the Karlsruhe Crucifixion; even His loincloth falls in meagre folds. The despair of the Mother and St. John is largely expressed through their hands. The Magdalen, without participating in the sorrowing of the Mother and St. John, conveys the fervent devotion of the spectator.

GUARDI, Francesco (1712–1793)

View on the Cannaregio, Venice   Plate 212
Canvas, 18¾ × 29¼ in. (No. 224)

Previously in the Chiesa collection, Milan. Samuel H. Kress Collection. A beautiful view of the town, flooded with light, and filled with lively figures—so characteristic of Guardi—both on the water and on shore.

LONGHI, Pietro (1702–1785)

Blind Man's Buff   Plate 211
Canvas, 19¼ × 24 in. (No. 175)

Previously in the Giovanelli collection, Venice, and then in the Samuel H. Kress Collection. One of Longhi's popular *genre* scenes which render episodes from daily life or from the theatre with natural gaiety and delicacy in handling.

MASTER OF ST. GILLES (active end of fifteenth century)

The Baptism of Clovis   Plate 197
Panel, 24⅜ × 19 in. (No. 83)

Together with its companion piece, the *Conversion of an Aryan by St. Remy*, it was formerly in the collection of Count Lestang-Parade and later in the collections of Baron E. de Beurnonville, Paris, and Mr. Watil, Paris. Samuel H. Kress Collection 1946.

Two panels in the National Gallery, London, illustrating the legend of St. Gilles, also belong to this series. A typically northern interior in which the figures, treated almost as portraits, seem to create the impression of a vast crowd. An important work of the Paris School of about 1500.

PISANELLO, Antonio (c. 1395–1455)

Profile Portrait of a Lady   Plate 194
Panel, 20⅜ × 14⅜ in. (No. 23)

From the Villeroy collection, Paris, it came into the Mackay collection, Roslyn, N.Y., and from there into the Mellon Collection in 1937.

Recent literature on this fascinating picture has tended to assume a French origin of about 1410–15, in view of the French court costume, the colouring and piquancy of conception. Paintings of this kind may have inspired Pisanello. The international character of European painting of this period explains the uncertainty of the attribution.

RAPHAEL (1483–1520)

Alba Madonna   Plate 202
Transferred from panel to canvas in 1837. Diameter 37¾ in. (No. 24)

In the sixteenth century this painting was apparently acquired by the Viceroy of Naples, Marchese del Caprio, from the Convent Monte Oliveto in Nocera and brought to Spain. For a long time it belonged to the Dukes of Alba, was later in the collections of Bourke and Coesvelt and since 1836 in the Hermitage, Leningrad. Mellon Collection 1937.

Preparatory drawings in Lille allow one to date this picture between Raphael's work in the first and second Stanza of the Vatican. Fischel drew attention to the fact that the picture is not only contained within the tondo form, but that the landscape too sweeps round the Madonna and fully encircles her.

REMBRANDT (1606–1669)

Portrait of a Lady with an Ostrich-Feather Fan
          Plate 207
Canvas, 39¼ × 32⅝ in. (No. 664)

From the collection of Prince Youssoupoff, Leningrad, it came into the Widener Collection.

A pendant to the portrait of a gentleman with gloves is in the same collection, but no inner connection between the two sitters is expressed. The distinguished lady gazes with great indifference in front of her. A masterpiece of the artist's late period.

RENOIR, Auguste (1841–1919)

Bather Arranging her Hair   Plate 218
Canvas, 35½ × 29 in.

Prince de Wagram; Chester Dale Collection. Belongs to the last period in Renoir's *œuvre*, having been exhibited on the Salon d'Automne in 1906. Figure and surroundings are given equal emphasis and picturesquely fill the picture space.

ROGIER VAN DER WEYDEN
(c. 1400–1464)

Portrait of a Lady   Plate 196
Panel, 14½ × 10¾ in. (No. 44)

From the collection of Prince Anhalt-Dessau, in Woerlitz, it came into the Mellon Collection. The identity of the lady, painted with a surprising freshness and simplicity, is not certain. It has been suggested that she is Marie de Valengin, a natural daughter of Philip the Good of Burgundy.

ROMNEY, George (1734–1802)

Mrs. Davenport   Plate 210
Canvas, 30 × 25 in. (No. 105)

The entries for the sittings, recorded in Romney's diary, extend over the period 1782–84. From the collection of Sir William Bromley Davenport, it passed into the Mellon Collection.

The most British of British portraits, contrasting strongly with contemporary French portraits of ladies of society. The hairstyle is natural, the dress rural and the expression unaffected and frank.

RYDER, Albert P. (1847–1917)

Siegfried and the Rhine Maidens   Plate 215
Canvas, 19⅞ × 20½ in. (No. 886)

Exhibited in New York in 1902. From the Sir William van Horne collection, Montreal, it passed to Chester Dale and then to the Mellon Collection. The picture, typical of Ryder's romanticism, was according to his own statement painted in 48 hours without a break, under the inspiration of a performance of Wagner's 'Götterdämmerung'.

SASSETTA (1392–1450)

The Meeting of St. Anthony and St. Paul
Plate 198
Panel, 18 × 13⅝ in. (No. 404)

Viscount Allendale collection, London; Samuel H. Kress Collection 1939. The panel originally belonged to a large altarpiece representing St. Anthony Abbot and scenes from his life.
In the background St. Anthony is seen on his pilgrimage, in the middle distance he asks the way of a centaur, and in the foreground he is embracing St. Paul, the even older hermit.

STUART, Gilbert (1755–1828)

The Skater
Plate 213
Canvas, 96⅝ × 58⅛ in.

A portrait of William Grant of Congalton skating in St. James's Park in 1782. Remained in the possession of his family in England until 1950, when it came into the Mellon Collection. This picture is supposed to have been the first to make Stuart well known after his studies under Benjamin West. It was exhibited in the Royal Academy in 1782. The main emphasis is placed on the portrait, which almost fills the entire picture, and not on the *genre* element, which is only hinted at in the landscape with small figures.

TINTORETTO, Jacopo (1518–1594)

Christ at the Sea of Galilee
Plate 205
Canvas, 46⅛ × 66½ in.

Collection Count J. Galotti; Arthur and Alice Sachs, New York. Samuel H. Kress Collection. The subject is represented as described in St. Matthew, 14, 22–31 rather than as in St. John 21, 4–7.
All scholars ascribe this painting to Tintoretto, but their opinions as to its date vary greatly.

No analogy with this painting can be found amongst Tintoretto's early or late certain works. Various elements in this overpowering and magnificent work make an attribution to El Greco, about 1578, plausible.

TITIAN (c. 1485–1576)

Venus with a Mirror
Plate 201
Canvas, 49 × 41½ in. (No. 34)

Titian's son sold it to the Barbarigo family, with whom it remained till it was sold to the Hermitage in 1850. Mellon Collection.
Several versions of this composition exist; the present one is probably the original, which remained in the studio as prototype, and was probably completed when sold to the Barbarigo family.

TURNER, Joseph Mallord William (1775–1851)

Venice: Dogana and San Giorgio Maggiore
Canvas, 36 × 48 in. (No. 681) Plate 217

Commissioned in 1834 by Henry McConnel, Manchester; 1849 in the collection of John Naynor, Leighton Hall; Widener collection.
A sun-drenched seapiece with festively dressed figures.

VERMEER, Jan (1632–1675)

A Woman weighing Gold
Plate 208
Canvas, 16½ × 14 in. (No. 693)

First mentioned in an auction at Amsterdam in 1696; in 1826 in the collection of the King of Bavaria as by Metsu; 1830 in the collection of Casimir-Périer; later in the collection of the Comtesse de Ségur. Widener Collection.
The composition, with the painting on the wall at the back emphasizing the picture plane, and the light falling from the left, is characteristic of the artist. Also typical of him are the glistening silks and the detached calm mood of the model.

THE FINE ARTS MUSEUMS OF
BUDAPEST AND BRUSSELS

IN THE INTRODUCTION it was pointed out that there are other
Galleries besides the eight dealt with in detail, all of which are called
National Galleries, or are at least ambitious to be regarded as such,
yet whose lack of money or too short lifespan have so far prevented them
from reaching their goal. Some of them come so near it that they may
well ultimately arrive in the top flight; in particular, two of them may
claim mention in these final chapters—Budapest and Brussels. The two
Galleries started under quite different conditions, since the one in Budapest was originally a princely collection, while the Brussels Gallery grew
into a National Gallery from being a place of shelter for Belgian works of
art which had no proper home.

The kernel of the Budapest Gallery was not the collection of a reigning
dynasty, as was the case with so many of the older Galleries, but one
originally belonging to a member, or leader rather, of the Hungarian
aristocracy. The Eszterhazy family had always rivalled the Kings of
Hungary in wealth, consequence and national consciousness. The earliest
of them to be known as a collector was the Prince Palatine Paul (1635–
1712), who began to assemble a collection of pictures in his Castle Frak

ó
after the liberation of his country from the Turks, and these modest
beginnings were carried further by Prince Nicholas, known to the
Hungarians as 'the Splendid'. He made his newly built Castle Eszterhaza
—later famous through Haydn's long residence there—into the home of
the growing collection. In 1748 the Gallery in the castle contained 348
pictures, mostly decorative in intent, and it was only under Nicholas,
grandson of Nicholas the Splendid, that purchases in Italy or from
Viennese dealers raised the status of the collection to that of a proper
Gallery. A second collection was created in another Eszterhazy castle,
at Pottendorf and formerly a Royal residence, and this collection,
together with a part of the Eszterhaza pictures, amounted to 528 works
by 1812, the date of the first Catalogue. In the troubled years at the
beginning of the nineteenth century the collection was moved several
times, until it settled in 1814 in the Summer Palace of Prince Kaunitz in

Vienna. The groundwork of a Spanish section was laid in 1822 with the purchase of 22 pictures from the Burke Collection, and this School has always been collected with special care by Budapest.

The collection now contained 636 pictures and thus it remained until Paul Eszterhazy, influenced by the rise of Hungarian national sentiment, transferred it to Budapest in 1865 and established it in the Hungarian Academy. Six years later it was bought by the Hungarian Government, which had been stressing its independence ever since the Covenant with Austria in 1867, and it was officially proclaimed the National Gallery of Hungary. The basis of the new Gallery consisted of 463 exhibited pictures from the Eszterhazy Collection, probably the finest in the Gallery, but the next year saw the arrival of Bishop Arnold Ipolyi's collection of about 400 pictures, including many Italian Trecento works coming mostly from the Ramboux Collection in Cologne. A little later there followed the collection of another Hungarian prelate, Archbishop Ladislaus Pyrker von Erlau, who had bought pictures when he was Patriarch of Venice, and who bequeathed them to the National Museum in 1836. They were made over to the National Gallery in 1875 and 1877, and with their arrival such masterpieces as Giorgione's *Broccardo* (Plate 220), Gentile Bellini's *Caterina Cornaro*, a male portrait by Lorenzo Lotto and Memling's *Crucifixion* entered the new Gallery. The Gallery grew rapidly in spite of the slender means at its command, thanks to the patriotic support of the public and the activity of Carl von Pulszky, who was Director from 1881 to 1896, and who was able to give the Gallery an international character by his purchases. To his efforts the Gallery owes such works as Gerard David's *Nativity*, Barent van Orley's *Charles V*, Jan Siberechts' *Ford*, as well as the interesting collection of Italian frescoes from the Trecento to the Cinquecento and the enrichment of the Spanish section by such pictures as Careño's *St. James fighting the Moors*.

When the new Museum building was opened in 1906 the Gallery contained almost a thousand pictures and the numbers continued to rise. The most important of the collections to be bequeathed to the Gallery was that of Johann, Count Palffy, in 1912, with 121 old pictures.

It is impossible for us to know to what extent the Gallery has been enriched by the political changes and the nationalization of private collections in Hungary, but it seems in the highest degree probable that the most important of these collections in the capital or outside it have entered the National Gallery, unless they have been smuggled out of the country.

Before all these upheavals the Gallery had attained a manysidedness and a level of quality which entitled it to claim a place among the other National Galleries. It possessed Italian pictures, mainly from the former Eszterhazy Collection, such as Raphael's *Eszterhazy Madonna*, the latest in date of his Florentine *Madonnas*, which was a gift from Pope Clement XI to the wife of Charles VI, the Empress Elizabeth, from whom it passed to Count Kaunitz and then to the Eszterhazy family. Among others there were Boltraffio's fine *Madonna and Child* (Plate 221); Correggio's so-called *Madonna del Latte*, Giorgione's portrait of Broccardo, charged with expression and feeling (Plate 220), which many people believe to have been finished by another hand, and G. B. Tiepolo's *St. James of Compostela* (Plate 222). The most outstanding of the Netherlandish pictures are Gerard David's *Adoration*, Van Dyck's early double portrait of a man and his wife, and Vermeer's portrait of a woman. In the Spanish section, specially cultivated in Budapest, the most important pictures are Careño's *St. James*, El Greco's *Annunciation*, Goya's *Girl with a Jug of Water* (Plate 223) and the portrait of the wife of Céan Bermudez.

Apart from the Spanish School, the Gallery was particularly anxious to build up an English section, perhaps because of the Anglomania which was a feature of Hungary in earlier years, and this made it rather an exception on the Continent. Naturally the Hungarian painters from the fifteenth to the eighteenth centuries were collected with particular zeal. The stormy history of the country up to the end of the seventeenth century and its close connection with Austria from then onwards did not allow much scope for the development of an individual School of painting. All the efforts made by King Mathias Corvinus, in the second half of the fifteenth century, to link up with the Renaissance in Italy were rendered vain by the events of later years, and the only slight reminiscence of this episode in the country's history is the *Ceres* by the Hungarian painter Michel Pannonius, who worked in Ferrara. The work of later painters, mostly portraits, was therefore all the more eagerly sought out and preserved in the National Gallery.

If its origin in a princely collection and the rarity of old works of the native School gave the Hungarian National Gallery an international outlook, the history of the Brussels Gallery was determined by the richness of the native School and the need to prevent it from being looted. It arose from a measure of protection, for, in 1795, the Committee of Public Safety in Paris despatched Citizens Leblond and Dewailly to Belgium with orders to remove—by force if necessary—all pictures in public buildings which seemed worthy of a place in the collection of the French Republic. No major picture escaped these Commissioners, and pictures which did not seem good enough to be sent to Paris were assembled from 1797 in the central Academy of Art in Brussels; it was from this that the idea of a Museum arose. It was first proposed by La Serna Santander, to whom Brussels also owes the foundation of the National Library, and it was carried out by G. J. de Bosschaert, later the first Keeper of the Gallery. When, in 1799, the French Republic decreed the creation of fifteen provincial museums, Brussels was one of them.

The principal efforts of the new Gallery were at once concentrated on recovering as many as possible of their pictures. An appeal to Napoleon succeeded in getting 43 pictures returned, most of them worthless, but shortly after, in 1802, they managed to secure the return of four works by Rubens—the *Adoration of the Magi*, the *St. Francis*, the *Coronation of the Virgin* and the *Martyrdom of St. Lievin*, a masterpiece painted for the High Altar of the Jesuit Church in Ghent, which had been sold to Louis XVI in 1777 for 112,000 francs. These additions encouraged the Gallery to open its doors and display the 251 pictures it then contained. The main emphasis lay on the seventeenth century, with the earlier pictures merely tolerated guests: the earliest Catalogue describes them as 'certain pictures which are hardly worth hanging, but which are admitted as the earliest experiments of an art which required much time and labour for its development'. During the next few years Flemish pictures came in in ones and twos and in 1811 the French Government sent 31 pictures, including Tintoretto's sketch for the *Miracle of St. Mark*, these being the usual overflow which Paris was accustomed to pass on to the provinces, and when the next Catalogue appeared the number of pictures had risen to 305, eighty-one of which were by painters who had lived before the seventeenth century. There was a most important increase in 1815, after the fall of Napoleon, when more than a hundred of the 271 pictures taken from Belgium in his time were returned. They included major works by Rubens, such as the *Assumption of the Virgin* from the Carmelite Church in Brussels, and the *Bearing of the Cross*, painted in 1636 for the Abbey Church of Afflighem (Plate 229). When the pictures were returned Bosschaert had to justify the Museum's claims to them against their former owners, but in the majority of cases he succeeded in carrying his point that what had once been confiscated remained confiscated.

The Gallery was at this time the property of the city, not the State, and had only limited means to carry on its work. In 1841 the collection of the Princes of Orange was transferred from The Hague to Brussels and at the same time the Gallery in Brussels was raised to the rank of the Belgian National Gallery. From now on it grew steadily and by 1887 it became necessary, because of increasing shortage of space, to move into the new Museum. Both before and after this date there was a lively flow of works into the Gallery and from 1907 onwards this was increased by the activities of the Société des Amis des Musées Royaux. Systematic arrangement of the pictures according to Schools was introduced by the Director, Wauters, in 1896. This makes the overwhelming preponderance of the native School particularly clear, since it is now represented in exceptional fullness by superb examples of all periods. The purpose of the Museum as a means of preserving Flemish pictures for their homeland has proved fully effective and it is not necessary to mention individual works.

The Brussels Gallery seeks to meet its responsibilities as a National Gallery by a systematic education of the public taste as well as by its buying policy. Fierens-Gevaert was the first Director who sought to make the Gallery accessible and useful to the broad mass of the public as well as to the specialist and the amateur, and his educational efforts were carried further in Brussels than is usual in most similar European institutions, the result being an unusually high number of visitors by European standards. Following and extending this policy, during Leo van Puyvelde's directorate the step was taken—significant for the future of Museum policy—of making a clear distinction between those works which are masterpieces of general significance and appeal, and those which, though more numerous, are of interest mainly to the art-historian. Both types are kept on permanent exhibition, the former in the main rooms, which, by the disposition of the Gallery, lead the majority of visitors naturally from one main room to the next, while the secondary works are exhibited in secondary rooms, opening off the main rooms and containing works which parallel, extend, interpret and emphasize the masterpieces on view in the adjoining main room, so that in every case the curious visitor is able to study each major work in the light of the works which preceded it and those which were influenced by it. Every museum nowadays must face for itself the problem of preventing the enjoyment of works of the highest quality from being stultified by the boredom which accompanies the large numbers of pictures necessary in a big Gallery.

NOTES ON THE ILLUSTRATIONS

BUDAPEST

BOLTRAFFIO, Giovanni Antonio (1467–1516)

Madonna and Child   Plate 221
Panel, 32⅝ × 24¾ in. (No. 115)

From the Eszterhazy Collection, where it was called Leonardo. It has been attributed to various Lombard artists since. Mother and Child turn to the left, where the vase may originally have contained a plant.

GIORGIONE (c. 1477–1510)

Portrait of Antonio Broccardo   Plate 220
Canvas, 28¾ × 21¼ in. (No. 140)

Traces of a later inscription: Antonius Brokardus . . . Marii.
Ladislaus Pyrker presented it to the Museum in 1846. This painting has also been attributed to other North Italian artists. If it is by Giorgione, it must date from his last years.

GOYA, Francisco de (1746–1828)

The Girl with a Water Jug   Plate 223
Canvas, 26¾ × 20½ in. (No. 313)

Acquired by Count Kaunitz in Vienna in 1812 and came into the Eszterhazy Collection before 1835. A popular subject with Goya; it is the companion piece to the *Knife-Grinder* also in Budapest. A charming *genre* figure of a young peasant girl taking a basket of food and drink to the fields.

TIEPOLO, Giovanni Battista (1696–1770)

St. James of Compostela   Plate 222
Canvas, 124¾ × 63¾ in. (No. 227)

Painted for the monastery of Aranjuez. The miraculous victory over the Moors is represented by the dominant figure of the Saint on horseback to whom a Moor is seen surrendering in the left foreground.

BRUSSELS

BOUTS, Dirk (c. 1415–1475)

The Justice of Emperor Otto   Plate 225
Panel 127⅝ × 71⅝ in. (No. 66)

Commissioned in 1468 by the magistrates of Louvain for the town hall. Acquired in 1861. Together with its companion piece (also in Brussels) it formed a typical decoration for a room in which justice was administered. In spite of the dramatic content, both pictures have a calm and quiet atmosphere.

BRUEGEL, Pieter, the Elder (c. 1530–1569)

Landscape with the Fall of Icarus   Plate 228
Canvas, 29¼ × 44⅛ in. (No. 800)

Acquired from the Sackville Gallery, London, in 1912. An idyllic landscape, typical of Bruegel and similar to the series of *Seasons of the Year*. Nothing is seen of the mythological episode, except the leg of the drowning Icarus.

DAVID, Louis (1748–1825)

Marat Stabbed in his Bath   Plate 230
Canvas, 65 × 50¾ in. (No. 169)
Inscribed: 'A MARAT DAVID l'an deux'
(1793).

Presented by David to the Convention
Nationale in 1793 and returned to the artist in
1796. In the David Sale of 1835 it was acquired
by Jules David and in 1893 it was presented to
the Museum.
In 1793 Charlotte Corday murdered Marat in
his bath while he was reading her petition.
The picture illustrates David's striving for
increased plasticity, characteristic of his style
in the 1790s.

MASTER OF THE ANNUNCIATION
OF AIX (Active *c.* 1440)

The Prophet Jeremiah   Plate 224
Panel, 59⅞ × 33⅞ in. (No. 950)

On the reverse a fragment of Christ appearing
to the Magdalen.
The right wing of the Annunciation altar of
the church of St. Magdalen in Aix-en-Pro-
vence. (The left wing showing Isaiah is in the
Van Beuningen Collection in Holland.)
The prophet, though portrayed as a living
being, reminds one of sculpture by his position
on a pedestal. The excessively emphasized still
life in the niche above the prophet contrasts
with the bare walls surrounding him.

MEMLING, Hans (*c.* 1430–1494)

Portrait of Guillaume Moreel, Mayor of Bruges
Plate 226
Panel, 14 × 9⅞ in. (No. 292)

A pendant, the portrait of the Mayor's wife,
is also in the Brussels Gallery. Because the
portrait is one of a pair, the sitter is represented
in profile to the right. Both are shown seated
before windows of equal construction, both
are shown with folded hands. But although they
face one another, their eyes do not meet: they
are linked by the same devout attitude.

RUBENS, Peter Paul (1577–1640)

The Bearing of the Cross   Plate 229
Canvas, 224 × 139¾ in. (No. 374)

Painted for the Abbey of Afflighem in 1636–7.
Confiscated by French commissioners, it was
returned by the French Government in 1815.
The movement of the procession from the right
foreground to the left background gives the
impression of a steep laborious ascent, arrested
only for a moment by Christ's fall between
Veronica and Nicodemus.

SNYDERS, François (1579–1657)

Stag Hunt   Plate 227
Canvas, 86⅝ × 165 in. (No. 437)

The movement towards the left creates the
impression that the second stag, too, cannot
escape.

THE PICTURE GALLERIES OF
MUNICH AND DRESDEN

AT THE TIME when the Berlin Gallery was taking its first hesitant steps, there were already two world-famous picture galleries in Germany—in Dresden and in Munich. The reason why neither of them ever rose to the rank of a National Gallery, in spite of their age, their scope and their possessions, is probably to be found in the political circumstances of the time, and the developments which led to the capital of Prussia becoming the capital of the Empire, thus giving the collections there a moral and material support which is usually accorded by the State to only one place. In any case, the Galleries in Dresden and Munich remained rich provincials, looking down their Saxon and Bavarian noses at the Prussian upstart, whose towering ambition they could not dispute.

The two Galleries developed along much the same lines, beginning with an art-loving Renaissance prince, on the modest remains of whose collection one of his descendants in the Baroque period built up a gallery of European rank; in both cases the nineteenth century added to it and systematized it without altering its main essentials. These general similarities are countered by some sharp contrasts, for the Dresden Gallery is mainly the creation of one passionate collector-prince, while the Munich Gallery is largely the result of repeated inheritance of independent collections formed by other branches of the ruling family, which died out and left their collections to Munich. In spite of the dominant role of the Elector Max Emanuel, the Munich Gallery is the creation of the whole House of Wittelsbach and not of any one man. The Dresden Gallery is the work, and the monument, of King Augustus III. A further difference between them is the fact that Augustus's predominance rather hindered the later development of the collection, while even at the beginning of the nineteenth century, the Munich Gallery was modernized by the Crown Prince, later King Ludwig I of Bavaria, and the consequences of this lasted all through his reign, so that the Munich Gallery lived in the present, whereas the Dresden Gallery rested on its laurels.

From the first, Munich showed an inclination towards contemporary works. The first patron of art there, Duke Wilhelm IV (1493–1550), employed all the artists of any repute in his domains—Altdorfer, Beham, Burgkmair, Breu, Schöpfer, and so on—and several of the big historical pictures painted for him are still in the Gallery, in particular Altdorfer's *Alexander's Battle* (Plate 234), Burgkmair's *Esther* and Jörg Breu the Elder's *Lucretia*; Cranach's *Lovers* and Schöpfer's *Judgement of Paris* also go back to this Renaissance Cabinet. The step from giving commissions to collecting was taken by Albrecht V (1550–79), a passionate collector of elaborate goblets and of antiques, who was also interested in pictures, and the Inventory drawn up shortly after his death already records Dürer's *Lucretia* and Altdorfer's *Susanna*. The taxpayers regarded their Prince's interests as a costly luxury, and under the next Duke, Wilhelm V (1579–97), there were official requests to give up 'the pernicious purchase of curious and useless things' and even to sell the collections. It did not come to that; indeed, Maximilian, the first Elector, bought works of art on an even grander scale than any of his predecessors. He was the great collector of Dürer's works, buying the *Paumgärtner Altar* in 1613, the *Heller Altar* in 1614 (burnt in the Residenz in 1729), and the *Four Apostles* in 1627 (Plate 231); but he also recognized the genius of Rubens, who painted the large *Lion Hunt* for him, as we know from a letter from the painter to Sir Dudley Carleton of April 28, 1618.

All these early achievements were surpassed by Max Emanuel (1679–1726), who built Schleissheim in 1684 to hold his Gallery. He had used his opportunity, as Regent of the Netherlands (just as the Archduke Leopold Wilhelm had done) to make a great number of purchases, the greatest of which was made in Antwerp on September 17, 1698, when he paid 90,000 Brabant guilders for 105 pictures, twelve of them by Rubens and including the *Hélène Fourment and her eldest Child* and the *Walk*, and fifteen by Van Dyck. The Schleissheim Inventory of 1761 lists 1016 pictures and there were still more in the other castles.

In 1777, the main branch of the Wittelsbach family died out and the Bavarian territories passed to the Prince Palatine, Karl Theodor von der Pfalz, who left a gallery of his own at Düsseldorf and built a gallery, accessible to artists and dilettanti, on the north side of the garden at Munich and filled it with pictures taken from the stores at Schleissheim and the Residenz at Munich. In the last year of his life he decided to bring his pictures from Mannheim to Munich, which meant that a number of good Dutch pictures went there. A still larger amount of new material came to the Gallery when the Bavarian throne passed to the

Pfalz-Zweibrücken family in 1799, under Max Joseph, and the Zwei-brücken Gallery of about 2000 pictures, many of them French, went to Munich.

Many pictures went to Paris as a result of the Napoleonic Wars, and only twenty-eight of them returned in 1815, but they included Titian's *Crowning with Thorns*, Altdorfer's *Alexander's Battle* (said to have been a particular favourite of Napoleon's), and Rubens's *Meleager and Atalanta*. Those pictures which had been sent to French provincial towns were specifically renounced by Munich, and it is for this reason, for example, that Rubens's *Adoration of the Magi* is still in Lyons, Munich having already found a substitute for it. Much ecclesiastical property was secularized in 1803 and this brought in many old German pictures, as well as Tiepolo's *Adoration of the Magi* from Schwarzach and Rubens's *Trinity* from the cathedral foundation at Freising. The great influx of works by Rubens is due, however, to the incorporation, at long last, of the Düsseldorf pictures, which included forty Rubenses and seventeen Van Dycks in the total of 348. Another highlight in this Gallery was the series of the Passion, painted by Rembrandt in 1633–39 for Prince Frederick Henry of Orange—the only commission Rembrandt is known to have received from a ruling prince (Plate 237). The Düsseldorf pictures also included Andrea del Sarto's *Holy Family* and Raphael's *Canigiani Madonna*, which once belonged to the Medici and came to Munich as a wedding-present on the occasion of the marriage between the Elector Palatine Johann Wilhelm von der Pfalz and one of the daughters of the Grand Duke Cosimo III.

Acquisitions such as these are still part and parcel of the old type of Court collection, but at the same time, at the beginning of the nineteenth century we find new ideas underlying some of the single purchases. The *Self-portrait* of 1500 by Dürer and the portraits of his brother Hans and his master Wolgemut, or the *St. Sebastian Altar* by Hans Holbein the Elder were highly thought of for the reasons defined by Christian von Mannlich, the Director of the Gallery, in his Catalogue of 1805, when he said that the basic principle of such a gallery should be to increase the pride felt by everyone in belonging to so gifted a nation as that which had produced these works. This feeling for the national past was only one of the elements in the slow development of the Romantic Movement. At the instance of the Crown Prince Ludwig, Italian pictures of the fifteenth and sixteenth centuries were bought, among them the portrait of a young man which was then thought to be a portrait of Bindo Altoviti by Raphael, although nowadays both attribution and identification are doubted. The great purchases in Paris, however, after the Peace of 1815, show some uncertainty in both selection and valuation; for Titian's beautiful late *Madonna* 40,000 francs was paid, for Murillo's *St. Thomas of Villanueva* 20,000 francs, for Francia's *Madonna in the Rose Garden* (Plate 232) 15,000 francs, and at the same time Albani's *Venus in a Landscape* was bought for 24,000 francs.

After the accession of Ludwig I, the Gallery began to follow a definite course, with Pre-Raphaelitism triumphant thirty years before it carried the day in London. Munich bought paintings by the two Lippis, Botticelli and Ghirlandaio and the two Raphaels were also bought—the *Madonna della Casa Tempi* in 1829, and the *Madonna della Tenda*. The Northern counterpart of these acquisitions was the purchase of two great collections of German and Netherlandish Primitives; one of them, the one assembled by the Boisserée brothers in opposition to the taste of their own days, for 240,000 gulden and the other, that of Prince Wallerstein, for 80,000 gulden. The number of important pictures of the fifteenth and sixteenth centuries, especially of the Rhenish and Netherlandish Schools, which came in with these two collections gave Munich a lead which no other Gallery was able to overtake.

The enlarged collection now needed a home worthy of it and of the ambitious capital in which it was situated. The new building was projected in 1803; in 1823 Leo von Klenze began to build it, and in 1836 the collections were moved into this rather frigid product of Munich Classicism. In this, the Alte Pinakothek, the well-directed and steadily growing collection of old masters was housed for more than a hundred years, until it, too, fell a victim to the War. The art of the nineteenth century was housed in the Neue Pinakothek, and that of the twentieth century in the Staatsgalerie, but the Alte Pinakothek was so badly bombed that even now, ten years later, ways and means of restoring it are still a subject of controversy. The skeleton of the building admits of reconstruction, but can a building which adumbrated new ideas in its day be made to serve contemporary practical and aesthetic needs by a simple repetition of its original forms? A committee has been set up to try to find an answer to these fundamental questions.

Whether the new building will be a re-creation of the Alte Pinakothek, in whose shadow Munich grew to be a German artistic centre, or whether it is decided to rebuild in a more modern style, the collection housed in it will always bear the impress of the mixture of Baroque and Romantic which is its history. The combination of its incomparable Rubens collection with the equally unique riches of the Boisserée Collection, both of them surrounded by the inheritance of dynastic interest in art in the sixteenth century and by the evidence of pioneering in the arts in the nineteenth, testify to a tenacity and vitality which augurs well for the future of the Alte Pinakothek.

The history of the Dresden Gallery does not end on so optimistic a note. Like the Munich Gallery, its beginnings go back to the patronage of the arts of the country in the early sixteenth century, for Frederick the Wise, Luther's patron, was also the patron of Dürer, Cranach and Jacopo de' Barbari, and some of their works remained in the possession of the House of Wettin. As the years passed, this activity was diverted into the mere assembling of a Cabinet of Curiosities which contained only a few pictures. Not until the second half of the seventeenth century was there a revival of interest in them, when the Dresden collection was enriched with Dürer's *Wittenberg Altar* and Cranach's *Torgau Altar*, as well as with works by contemporary Italian painters. Under Augustus II 'the Strong', more purchases were made, since he had spent two years on a Grand Tour of Germany, France, Spain, Portugal and Italy, and had thus acquired a taste for collecting as well as the opportunity to gratify it. The war with Sweden, in which Augustus was involved as King of Poland, hindered him at first, but he was able to buy fifteen pictures from the dealer Le Roy in 1699, and one of them was Giorgione's *Sleeping Venus* (Plate 245). After the Peace of Altranstadt of 1707, which freed Saxony from the Swedes, Augustus became more active in collecting and was advised by the Flemish architect, Reymond Le Plat, and by Count August Christian von Wackenbarth. In 1722, he had an Inventory drawn up of all the pictures belonging to the Crown, in the Cabinet of Curiosities, castles and churches, and 1938 of them were chosen from this Inventory for the Gallery.

All this formed the prologue to the activities of Augustus the Strong's son and successor, Augustus III, the real creator of the Dresden Collection, who, according to Winckelmann in his first book, published in 1755, 'brought the arts to Saxony'. His only interests were hunting and art, and he poured out money on the arts although his Treasury was invariably empty, encouraged by his Minister, Count Heinrich Brühl, himself a collector on the grand scale, and Director from 1733 onwards of all the Royal undertakings in the arts. It would be wearisome to relate all the purchases made by Augustus III, and Hans Posse's big Catalogue of the Gallery contains a mass of material relating to their history, so that a few of the high-lights suffice.

Count Francesco Algarotti was sent to Italy in 1743 with special instructions, and there he bought twenty-one pictures for 3000 ducats, including Palma Vecchio's *Three Sisters*, the *Madonna of Burgomaster Meyer*, then believed to be Holbein's original, Liotard's *Chocolate Girl* (Plate 246), and Tiepolo's *Banquet of Antony and Cleopatra*. Incomparably more sensational was the purchase, soon afterwards, for 100,000 zecchini, of the collection of the Duke Francesco V of Modena, which was crammed with Italian masterpieces: four altarpieces by Correggio, several Titians, including the *Tribute Money* (Colour Plate XXIII), the four Cuccina pictures by Paolo Veronese, almost all the Ferrarese pictures owned by the Dresden Gallery, and also Andrea del Sarto's *Sacrifice of Isaac*, Tintoretto's so-called *Widow*, all the seventeenth-century masterpieces, and, by non-Italian painters, Holbein's portrait of Morette, three portraits by Velazquez, and the *St. Jerome* by Rubens, one of his few signed pictures.

These did not by any means satisfy the King's appetite. He opened negotiations with the church of Sta Anna in Foligno for the purchase of Raphael's *Madonna di Foligno*, but the Cardinal-Procurator put a stop to that. It was as a substitute for this that Raphael's *Sistine Madonna* (Plate 243) was bought in 1754, with the assistance of the Bolognese painter Carlo Cesare Bianconi in the negotiations. It came from the Benedictines of San Sisto in Piacenza and the price paid, 20,000 ducats, was a record for the time; but, at least, the picture was reckoned one of the greatest achievements of art by the Royal collector, and for many generations afterwards. It is said that he had his throne moved out of the way 'to make room for the great Raphael'.

His successes in the field of Italian art did not prevent Augustus III from seeking after Northern art as well, and in 1741 he bought the collection of Count Wallenstein at Dux, and in 1742 and 1749 he bought 84 and 69 pictures from the Imperial Gallery, including Rubens's *Boar Hunt*, Van Dyck's *Henriette of France*, Matsys's *Selling the Bird*, as well as Bartolommeo Veneto's *Salome* and pictures by Tintoretto, Bassano and Palma Giovine. At about this time—1742—Rubens's *Mercury and Argus* and the *Lion Hunt*, and Rembrandt's *Saskia with a Red Flower* were bought in Paris, followed by the purchase of Rembrandt's *Self-portrait with Saskia* in Amsterdam in 1749.

The outbreak of the Seven Years War, which brought much suffering in Saxony, put an end to this intoxicating sequence of purchases, and an acute shortage of money, which lasted well into the nineteenth century, prevented any resumption. From time to time there were exceptions, as for example the purchase of fifteen Spanish pictures from the collection of Louis Philippe, the *Crucifixion* attributed to Dürer, from the Böhm

Collection in Vienna, or the *Legend of St. Ursula* by Jörg Breu, which was then given to Burgkmair. In 1873, some money was made available from the Franco-Prussian War indemnity, and with this Antonello da Messina's *St. Sebastian* (Plate 242) and Lorenzo di Credi's *Madonna and Saints* were bought from the Charles Eastlake Collection in London, as well as Barent van Orley's *Holy Family* shortly afterwards. On the whole, despite the lack of expert direction, the Gallery lived on its traditions and was also able to carry out extensive work on restoration, Pietro Palmaroli being specially brought from Rome for this.

Under the Directorship of Julius Schnorr von Carolsfeld, from 1848 onwards, the long overdue move to a new building was carried out; previously, pictures had been standing on the floor or were propped up against the walls. The new gallery, built by Gottfried Semper between 1847 and 1855, held 2202 pictures, leaving about 700 over. These were disposed of by selling off 566, mostly seventeenth and eighteenth century works and by using 75 others to decorate the Royal palaces. From 1885 onwards, occasional purchases were made with the restricted means available, in order to fill gaps, but they did not affect the general character of the collection, which, even down to the uniformly carved frames, remained that of Augustus III, an absolute ruler in the grip of an uncontrollable passion for collecting.

This creation of a far distant epoch was largely carried off to Russia at the end of the Second World War. Whether the pictures suffered any damage at the time—or had previously suffered any—where they are now and what it is planned to do with them, are all questions to which there has never been a single word in answer from official sources. For art lovers all over the world who knew and loved it as one of the great collections, it will always remain, even in exile, the Dresden Gallery, which gave its city the nickname of the Florence on the Elbe, and which, in all essentials, is the same Gallery as the one that overwhelmed the student Goethe in 1768.

NOTES ON THE ILLUSTRATIONS

MUNICH

ALTDORFER, Albrecht (1480–1538)

The Battle of Alexander Plate 234
Panel, 62¼ × 47¼ in. (No. 688)

Signed in monogram and dated 1529, it bears a long inscription on a tablet high up in the picture, which relates to the battle between Alexander and Darius.
Since the sixteenth century in the Ducal collection in Munich. One of Napoleon's favourite pictures, it hung in St. Cloud, but was returned by France in 1815. It belongs to a series of historical pictures painted for Duke William IV, four of which are still in Munich. Above the turmoil of the battle raging in the foreground, the eye is drawn into a distant richly detailed landscape under a dramatic cloudy sky.

BRUEGEL, Pieter, The Elder (c. 1530–1569)

Head of a Peasant Woman Plate 235
Panel, 8⅝ × 7⅛ in. (No. 7057)

In 1804 in Castle Neuburg on the Danube. In 1912 it came to Munich from the Germanische Museum.
A caricature-like study.

DÜRER, Albrecht (1471–1528)

The Apostles Paul and Mark Plate 231
Panel, 84¼ × 29⅜ in. (No. 540)

In 1526 Dürer presented it to the Nuremberg Councillors, together with its companion piece, *The Apostles John and Peter*, also in Munich. In 1627 it was left to the Elector Maximilian I. These two panels are Dürer's most mature work and at the same time a confession of his deeply felt religious views, also expressed in a long description. Maximilian ordered this to be cut and then sent it back to Nürnberg with copies of the paintings. (Now it has again been returned).

DYCK, Anthony van (1599–1641)

Self-Portrait Plate 238
Canvas, 32 × 27 in. (No. 405)

FRANCIA, Francesco (1450–1518)

Madonna and Child in the Rose Garden
Plate 232
Panel, 68⅞ × 52 in. (No. 994)

Signed Francia Aurifex Bonon.
From the Capuchin church in Modena it came to the Academy in Mantua in 1786. At the beginning of the nineteenth century it belonged to the Danish Ambassador and then to Empress Josephine in Malmaison. In 1815 it was acquired by Crown Prince Ludwig.
The Virgin Mary, youthful in her unbound hair, is adoring the Infant lying on the ground as in St. Bridget's vision of the Nativity. The Child greets His mother with a gesture of blessing. In spite of much symbolism the picture is enchantingly naive in feeling.

EL GRECO (1541–1614)

The Disrobing of Christ Plate 236
Canvas, 65 × 39 in. (No. 8573)

Abreu Collection, Seville. Acquired in 1909 on the French art market.
The final version—of about 1583—of the famous composition invented first for the altar painting of 1579, for the main sacristy in Toledo.
The emphasis on the figure of Christ, clad in red, is increased by cutting the figures in the foreground or showing them bending down.

GRÜNEWALD, Matthias (died c. 1530)

The Mocking of Christ Colour Plate XXII
Panel, 42⅞ × 28¾ in. (No. 2)

In 1803 brought into the picture gallery from the Carmelite monastery in Munich. In 1809 lent to Landshut University and with it transferred to Munich. Since 1910 in the Pinakothek.

In this early work, probably painted about 1503, the main group is perhaps inspired by Italy (Pesellino).

Two crossing diagonals hold the composition together, the weaker one ending in the pathetic figure of the mocked Christ.

MASTER OF THE ST. BARTHOLOMEW ALTARPIECE (Active *c.* 1500)

St. Agnes Plate 233

Panel, 47¼ × 63⅜ in. (No. 579)

Detail of the central panel of an altarpiece representing St. Bartholomew between St. Agnes and St. Cecilia.

Acquired by S. Boisserée in 1809, from the Church of St. Columba in Cologne and came to Munich with his collection. The anonymous master has been named after this altarpiece, whose wings are in the galleries at Munich, Mainz and London. In the figure of St. Agnes

the artist develops his personal style of late Gothic gracefulness and subtle treatment of costume and gesture.

REMBRANDT (1606–1669)

The Descent from the Cross Plate 237

Panel, 36⅝ × 26¾ in. (No. 395)

Painted in 1633 for Prince Frederick Henry, Stadtholder of the Netherlands. A composition, frequently varied by Rembrandt both in his paintings and etchings. As in many of his early works, he employs strong contrast of light and shade.

RUBENS, Peter Paul (1577–1640)

Self-Portrait with his first Wife in the Honey-suckle Arbour Plate 239

Canvas on panel, 68½ × 52 in. (No. 334)

Painted at the time of his marriage in 1609. The young couple, in their best finery, happily regard the spectator from their arbour. An artistic precursor of the wedding photograph.

DRESDEN

ANTONELLO DA MESSINA (1430–1479)

St. Sebastian Plate 242

Panel transferred to canvas, 67⅜ × 33¾ in. (No. 52)

A late work by the artist, in which the two dominant influences of this period, those of Piero della Francesca and Giovanni Bellini, are united. The figure of the Saint seen from close viewpoint, fills nearly the whole height of the picture; smaller figures in the background add depth.

CORREGGIO, Antonio (Allegri) (*c.* 1489–1534)

Holy Night Plate 244

Panel, 101 × 74 in. (No. 152)

Commissioned in 1522, but probably not painted before 1530. In 1640 it was acquired by force for the gallery in Modena, from where it was purchased in 1746.

The figures are arranged in two wedge-shaped

groups which meet in the figures of the Madonna and Child. This construction is further emphasized by the treatment of light.

GIORGIONE (1477?–1510)

Venus reclining in a Landscape Plate 245

Canvas, 42¾ × 68⅞ in. (No. 185)

This picture had been accepted as a work by Giorgione since Morelli had identified it with the 'Venus by Giorgione completed by Titian' which Marcantonio Michiel had seen in the house of Domenico Marcello in 1525. Recently, however, it has again been doubted and ascribed to Titian.

Acquired as a Titian by Augustus the Strong in 1699 in Paris. In the nineteenth century it was thought to be a work by Sassoferrato.

In contrast with the realism of Titian's *Venus of Urbino* (Plate 52) this is an idealized representation of a heavenly being and has no direct link with the spectator. This motif strongly influenced later Venetian painting.

LIOTARD, Jean-Etienne (1702–1789)

The Chocolate Girl   Plate 246

Pastel on parchment, 32½ × 20¾ in. (No. 161)

Purchased in Venice in 1745. This picture with its delicate colours and reticent pose of the girl, carrying a tray towards the right, that is away from the onlooker, equals in popularity the Sistine Madonna in this gallery.

RAPHAEL (1483–1520)

The Sistine Madonna   Plate 243

Canvas, 104⅛ × 77⅛ in. (No. 93)

Painted for the Benedictine monastery of San Sisto in Piacenza *c.* 1515–1519. In 1754 it was sold to King Augustus III for 20.000 ducats.
The curtains are drawn aside and the Mother and Child approaching on the clouds are seen in full view, flanked by the adoring St. Barbara and Pope Sixtus. The two angels below form repoussoir figures to this cloud setting. Surely the most popular of all religious paintings and in its effect comparable to the most popular portrait, the Monna Lisa (Colour Plate XII).

REMBRANDT (1606–1669)

The Rape of Ganymede   Plate 241

Canvas, 67⅜ × 51⅛ in. (No. 1558)

Signed: Rembrandt Ft. 1635.
The emphatic realism of this picture, bordering almost on caricature, contrasts greatly with the usual idealization of such mythologies, particularly in the seventeenth century.

RUBENS, Peter Paul (1577–1640)

Bathsheba receiving King David's Letter
    Plate 240

Panel, 68⅞ × 49⅝ in. (No. 965)

The painting was in the sale of the artist's effects. In 1749 it was acquired in Paris.
The scene contains much architecture and draperies and the story is told very explicitly, with King David appearing on the balcony in the background and the messenger delivering his letter in the foreground. This contrasts greatly with Rembrandt's interpretation of the same subject (see Plate 72).

TITIAN (*c.* 1485–1576)

The Tribute Money   Colour Plate XXIII

Panel, 29½ × 22 in. (No. 169)

Signed Ticianus f.
Painted for Alfonso d'Este who used the Biblical passage illustrated in this picture as his device on his gold coins. Vasari saw the painting in Ferrara, forming the door of a cupboard. In 1746 it was sold to Dresden with the Modena collection. This picture dates from Titian's giorgionesque period. He sharply contrasts the radiant figure of Christ with the sombre figure beside Him, by the juxtaposition of simple areas of colour. By making them half-length figures he increases the expressiveness of the scene.
The political allusion to the then precarious relation between Alfonso and the Pope is not noticeable.

THE BRERA IN MILAN
AND THE ACADEMY IN VENICE

ALL THE MOST IMPORTANT EUROPEAN MUSEUMS
have in common the fact that they grew out of earlier cultural
activities; either, like the Galleries at Dresden and Munich and
several other of the greatest, from the rulers' desire for prestige, so that the
fulfilment of this official function came to form a large part of their duties,
or else they arose from a re-awakened interest in the monuments of the
nation's past and a wish to protect them from dispersal or destruction.

The far-reaching changes which the late eighteenth century saw
created a favourable ground for such self-consciousness. In every country
there were a few enthusiasts who looked back into the past and discovered
fragments of the history of their country which they did not wish to see
disappear. In France, Alexandre Lenoir collected every record of the
national past, and in Germany the Boisserée brothers and Wallraf
rescued whatever seemed worthy from the wreckage of suppressed
churches and convents. In Italy, collecting points were established by
official bodies, or on the initiative of local patriots, for the reception of
those works of art rendered homeless by the secularization of hundreds
of ecclesiastical institutions. Many of these places subsequently became
important museums and the Brera in Milan and the Accademia in Venice
are particularly good examples of this development from modest
beginnings.

After the suppression of the Jesuit Order, the Empress Maria Theresa
decided, in 1772, to use their former Palace of the Brera in Milan as the
headquarters of various educational and learned bodies. When, in 1787,
some pictures by Cesare da Sesto and Perugino were in need of a home it
seemed only logical to put them into the Brera, but by 1790 they had
been taken back again and sold. Many ecclesiastical houses were closed
down between 1796 and 1799, but the Brera did not immediately gain
from the pictures thus released. Order was not introduced into the ruling
chaos until Carlo Bianconi and later Giuseppe Bossi, under the aegis of
the leading Milanese painter of the time, Andrea Appiani, really set
about making a proper museum in the new capital of the French Italian

province. After 1802, every picture uprooted in Lombardy, or even in other parts of Italy, came into the Brera, where all these acquisitions were examined by the Viceroy, Eugène de Beauharnais, who took some of them for the decoration of his palace. Yet he helped in building up the Gallery and we learn that he expressly approved the purchase of five pictures in 1806—as well he might, seeing that one of them was Raphael's *Marriage of the Virgin* (Colour Plate VIII), which the town council of Città di Castello had been forced to cede to General Giuseppe Lecchi, the commander of a French brigade stationed in the town in 1798. The Viceroy may also have had a hand in the transfer, through the Ministry of Finance, of another five pictures, including Bramantino's *Crucifixion* and Borgognone's *Assumption*, but the importance of these acquisitions in ones and twos is completely overwhelmed by the stream of pictures from the provinces, made over to France under the Treaties of Tolentino (1797) and Pressburg (1805), the contributions from the Veneto being particularly comprehensive.

Not content with the official transfers, the Brera Gallery, open to the public since 1805, paid 344,000 francs for part of the Sampiero Collection in Bologna, thus gaining a large number of important pictures of the Bolognese seventeenth century; at the same time they received eighteen pictures from the Archiepiscopal Museum founded in 1650 by Cardinal Monti, which included Carpaccio's *Sposalizio* and *Presentation in the Temple*. In 1811 Beauharnais presented Giovanni Bellini's *Pietà* (Plate 250), which also came from the Sampiero Collection, and in the following year an exchange was arranged with Paris, by which some Lombard pictures were given up in favour of five important works of the Northern School, so that the Brera now had a more international flavour. The pictures were Rembrandt's portrait of his sister, Rubens's *Last Supper*, Van Dyck's portrait of Amalia von Solms and his *Madonna and St. Antony*, and Jordaens's *Sacrifice of Isaac*. Not all exchanges of this kind were as successful, and in 1823 Crivelli's *Annunciation*, of 1486, left the Brera to end up, after long wanderings, in the National Gallery in London (Plate 172).

Before this time the Gallery which, as the collecting point for pictures from all over Italy, had expanded enormously, had been forced to disgorge many of them. On the one hand, thanks to the energetic intervention of Canova and Bossi, the pictures taken to Paris from the Brera were returned after the fall of Napoleon; but on the other hand, the Brera also had to return many pictures to other Italian cities, especially to the States of the Church—pictures which had helped to make it so

VIII. Raphael: *The Marriage of the Virgin*. Milan, Brera

rich a collection. These acts of restitution were resisted as far as possible but these were years when great pictures were constantly on the move. Paolo Veronese's fine *Supper of Pope Gregory the Great*, sent to Milan in 1811, was returned to the church of Monte Berico in Vicenza in 1817, although Domenichino's altarpiece from S. Petronio dei Bolognesi in Rome remained in the Brera.

After the relatively brisk period of acquisition which ended in 1839, there followed a half-century of inactivity, broken only by the bequest of fifty Italian and thirty foreign pictures from Cavaliere Pietro Oggioni in 1855 and by King Vittorio Emmanuele II's gift of three Lotto portraits in 1860. A new phase of activity began with the appointment of Bertini as Director in 1883, followed by a number of competent Directors. All of them, naturally, stressed the Lombard School in their buying policy, but they did not forget the other Italian Schools or the general European outlook of the Gallery, which, like Milan itself, has a cosmopolitan flavour to its essentially Lombard character. Originally the pictures were exhibited anyhow, but in 1850 a beginning was made with the modernization of their arrangement, which was made to emphasize aesthetic qualities that in many other Galleries are a matter of indifference. In 1882, the Gallery was separated from the Academy and made into an independent institution and since then the appearance of the collection has improved continually. The risks, and even the extensive damage to the building, caused by the Second World War were turned to good account, so that the evacuated pictures could be shown to even better advantage on their return. The present arrangement, completed by Dr Fernanda Wittgens in 1950, may well be reckoned one of the most elegant solutions to the problem of museum arrangement.

The Gallery in Venice came into being, like the Brera, as a home for uprooted pictures of the local School, but unlike the Brera, never extended its activities to cover all the Italian Schools and it has remained a purely Venetian institution. In 1807 the Napoleonic government ordered a selection to be made of the best works from the churches, convents and official buildings which had been closed since 1798, and these pictures were then to be divided between the Academies of Milan and Venice. The importance of the works received from Venice and the Veneto has already been mentioned in connection with the Brera: the share received by Venice was relatively smaller but more of a unity. Together with the pictures belonging to the Academy (founded in 1767), mostly examples of the Venetian Rococo, they formed a core which acted like a magnet to the artistic heritage of the territories once ruled by the Serenissima, and pictures which came back from Paris after the Napoleonic interlude were entrusted to the Gallery of the Accademia, as for example Titian's *Assunta*, which remained in the Gallery for more than a hundred years until it was replaced in its original position on the High Altar of Sta Maria dei Frari in 1919. Under Austrian rule whole collections were bought or inherited—Molin in 1813, Parisi in 1821, Bertrand-Renier-Hellman in 1833, Contarini in 1838, Manfrin in 1865—and after the First World War 156 pictures, with three exceptions all Venetian, which had been transferred to Vienna in 1816 and 1838 from the enormous depots in Venice, were returned to Venice, in spite of the fact that Italy had renounced all claim to them in a treaty of 1868. Many of these pictures, which represented a considerable addition in numbers to the collection, were hardly worth exhibiting, and were not in fact exhibited, but others are still among the most precious possessions of the Gallery, as for example Cima's *Madonna under the Orange Tree*.

In this sense of completing the representation of the School, Giorgione's *Tempesta* (Plate 257) is still more important. It was given in 1932 by the State to the City of Venice, where it had been recorded as early as 1530 by the celebrated connoisseur Marcantonio Michiel, who saw it in the house of Gabriele Vendramin. This, the best documented work by that mysterious master, was the finishing touch to a collection which surpasses all others as a treasure house of Venetian painting. Other Galleries no doubt possess splendid examples of this School, which has been eagerly sought after by all the great collectors from the sixteenth century on-wards, but nowhere else is there so consistent a series of first-rate and soundly documented examples of the School from the Primitives up to the painters of the Rococo. It is only in the seventeenth century that links are missing from the chain, or at least appear to be missing, since lack of space makes it difficult to give an exhaustive representation to this chapter of Venetian painting, which is, in a certain sense, the least deeply rooted in its native soil of all the phases of a long development.

The typically Venetian impression made by the Gallery is heightened by the fact that it shares with the Academy of Fine Arts the buildings of the church and the great Scuola of the Carità, a series of inter-dependent buildings characteristic of the general appearance and the history of old Venice. The building still retains, in spite of severe damage and other drawbacks, a certain atmosphere which the Gallery is able to use to stress the specifically Venetian nature and charm of the contents of some of the rooms. The most successful of these evocations of the past is in the little room which was once the private room of the head of the Scuola, with its richly carved and painted ceiling of about 1500 testifying to the love of splendour common to all these old charitable brotherhoods. Here, where their Relics were kept, there now stands the Reliquary of the Holy Cross given to them by Cardinal Bessarion in 1463, next to the contemporary portrait of the Cardinal holding the reliquary. Here, too, though not quite in its original place, is the large triptych of 1446 by Antonio Vivarini and Giovanni de Alemagna, one of the incunabula of Venetian painting, and over the door, in the very place for which Titian painted it in 1538, is one of the most splendid examples of the School in its maturity, Titian's *Presentation of the Virgin* (Plate 258).

The old church is used to exhibit altarpieces and other pictures, some of which originally belonged to the Scuola, and the Gothic interior is used to give a general feeling of its former character without any attempt at a bogus historical setting. The specific impression of a Scuola is conjured up, with modern means, in the two rooms which contain the two great cycles from other Scuole. The pictures of the *Legend of St. Ursula* were painted between 1489 and 1498 for the ancient Scuola under her patronage; in them Vittore Carpaccio unfolds his teeming imagination and his unrestrained joy in story-telling, using the romantic and charming episodes of the legend as an excuse to evoke a fairy-tale Venice with an inner, poetic truth of its own, which transcends reality (Plate 255). The other cycle, the large canvases of the *Miracles of the Holy Cross*, comes from the great Scuola di San Giovanni Evangelista, for which it was painted between 1494 and 1501. In the execution of this cycle Gentile Bellini, Carpaccio and Mansueti all took part, and the Venice of their day, in all its richness and vivacity, is shown in these great documents. In Gentile's *Procession in the Piazza di San Marco* (Plate 254) we can see that characteristically Venetian mixture of religious and secular motives, set out in the most beautiful piazza in the world; in his *Miracle of the Reliquary recovered from the Canal*, and in Carpaccio's *Miracle on the Rialto Bridge*, we see the swarms of people on the bridges and the canals, just as we see the luxury of the interior of a Venetian palace in one of Mansueti's pictures. The fidelity of the views—not confined to the façade of St. Mark's, but also to be found in the intimate glimpses of the church of S. Lio or the bridge of S. Lorenzo—the bright colours and exact rendering of the costumes, the number of figures and the faces of both local people and exotic visitors, all bring the Venice of the Golden Age before our eyes, as an enduring yet ever-changing background of all that art which is brought together in the Accademia.

NOTES ON THE ILLUSTRATIONS
MILAN

BELLINI, Giovanni (*c.* 1430–1516)

Pietà   Plate 250
Panel, 33⅞ × 42¼ in. (No. 214)

In 1811 Viceroy Eugène Beauharnais presented it to the Brera.
Usually dated shortly after 1470. A magnificent composition of the three figures cut by the parapet. A gesture of infinite tenderness links Christ to His mother and isolates Him from the rest of the world, even from His favourite disciple.

BRAMANTE (1444–1514)

Christ at the Column   Plate 248
Panel, 36⅝ × 24⅜ in. (No. 816)

From the Abbey of Chiaravalle.
The humiliation of the scene is contrasted with the dignity of the tortured Christ. The exquisitely carved pillar heightens this impression. The chalice on the parapet is a symbol of the Eucharist.

COSSA, Francesco (1435–1477)

St. John the Baptist   Plate 247
Panel, 44¼ × 21¾ in. (No. 449)

Together with its pendant, *St. Peter*, also in the Brera, it formed part of a large polyptych. Previously it was attributed to Marco Zoppo. A huge red mantle drapes the emaciated figure of the Saint.

LUINI, Bernardino (*c.* 1475–1532)

The Soul of St. Catherine borne by Angels
                 Plate 251
Fresco, 47⅝ × 89 in. (No. 288)

Inscribed: C.V.S.X. (Caterina Virgo Sponsa Christi).
Originally painted on the door of the chapel of the summerhouse of the Pelucchi, near Monza, in 1520/25. It was detached in 1821, was first kept in the Royal Palace in Milan and hung in the Brera in 1911. One of the most enchanting and popular Lombard mural paintings preserved in the Brera.

PIERO DELLA FRANCESCA (1416?–1492)

Madonna and Child enthroned with Angels and Saints, adored by Duke Federigo of Urbino
                 Plate 249
Panel, 97⅝ × 66⅞ in. (No. 510)

Acquired in 1811 from S. Bernardino, Urbino. According to Meiss, the earliest Italian example of the Madonna and Saints in a church interior. The Madonna is perhaps an idealized portrait of Federigo's deceased wife, Battista Sforza; the Child and angels possibly portraits of their children.

RAPHAEL (1483–1520)

The Marriage of the Virgin
                Colour Plate VIII
Panel, 66½ × 44⅞ in. (No. 472)

Signed and dated: Raphael Urbinas MDIIII. Painted for San Francesco in Citta di Castello, it was handed over to the French General Giuseppe Lecchi in 1798, who in 1801 sold the picture to Giacomo Sannazaro, Milan. The latter bequeathed it to the hospital in 1804, from where it was sold to the Government in 1806. Still deeply rooted in the Umbrian tradition. The special clarity and the grouping of the figures already show the trend the young artist was to pursue in his Roman frescoes.

TINTORETTO, Jacopo (1518–1594)

The Finding of the Body of St. Mark
                Plate 252
Canvas, 159½ × 159½ in. (No. 143)

One of the three paintings from the legend of St. Mark commissioned in 1562 for the Scuola di San Marco in Venice. Acquired by the Brera in 1811, but until 1847 it was in San Marco in Milan.
St. Mark himself identifies the body being lowered from the sarcophagus as his own. The vast crypt, shown in daring perspective, with the numerous sarcophagi, convinces the spectator that without miraculous intervention it would have been impossible to identify the body of the Saint.

VENICE

BELLINI, Gentile (1429–1507)

The Corpus Christi Procession in the Piazza di San Marco   Plate 254

Canvas, $144\frac{1}{2}$ × $293\frac{1}{2}$ in. (No. 567)

Signed and dated: MCCCCLXXXXVI Gentilis Bellini Veneti Equitis Crucis Amore Incensus Opus.

Painted for the Scuola di San Giovanni Evangelista as part of a series in which other artists also had a share. The artist places particular emphasis on the procession, which is shown in its accurately rendered town setting. San Marco in the background shows the mosaics which no longer exist. The main event taking place behind the baldacchino is the thanksgiving of a certain Jacopo de Salis for the healing of his son, but this is almost lost in the crowded scene.

BELLINI, Giovanni (c. 1430–1516)

Madonna and Child between SS. Catherine and Mary Magdalene   Plate 256

Panel, $48\frac{1}{8}$ × $62\frac{3}{4}$ in.   (No. 613)

Usually dated between Bellini's San Giobbe and Frari Altarpieces. Antonello da Messina's influence can still be felt in this silent and peaceful communion of the three women.

CARPACCIO, Vittore (c. 1455–1526)

The Dream of St. Ursula   Plate 255

Canvas, $107\frac{7}{8}$ × $105\frac{1}{8}$ in. (No. 578)

The signature and date, if not entirely apocryphal, were certainly repainted during a restoration in 1752.

Part of a series devoted to the legend of St. Ursula, which was originally placed in the Scuola dedicated to her. The angel appearing to the saint announces her martyrdom. In spite of the minute rendering of the furnishings of a Venetian bedroom, an atmosphere of calm pervades this picture.

GIORGIONE (c. 1477–1510)

The Tempest   Plate 257

Canvas, $32\frac{1}{4}$ × $28\frac{3}{4}$ in. (No. 915)

Marcantonio Michiel saw it in 1530 in the house of Gabriele Vendramin, and later it was in the collections of Manfrin and Giovanelli; acquired from the latter by the Italian Government in 1932.

The early confirmation of its authorship as well as its high quality make this entirely autograph work the typical Giorgione. In spite of numerous attempts, the subject of this picture has never been explained satisfactorily; a natural phenomenon—a thunderstorm—appears as the dominant motif.

JACOBELLO DEL FIORE
(c. 1370–1439)

Paradise   Plate 253

Panel, $111\frac{3}{8}$ × $79\frac{7}{8}$ in. (No. 1)

Commissioned by Antonio Carraro, Bishop of Ceneda, for the Cathedral of that town. Acquired by the Academy in 1882. This subject is often treated in Venetian painting. The local Byzantine predilection for solemn pomp is here somewhat relaxed through the influence of the so-called International Style of the early fifteenth century.

TITIAN (c. 1485–1576)

The Presentation of the Virgin in the Temple
                           Plate 258

Canvas, $135\frac{1}{8}$ × $305\frac{1}{8}$ in. (No. 626)

Painted 1534–8 for the Scuola della Carità, which now houses the museum, and thus it is still in its original position. It forms a clear-coloured wall decoration above the entrance door. All compositional elements serve to clarify the narrative. For instance: the movement of the dense crowd of figures, and the treatment of the steps whose lighting seems to slow down any movement, give the impression that the little girl is only slowly ascending towards the High Priest awaiting her.

THE VATICAN GALLERY IN ROME
AND THE METROPOLITAN MUSEUM
OF ART IN NEW YORK

SEVERAL OTHER GALLERIES have been grouped around the leading ones: Brussels and Budapest, which are called—and are—National Galleries, even though they do not attain the rank of the greatest; Munich and Dresden, which possess the quality necessary for a National Gallery, but which never had the ambition or the opportunity to take the decisive step; Milan and Venice, which have attained world-wide fame in spite of their being limited to the art of their own regions. One more pair may be added to this list—the new Vatican Gallery and the Metropolitan Museum in New York, although at first glance they may seem strange yokefellows. This pairing is due not only to the fact that the material they contain, whether splendid or fortuitous, is of varied origin and of interest to the whole world because of its artistic worth; what determined the treatment in this chapter of the two together is the fact that they did not grow organically so much as they arose from the special position occupied by their founders and owners, the one being at the centre of the Catholic Church and the other at the point where the greatest wealth flowed, a circumstance which had to have proper expression, even in art.

The Vatican Gallery is a comparatively new creation, for all that it belongs to an age-old institution. It was formed at the instance of Pope Pius X, and was compounded of the old Pinacoteca Vaticana—the Byzantine and early Italian pictures, mostly rather small in size, which belonged to the Vatican Library or the Museo Cristiano—and of works of art scattered in various Papal palaces; this new gallery was opened on March 28, 1909. To some extent the eighty Byzantine icons and the 260 Italian Primitives had always been there, for we read that the early Renaissance Pope, Paul II, a Venetian, brought small Greek panel paintings with him to the Vatican, and others followed as gifts to his courtiers. Like the early Italian pictures acquired in the same way, they would have been carefully stored away but nobody would have taken any particular interest in them. As a matter of fact, both these constituent elements are among the most important of their kind, but their early history is unknown. Some of the Italian pictures were systematically gathered together by the Library in the mid-nineteenth century from various small Italian towns, mostly in Tuscany and the Romagna, but no particular note was taken of where they came from. As a result, they have had to be arranged solely on criteria of style-criticism, the ground-work for which was laid by the two splendid catalogue volumes by Pietro d'Achiardi and A. Muñoz.

The other constituent, the 'Old Pinacoteca', was almost equally for-tuitous. The basis of it consisted of the works belonging to the States of the Church, which, under the Treaty of Tolentino of 1797, were taken by Napoleon: of the 100 he took, sixty-seven were returned after his fall, and by a specific decree of the Congress of Vienna they were not to be returned to their original homes, but were to be publicly exhibited in the Vatican. This exhibition had no fixed home and was moved about until it finished up in an inaccessible and unsuitable place on the top floor, in the apartments of Pope Gregory XIII. Other pictures were added, from time to time, from the stock in the Vatican or the Lateran, and occasion-ally a Pope bought a picture for personal reasons or felt himself obliged to buy a work from a suppressed convent in order to save it from being put on the market, as happened, for example, with Lucas Cranach's *Pietà* from the Swiss convent of Kreuzlingen in 1851. There was never any question of methodical purchasing, yet an important Gallery created itself because of the high quality of many of these pictures. When the New Pinacoteca was being formed a number of valuable new acquisitions were made by combing through the Papal palaces, and among them was one of the most popular of the Gallery's pictures—Federigo Barocci's *Rest on the Flight*, painted in 1573.

This is much more of a collection of single works than most of the collections in this book. It extends over a wide space of time, from the altarpiece of 1372, signed by Giovanni Bonsi, which is the only known work by this artist, up to the original altarpieces painted for St. Peter's by the great Baroque masters, which were later removed from the altars and their places taken by copies of them in mosaic. Most of the Italian and some of the foreign Schools are represented. Famous painters— Antonio Vivarini, Francesco Cossa, Perugino, Pintoricchio, Fra Bar-tolommeo, Raphael, with the *Madonna di Foligno* and the *Transfiguration* (Plate 260), Leonardo da Vinci, with the *St. Jerome*, Titian, with the great altarpiece from St. Niccolò dei Frari and the portrait of Doge

Marcello, Caravaggio, with the *Entombment* (Plate 262); all are represented and their works have come from many quarters, often under the oddest circumstances. One of the strangest circumstances is responsible for the presence of Leonardo's *St. Jerome*, which has no long and traditional attribution to Leonardo, although it is certainly an early work by him. It was found at the beginning of the nineteenth century by the well-known collector Cardinal Fesch, serving as the lid of a chest in a shop in Rome; the head, which was missing, was later discovered by the Cardinal in a shoemaker's shop and the reconstituted picture was later bought by Pius IX. At the opposite extreme to this foundling there is an original inhabitant of the Vatican, Melozzo da Forlì's fresco (transferred to canvas in the nineteenth century) commemorating the foundation of the Vatican Library by Sixtus IV in 1477, with portraits of the Pope, members of his family, and his Librarian Platina (Plate 261).

The division between the Vatican Gallery and the Metropolitan Museum in New York seems very wide, even enormous, but the relationship between them lies in the fact that they did not grow naturally out of preceding cultural activities but attained their present prominence on account of the importance of the centres of collecting in which they are situated. Their origin owes a lot to a sense of public spirit.

It is logical that they should both be late-comers. The Metropolitan Museum arose from the upsurge which the end of the Civil War brought to the United States, especially to the North. Museums had been founded already in a number of American cities, as well as in the enormously expanding city of New York itself, but an Independence Day speech in 1866 by the American Ambassador in Paris, John Jay, was the first public proclamation of the idea of the New York Museum and formulated clearly the novelty of this idea by comparing it with earlier attempts. In a speech at the first meeting of the executive committee, the poet William Cullen Bryant re-emphasized that the time had come for the American people to found a National Gallery for themselves, overcoming their provincialism by creating an institution which should be worthy of the metropolis of New York and of a great nation. In all these early proclamations, the speakers' eyes were fixed on Europe, whose ancient and famous foundations were to be rivalled and excelled; but for all their ambitions, the beginnings were modest enough. The Museum had a rapid succession of homes in Manhattan before it came to its final home in Central Park in 1880, where at first it had a medium-sized building, until the flow of material became so great that new wings had to be added in 1888, 1894, 1902, 1909, 1913, and 1916 to hold it all.

The quality of the new accessions could not always keep pace with their quantity, and the impossibility of refusing gifts without offending the donor was a constant theme of the Museum officials, so that as early as 1887 the Trustees expressed the desire to raise the general level of their possessions by removing the less important objects.

At first the main emphasis was on the archaeological side, on account of the long activity of its Director, General Cesnola, the discoverer of the antiquities of Cyprus, whose enormous collection was purchased by the Museum, and of Edward Robinson. In 1871, there was a purchase of 174 pictures *en bloc*, mostly Dutch, several of which, for example Frans Hals's *Malle Babbe*, are still exhibited. In 1886, a separate Department of Paintings was set up and was for long presided over by George H. Storey: the first major addition to the new department was the collection of Catharine Lorillard Wolfe in 1887, consisting of 148 works by contemporary European painters, followed in 1888 by the much more important group of 35 pictures collected by Henry G. Marquand. These included many of the Museum's most precious works—Vermeer's *Woman with a Jug*, Van Dyck's *James Stuart, Duke of Lennox*, and Rembrandt's *Bearded Man*. Yet Roger Fry, Story's successor in 1906–7, and later European advisor to the Department, characterized the collection very acidly when he said that there was only one group of paintings really well represented in the Museum, and that was the sentimental and anecdotic art of the nineteenth century. Otherwise it could offer only isolated peaks in the great sequence of European artistic activity. It had no Byzantine works, no Giotto, no Giottesques, no Mantegna, no Botticelli, no Leonardo, no Raphael, no Michelangelo. All the finest works were then shown in one room, known as the Marquand Gallery.

Fry's criticisms were made at the moment when the election of J. P. Morgan as President of the Museum opened a new era for it. It was not only that he lent the Museum a valuable part of his own celebrated collection, including twenty-nine pictures, most of which were given to the Museum by his son in 1916—and pictures like Raphael's *Colonna Madonna*, painted in 1504 for the nuns of St. Antony of Padua in Perugia, and Rogier van der Weyden's *Annunciation* were included in this gift. One of the predella panels from the Raphael altarpiece was later bought from the Clarence H. Mackay Collection with the proceeds of a sale of surplus works from the Museum.

Names like Morgan and Mackay bring us into the period of enormous fortunes in America, when the whole tempo of life was greatly accelerated, and there was a short-lived fashion for art collecting on the grand scale among the richest men in the country. Most of the collections which the multimillionaires of the time outbid each other to assemble have since been broken up or have passed into public collections. The Museum benefited from this, and there were so many gifts and bequests of whole collections or of single works that all the departments of the Museum were showered with them and Roger Fry's remarks could almost have been reversed. There is no need to repeat the long list of these donations here, and a few names must suffice to recall the scope and quality of them. One of the richest collections, including masterpieces from all the major European Schools, was bequeathed by Benjamin Altman in 1913 on condition that it should be exhibited as an undivided whole, and it is still so exhibited. Other collections followed—in 1915 that of Theodore M. Davis, in 1917 the Fletcher Collection, in 1920 that of W. K. Vanderbilt, in 1925 that of C. P. Huntington, and in 1929 the Havemeyer Collection; even the depression of 1929 did not bring the sequence to an end. The year 1931 brought the best parts of the fine collection of Michael Friedsam, 1941 the big collection of George Blumenthal, with some pictures as well as a great many *objets d'art*, 1943 the Maitland Griggs Collection with its precious Italian Primitives, 1945 the collection of Jules Bache, at first as a loan but made over to the museum a few years later, 1951 some masterpieces from the collection of Samuel H. Lewisohn. In 1940 and 1950 Edward and Mary Stillman Harkness gave several pictures as well as a collection of Egyptian antiquities, and from 1928 S. H. Kress began to make gifts to the Metropolitan Museum as he did to other museums. Such a stream of gifts had obvious advantages, but there were also some unavoidable snags in that some attributions to great artists were clung to with more tenacity than was desirable. A museum must give reliable information to the public, and although it is painful to have to alter attributions cherished by the donors it is sometimes made necessary by advances in knowledge. But a collection such as the Metropolitan was bound to suffer from these teething troubles.

Gifts of whole collections or of single pictures were not the only way in which the Museum benefited from the economic prosperity and the lavishness of its patrons, for it received at this time a number of richly endowed funds, some of which could be applied to the purchase of works of art. J. S. Rogers headed this line of benefactors in 1901 with a gift of nearly five million dollars, and he was followed by John S. Kennedy and Joseph Pulitzer, the Jesup Fund for American pictures and the Hearn Fund for contemporary art both in 1915, the gifts of J. D. Fletcher in 1917, Frank A. Munsey in 1925, Gwynne M. Andrews in 1931, and so on down to the most recent, the Rockefeller gift of ten million dollars for The Cloisters. The millions at the Museum's disposal have thus made it possible to round off the results of private collecting in a systematic way. In 1945 the Museum itself issued a list of ten works acquired in this way, which it regards as the most important; they are: Renoir, *Madame Charpentier and her Children* (1907); Paolo Veronese, *Mars and Venus* (1910); Vittore Carpaccio, *Meditation on the Passion* (Plate 265), (1911); Pieter Bruegel the Elder, *Harvest* (1919); Mantegna, *Adoration of the Shepherds* (1932); Michelangelo, drawing for the *Libyan Sibyl* (1924); Van Eyck, *Crucifixion* and *Last Judgement* (1933); Watteau, *Mezzetin* (1934); Fra Carnevale, *The Birth of the Virgin* (1935) and Titian, *Venus with the Lute Player* (1936). Although even this carefully selected list contains some works which have not quite come up to expectations, yet it does show a desire to counterbalance the erratic increase from donations by a policy which strives to fill up the gaps. Other single purchases of the Museum in the last few years show the same independence and responsibility.

In all these ways the collection of paintings, and all the other departments of the Museum, has grown to an extraordinary richness. Many chapters in the history of European art are splendidly represented, for instance, the Italian Quattrocento, the early Netherlandish Schools (Plate 263), Rembrandt (Plate 266), El Greco (Plate 267 and Colour Plate XXIV) and Goya (Plate 271); others, such as the French Impressionists (Plate 272), are so well represented that it has become impossible to obtain a thorough knowledge of them without a study of the Museum's possessions. Its financial strength makes it seem likely that it will become still more of a treasure house.

The Directors soon realized that the Museum had to be more than a mere follower and rival of European institutions, and they aimed at popular instruction on the largest scale. Since the Museum could not draw to any extent on a long-standing cultural tradition, it was necessary to find other ways of serving the public which helped to support it. Museum instructors, tours for classes of school children, popular publications—all were introduced at an early stage and have been extended by modern methods such as concerts, educational films and television. From time to time, even display methods have been adopted which were calculated to appeal to the widest public. This tendency, corresponding to the democratic structure of American society, is now stronger than ever. The present rebuilding, necessary for some time past, since the continual flow of materials has threatened to burst the old building at the seams, is designed to make the display of the Museum's treasures more easily comprehensible, for latterly the not very suitable building has made them confused and confusing. At the same time, it will throw into sharper relief the museum's function as a means of popular education. The problem of which the present direction of the Museum is fully conscious, is to develop beyond a mere repetition of the type of Museum developed in Europe in the nineteenth century and towards a Museum which will answer the needs of the specifically American mind and of our time. Thus it will fulfil the ideal already foreshadowed in that Independence Day speech of 1866—America's ideal of independence in this sphere.

The Metropolitan Museum of Art, New York

NOTES ON THE ILLUSTRATIONS

THE VATICAN GALLERY

ANGELICO, Fra Giovanni (1387–1455)

Two Miracles of St. Nicholas of Bari
Plate 259
Panel, 13 × 24¾ in. (No. 116)

Part of the predella of an altarpiece for St. Nicholas in San Domenico, Perugia. On the left the Saint is multiplying the corn, on the right saving a ship at sea. The landscape both separates and links the two scenes.

CARAVAGGIO, Michelangelo (1573–1610)

The Entombment
Plate 262
Canvas, 118¼ × 79⅞ in. (No. 245)

Painted for the family chapel of the Vittrici in Sta Maria in Vallicella in Rome (1601–4). From 1799–1815 in Paris. It was then acquired by the Vatican. This powerful composition, with its naturalistic detail and violent light contrasts, was felt to be a tremendous innovation and a reaction against the artistic currents of the time. It greatly influenced the whole of European painting.

MELOZZO DA FORLI (1438–1494)

Pope Sixtus IV and his Court
Plate 261
Fresco transferred to canvas, 145⅝ × 124 in. (No. 141)

Painted on the occasion of the founding of the Vatican library in 1476–7.
In a magnificent Renaissance hall, open towards the back, the librarian Platina is kneeling before the seated Pope, who is attended by four of his relatives. A real event is treated here with monumental ceremony.

RAPHAEL (1483–1520)

The Transfiguration
Plate 260
Panel, 159½ × 109½ in. (No. 333)

Commissioned by Cardinal Giulio de' Medici for a church in Narbonne, it was unfinished at the time of Raphael's death and the lower part was completed by pupils. On the High Altar of St. Pietro in Montorio until 1757. After its return from Paris in 1815 it came to the Vatican. The upper part of the picture illustrates the Transfiguration of Christ according to Luke IX, 28–32 and the lower half the healing of the possessed boy, which took place on the following day according to Luke 37–43. The two events are linked by the apostles placed opposite the boy, pointing to the scene of the Transfiguration above. The young man worshipping the Transfiguration suggests that the scene is a vision. In subsequent periods this painting was considered as the high water mark of classic composition.

THE METROPOLITAN MUSEUM

BOSCH, Jerome (c. 1450–1516)

The Adoration of the Magi
Plate 263
Panel, 28 × 22¼ in. (No. 1326)

Acquired 1912 from the Friedrich Lippmann collection, Berlin, through the Kennedy Fund. Usually taken to be an early work, but not accepted by Tolnay as autograph. The narrative is hesitant, pieced together from individual motifs and this may point to it being either an early work or by a follower.

CARPACCIO, Vittore (c. 1455–1526)

Meditation on the Passion
Plate 265
Panel, 27⅜ × 34 in. (No. 11.118)

False signature: Andreas Mantinea.
First mentioned in 1632. First recognized as a Carpaccio by C. Philips in 1911, when it was acquired from the Sir William Abdy collection through the Kennedy Fund. The aged St. Jerome and Onophrius have their solemn meditations crowned by a vision of the suffering Christ.

COPLEY, John Singleton (1737–1815)

Portrait of Joseph Sherburne   Plate 268
Canvas, 50 × 40 in.   (No. C.79–3)

Acquired from a direct descendant, Miss Mary Bowers Wheelwright, in 1923 (Lazarus Fund). Considered as painting alone, it is not a pioneering work, but it is the characteristic expression of New World middle-class self-assurance.

DAUMIER, Honoré (1808–1879)

In the Third Class   Plate 270
Canvas, 25½ × 35⅜ in. (No. 29.100.129)

Presented to the museum in 1929 with the O. Havemeyer bequest.
The subject was first treated in lithographs which date from 1855–58. One of Daumier's descriptions of contemporary petit-bourgeois life.

FRAGONARD, Jean-Honoré (1732–1806)

The Billet-doux   Plate 269
Canvas, 32⅝ × 28¼ in. (No. 49.7.49)

On the letter the inscription: A Monsieur mon Cavalier.
Collection Ernest Bardoc, and later Jules S. Bache. In the museum since 1949.
A charming picture of contemporary manners and at the same time a delightful example of the colourful lightheartedness and sweetness of French Rococo.

GOYA, Francisco de (1746–1828)

Women on a Balcony   Plate 271
Canvas, 76½ × 49½ in. (No. 29.100.10)

Acquired by the museum from the collection of Don Sebastian Gabriel de Bourbon and Duke of Marcena through the H. O. Havemeyer donation, 1929.
Painted *c.* 1810. Considered purely as painting it is a perfect jewel and greatly influenced French Impressionists. In subject matter a ruthless description of contemporary morals.

EL GRECO (1541–1614)

Portrait of the Grand-Inquisitor Fernando de Guevara   Plate 267
Canvas, 67¼ × 42⅜ in. (No. 29.100.5)

Signed in Greek letters.
In a monastery in Toledo and then in various Spanish collections. Donated to the museum with the Havemeyer collection in 1929.
In spite of the general use of strong colour, the face, and particularly the eyes dominate.

View of Toledo   Colour Plate XXIV
Canvas, 47¾ × 42¾ in. (No. 29.100.6)

Signed in Greek letters.
In the collection of Countess Anover y Castaneda, Madrid. It entered the museum with the H. O. Havemeyer collection in 1929.
The buildings typical of Toledo are not topographically accurate but are put together to achieve an artistic effect. The picture was perhaps part of a larger composition, probably of a *Crucifixion*. In its isolation it creates a concentrated, almost ghostly effect.

MANET, Edouard (1832–1883)

Woman with a Parrot   Plate 272
Canvas, 72⅞ × 50⅝ in. (No. 89.21.3)

Donation Erwin Davis, 1889.
Painted in 1866. The pinkish yellow of the citrus fruit and the dull yellow of the sand below the parrot set the colouristic tone of the picture, which is enriched by the warmer tone of hair and flesh and the restrained black of the necklace and shoe lace. The parrot supplies the complementary colour.

REMBRANDT (1606–1669)

Man with a Magnifying Glass   Plate 266
Canvas, 36 × 29¼ in. (No. 14.40.621)

Acquired by the museum with the Altman Collection in 1913. A pendant to the *Woman with a Carnation* also in the Metropolitan Museum. The sitters are sometimes identified as Rembrandt's son Titus and his wife, whom he married in 1668, and sometimes as Miguel de Barrios and Abigail de Pina, who were probably the models for the *Jewish Bride* (see Plate 126). A magnificent late work.

SASSETTA (1392–1450)

The Procession of the Three Magi   Plate 264
Panel, 9 × 12 in. (No. 43.98.1)

Marchioness of Crewe collection; Maitland F. Griggs bequest, 1943. Predella of a polyptych. A charming and colourful narrative, taking obvious delight in well observed natural detail. Miniature-like execution.

THE PLATES

1. GEERTGEN TOT SINT JANS: *The Finding of the Remains of Saint John the Baptist*

2. KONRAD LAIB: *The Crucifixion*

3. JAN VAN EYCK: *Portrait of Cardinal Nicolas Albergati*

POTENTISSIMVS MAXIMVS ET INVICTISSIMVS CÆSAR MAXIMILIANVS
QVI CVNCTOS SVI TEMPORIS REGES ET PRINCIPES IVSTICIA PRVDENCIA
MAGNANIMITATE LIBERALITATE PRÆCIPVE VERO BELLICA LAVDE ET
ANIMI FORTIDVDINE SVPERAVIT NATVS EST ANNO SALVTIS HVMANÆ
M CCCC LIX DIE MARCII IX VIXIT ANNOS LIX MENSES IX DIES XXV
DECESSIT VERO ANNO M D XIX MENSIS IANVARII DIE XII QVEM DEVS
OPT MAX IN NVMERVM VIVENCIVM REFERRE VELIT

4. ALBRECHT DUERER: *Portrait of Emperor Maximilian I*

5. HANS HOLBEIN: *Portrait of Jane Seymour, Third Wife of Henry VIII*

6. LUCAS CRANACH: *Stag Hunt of the Elector Frederic the Wise*

7. PIETER BRUEGEL: *The Return of the Herd*

8. Pieter Bruegel: *Children's Games*

IX. PIETER BRUEGEL: *A Peasant Wedding*. Vienna, Kunsthistorisches Museum

9. PIETER BRUEGEL: *The Tower of Babel*

10. MORETTO DA BRESCIA: *Saint Justina and a Donor*

11. GIORGIONE: *The Three Philosophers*

12. RAPHAEL: *The Madonna of the Meadow*

13. TITIAN: *Nymph and Shepherd*

14. Jacopo Tintoretto: *Susanna and the Elders*

15. TITIAN: *Ecce homo*

16. LORENZO LOTTO: *The Virgin and Child with Saints Catherine and James the Great*

17. TITIAN: *Portrait of Jacopo de Strada*

18. CORREGGIO: *Jupiter and Io*

19. VAN DYCK: *Portrait of an Officer*

20. RUBENS: '*Het pelsken*' (Portrait of Helène Fourment with a Fur)

21. RUBENS: *Saint Ignatius Loyola Driving out the Devil*

22. CARAVAGGIO: *The Madonna of the Rosaries*

23. JAN VERMEER VAN DELFT: *The Artist in his Studio*

24. REMBRANDT: *Portrait of the Artist's Son Titus*

25. VELAZQUEZ: *Portrait of Infante Baltasar Carlos*

X. RUBENS: *The Madonna Presenting Saint Ildefonso with his Chasuble.*
Vienna, Kunsthistorisches Museum

26. VELAZQUEZ: *Portrait of Infanta Margarita Teresa*

27. CIMABUE: *The Virgin and Child Enthroned, with Angels and Saints*

28. GIOTTO: *The Virgin and Child Enthroned, with Angels and Saints*

29. Gentile da Fabriano: *The Adoration of the Magi*

30. Albrecht Duerer: *The Adoration of the Magi*

31. HUGO VAN DER GOES: *The Adoration of the Shepherds*

32. LEONARDO DA VINCI: *The Adoration of the Magi*

33. Detail from Plate 32

34. ANDREA VERROCCHIO: *The Baptism of Christ*

35. ANTONIO POLLAIUOLO: *Hercules and Antaeus*

36. PIERO DELLA FRANCESCA: *Portrait of Federigo da Montefeltro, Duke of Urbino*

37. Domenico Ghirlandaio: *The Virgin and Child Enthroned, with Angels and Saints*

38. Fra Filippo Lippi: *The Coronation of the Virgin*

39. NICOLAS FROMENT: *The Raising of Lazarus*

40. ANDREA DEL SARTO: 'The Madonna of the Harpies' with Saints Francis and John the Evangelist

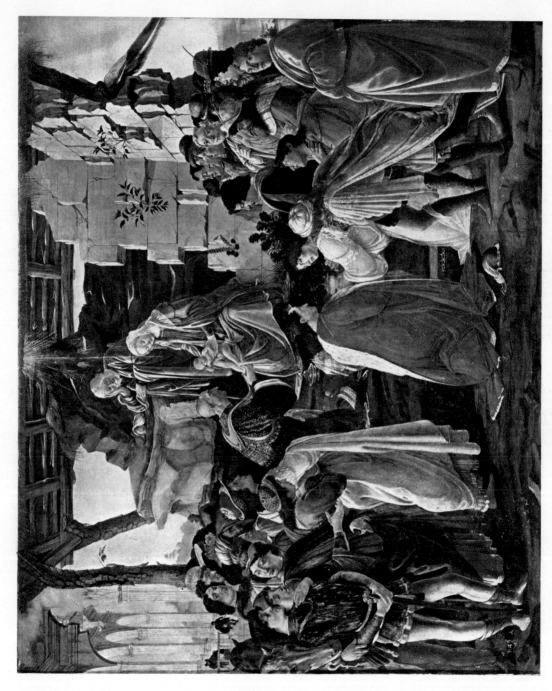

41. BOTTICELLI: *The Adoration of the Magi*

XI. BOTTICELLI: *The Birth of Venus.* Florence, Uffizi

42. BOTTICELLI: *Self-Portrait* (Detail from Plate 41)

43. BOTTICELLI: *The Madonna of the Pomegranate*

44. Detail from Plate 43

45. BOTTICELLI: *The Three Graces* (Detail from the 'Spring')

46. JACOPO DA PONTORMO: *Portrait of Cosimo de' Medici*

47. MARIOTTO ALBERTINELLI: *The Visitation*

48. MICHELANGELO: *The Holy Family*

49. ANGELO BRONZINO: *Portrait of Maria de' Medici*

50. TITIAN: *Portrait of Francesco della Rovere, Duke of Urbino*

51. GIOVANNI BELLINI: *Religious Allegory*

53. PIETRO PERUGINO: *Portrait of Francesco delle Opere*

54. RAPHAEL: *The Madonna of the Goldfinch*

55. ANDREA MANTEGNA: *The Circumcision of Christ*

56. Jean Fouquet: *Portrait of King Charles VII*

57. LEONARDO DA VINCI: *The Virgin of the Rocks*

XII. LEONARDO DA VINCI: *Portrait of Monna Lisa*. Paris, Louvre

58. JAN VAN EYCK: *The Virgin and Child Adored by the Chancellor Rolin*

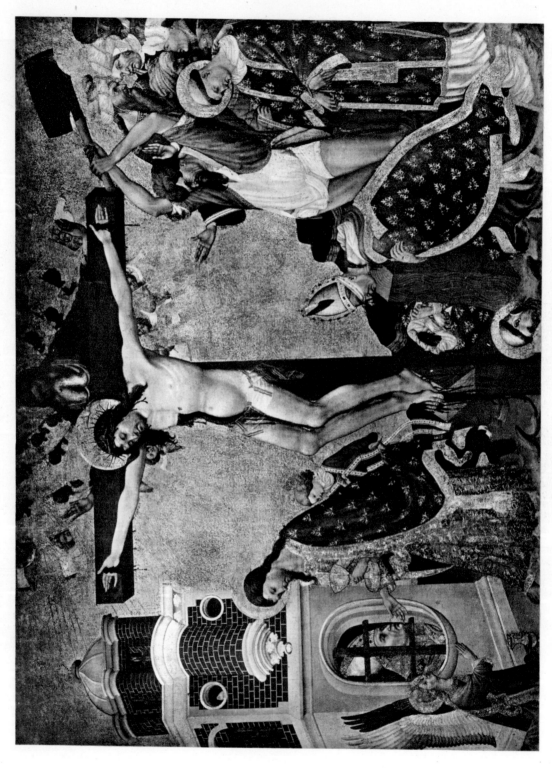

59. JEAN MALOUEL: *The Martyrdom of Saint Denis*

60. School of Avignon, 15th Century: *The Pietà of Villeneuve-lès-Avignon*

61. ANDREA MANTEGNA: *The Parnassus*

62. GIORGIONE: *Concert champêtre*

63. TITIAN: *Portrait of King Francis I of France*

64. RAPHAEL: *Portrait of Balthasar Castiglione*

65. QUENTIN METSYS: *The Banker and his Wife*

66. HANS HOLBEIN: *Portrait of Erasmus of Rotterdam*

67. RUBENS: *King Henri IV Receiving the Portrait of Maria de' Medici*

68. VAN DYCK: *Portrait of King Charles I of England*

69b. FRANS HALS: *The Gipsy Girl*

69a. ADRIAEN BROUWER: *The Smoker*

70. RUBENS: *The Flemish Kermesse*

71. REMBRANDT: *Self-Portrait at the Age of Fifty-Four*

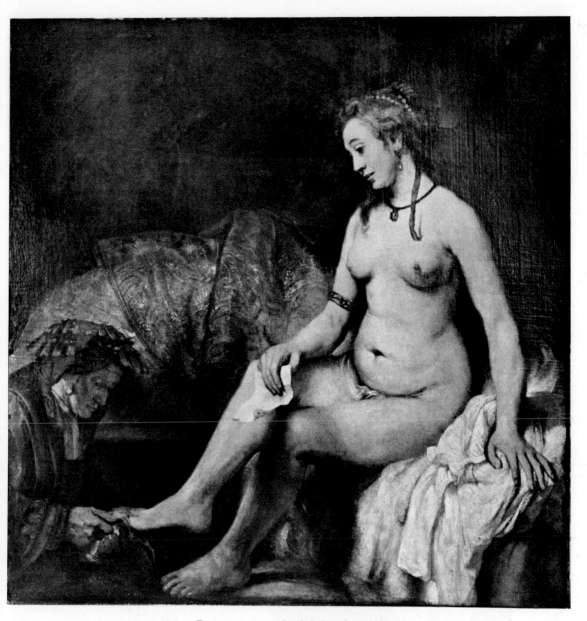

72. REMBRANDT: *Bathsheba after the Bath*

73. FRANÇOIS BOUCHER: *Diana after the Bath*

74. JEAN-HONORÉ FRAGONARD: *The Music Lesson*

XIII. ANTOINE WATTEAU: *The Actor Gilles*. Paris, Louvre

75. JEAN-BAPTISTE-SIMÉON CHARDIN: *Saying Grace*

76. NICOLAS POUSSIN: *The Deluge*

77. Antoine Watteau: *The Embarkation for Cythera*

78. GUSTAVE COURBET: *A Funeral at Ornans*

79. THÉODORE GÉRICAULT: *The Raft of the Medusa*

80. EUGÈNE DELACROIX: *The Massacre at Scios*

81. LOUIS DAVID: *Three Ladies of Ghent*

82. JEAN-AUGUSTE-DOMINIQUE INGRES: *The Turkish Bath*

83. AUGUSTE RENOIR: *Dance at the Moulin de la Galette*

84. Edouard Manet: *Olympia*

85. VINCENT VAN GOGH: *Portrait of Dr. Gachet*

86. PAUL CÉZANNE: *The Card Players*

87. EDGAR DEGAS: *Ballet Dancer on the Stage*

88. Claude Monet: *The Cathedral of Rouen*

89. CASTILIAN SCHOOL, 15TH CENTURY: *The Virgin and Child with Saints Thomas and Dominic,*
Adored by the King and Queen of Spain

90. FRANCISCO DE ZURBARÁN: *Saint Peter Nolasco's Vision of the Heavenly Jerusalem*

91. JOSÉ DE RIBERA: *Jacob's Dream*

92. ESTEBÁN MURILLO: *The Immaculate Conception*

93. EL GRECO: *The Resurrection*

XIV. VELAZQUEZ: *The Surrender of Breda* ('*Las Lanzas*'). Madrid, Prado

94. VELAZQUEZ: *The Dwarf Calabacillas* (known as '*Bobo de Coria*')

95. VELAZQUEZ: *Portrait of King Philip IV of Spain*

96. VELAZQUEZ: *The Maids of Honour* ('*Las Meninas*')

97. JEROME BOSCH: *The Temptation of Saint Anthony*

98. ALBRECHT DUERER: *Self-Portrait*

99. ROGIER VAN DER WEYDEN: *The Descent from the Cross*

100. TITIAN: *The Deposition*

101. RAPHAEL: *The Madonna with the Fish*

102. PAOLO VERONESE: *The Finding of Moses*

103. TITIAN: *Portrait of Emperor Charles V on Horseback*

104. TITIAN: *Portrait of King Philip II in Armour*

105. TITIAN: *The Worship of Venus*

106. RUBENS: *The Garden of Love*

107. RUBENS: *Adam and Eve*

108. RUBENS: *The Apostle Paul*

XV. Francisco de Goya: *An Episode of May 3, 1808 : The Execution of Rebels in Madrid.* Madrid, Prado

110. Francisco de Goya: *Nude Maja*

III. FRANCISCO DE GOYA: *The Manikin*

112. FRANCISCO DE GOYA: *Portrait of King Ferdinand VII*

113. EL GRECO: *Portrait of Julian Romero with his Patron Saint Louis*

114. MASTER OF THE SEVEN WORKS OF CHARITY: *Feeding the Hungry*

115. GEERTGEN TOT SINT JANS: *The Adoration of the Magi*

116. LUCAS VAN LEYDEN: *The Sermon*

117. ANTONIS MOR: *Portrait of Sir Thomas Gresham*

118. Jan van Scorel: *Saint Mary Magdalene*

119. WILLEM KALF: *Study of Still Life*

120. JAN ASSELYN: *The Enraged Swan*

121. BARTHOLOMEUS VAN DER HELST: *The Banquet of the Civic Guard in Celebration of the Peace of Munster, 1648*

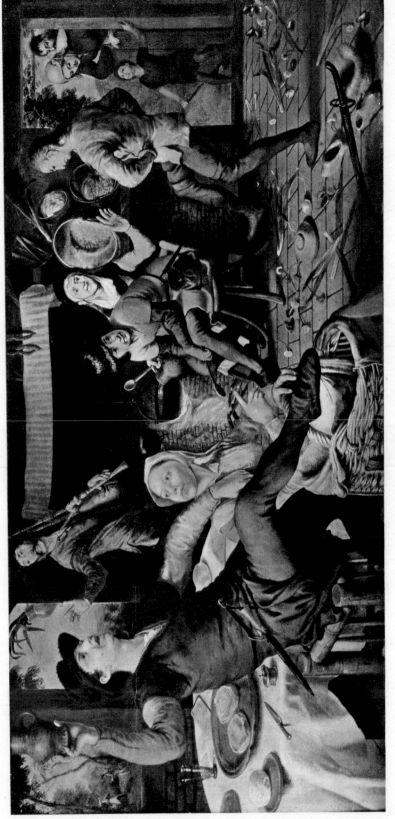

122. PIETER AERTSZ: *The Egg Dance*

123. GERRIT ADRIAENSZ BERCKHEYDE: *The Flower Market at Amsterdam*

124. JAN VAN GOYEN: *The Valkhof at Nijmegen*

125. JAN HACKAERT: *The Ash-Tree Avenue*

126. REMBRANDT: *The Jewish Bride*

XVI. REMBRANDT: *The Night Watch*. Amsterdam, Rijksmuseum

127. REMBRANDT: 'The Staalmeesters' (The Masters of the Clothmakers' Guild)

128. GERARD TERBORCH: *Portrait of Helena van der Schalcke*

129. VAN DYCK: *Portrait of Prince William II and his Young Wife, Princess Mary Stuart*

130. FRANS HALS: *Portrait of a Man and his Wife*

131. FRANS HALS: *The Jolly Toper*

132. HERCULES SEGHERS: *River in a Valley*

133. WILLEM VAN DE VELDE THE YOUNGER: *The Ij before Amsterdam*

134. JACOB VAN RUISDAEL: *The Castle of Bentheim*

135. ADRIAEN VAN OSTADE: *Travellers Resting*

136. JAN STEEN: *The Feast of St. Nicholas*

137. JAN VERMEER VAN DELFT: *The Little Street*

138. JAN VERMEER VAN DELFT: *Young Woman Reading a Letter*

139. PIETER DE HOOCH: *The Small Country House*

140. EMANUEL DE WITTE: *Interior of a Gothic Church*

141. GERARD DOU: *Self-Portrait*

142. Konrad Witz: *Solomon and the Queen of Sheba*

143. ANTONIO POLLAIUOLO: *David with the Head of Goliath*

XVII. Piero Pollaiuolo: *A Young Lady*. Berlin, Kaiser Friedrich Museum

144. JAN VAN EYCK: *Madonna in the Church*

145. JEAN FOUQUET: *Portrait of Etienne Chevalier with his Patron Saint Stephen*

146. PETRUS CRISTUS: *Portrait of a Girl*

147. ROGIER VAN DER WEYDEN: *The Adoration of the Child, with a Donor*

148. DIRK BOUTS: *Christ in the House of Simon*

149. ALBRECHT ALTDORFER: *The Nativity*

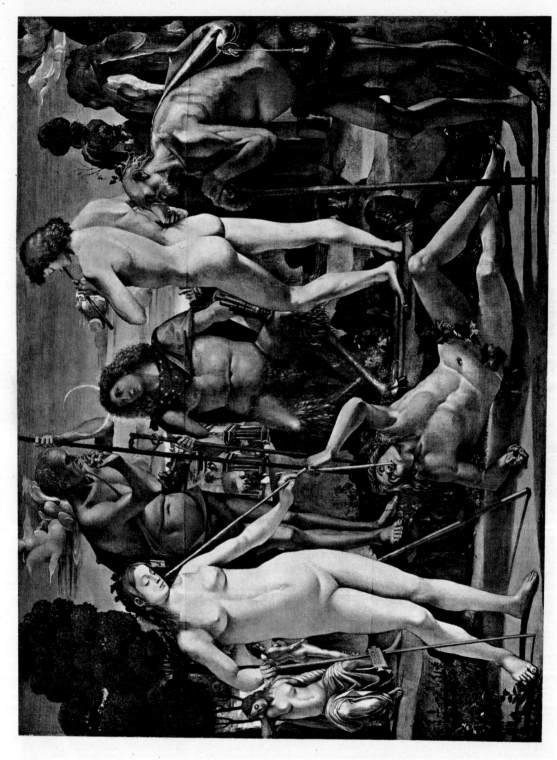

150. LUCA SIGNORELLI: *Pan and his Court* (destroyed in 1945)

151. CORREGGIO: *Leda and the Swan*

152. LUCAS CRANACH: *The Rest on the Flight into Egypt*

153. ALBRECHT DUERER: *Portrait of Hieronymus Holzschuher*

154. HANS HOLBEIN: *Portrait of Georg Gisze*

155. Lorenzo Lotto: *Portrait of an Architect*

156. Francesco Cossa: *Allegory of Autumn*

157. TITIAN: *Self-Portrait*

158. GEORGES DE LA TOUR: *Saint Sebastian Lamented by Saint Irene*

159. CARAVAGGIO: *Saint Matthew and the Angel*

160. ANDREA SACCHI: *Portrait of the so-called Borro*

XVIII. JAN VERMEER VAN DELFT: *A Lady with a Pearl Necklace*. Berlin, Kaiser Friedrich Museum

161. JAN STEEN: *Garden of an Inn*

162. FRANS HALS: *Malle Babbe, the Witch of Haarlem*

163. REMBRANDT: *Samson Threatening his Father-in-Law*

164. REMBRANDT: *The Vision of Daniel*

165. ADAM ELSHEIMER: *Landscape with Saint Mary Magdalene*

166. REMBRANDT: *The Man with the Gold Helmet*

167. Antoine Watteau: *The Italian Comedy*

168. WILLIAM HOGARTH: 'Shortly after the Marriage'

169. FRENCH OR ENGLISH SCHOOL, ABOUT 1395: *The Virgin and Child with Eleven Angels*
(Right Half of the '*Wilton Diptych*')

170. JAN VAN EYCK: *Portrait of Giovanni Arnolfini and his Wife*

171. Antonello da Messina: *Saint Jerome in his Study*

172. CARLO CRIVELLI: *The Annunciation*

173. BOTTICELLI: *Mars and Venus*

174. PAOLO UCCELLO: *The Rout of San Romano*

175. PIERO DELLA FRANCESCA: *The Nativity*

176. MICHELANGELO: *The Entombment*

IOANNES BELLINVS

177. GIOVANNI BELLINI: *Portrait of Doge Leonardo Loredan*

XIX. Antonio Canaletto: *The Piazza, Venice, seen through an Archway*. London, National Gallery

178. JACOPO TINTORETTO: *Saint George and the Dragon*

179. HANS HOLBEIN: *The French Ambassadors to the English Court*

180. HANS HOLBEIN: *Portrait of Princess Christina of Denmark, Duchess of Milan*

181. TITIAN: *Bacchus and Ariadne*

182. RUBENS: *The Triumph of Silenus*

183. Detail from Plate 182

184. RUBENS: *'Le chapeau de paille'*: *Portrait of Susanna Fourment*

185. RUBENS: *The Château de Steen*

186. Meindert Hobbema: *The Avenue, Middelharnis, Holland*

187. CLAUDE LORRAINE: *Seaport: The Embarkation of the Queen of Sheba*

188. VELAZQUEZ: 'The Rokeby Venus'

189. REMBRANDT: *Portrait of Margaretha Trip*

190. REMBRANDT: *The Woman Taken in Adultery*

191. REMBRANDT: *A Woman Bathing*

192. SIR JOSHUA REYNOLDS: *Portrait of Lord Heathfield, Governor of Gibraltar*

193. JOHN CONSTABLE: *The Cornfield*

XX. PAUL CÉZANNE: *Old Woman with Rosary*. London, National Gallery

194. PISANELLO: *Profile Portrait of a Lady* (Mellon Collection)

195. JAN VAN EYCK: *The Annunciation* (Mellon Collection)

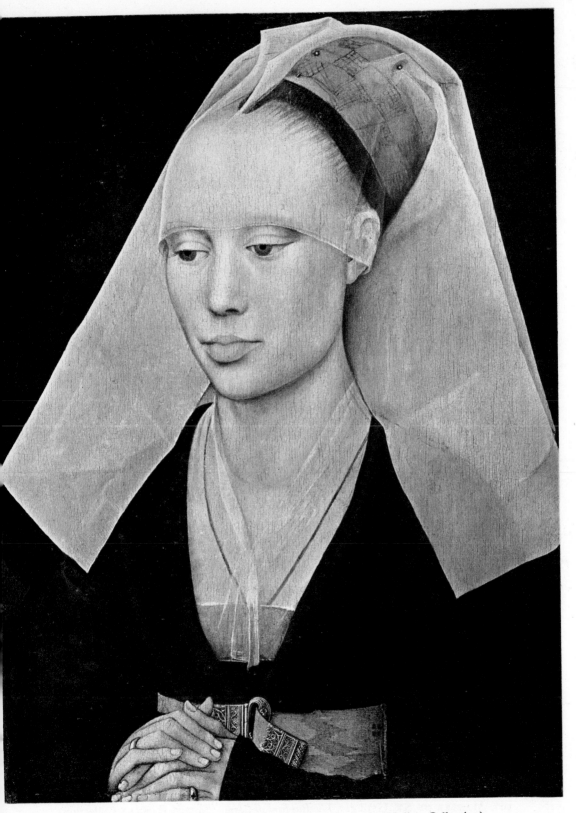

196. ROGIER VAN DER WEYDEN: *Portrait of a Lady* (Mellon Collection)

197. MASTER OF ST. GILLES: *The Baptism of Clovis* (Samuel H. Kress Collection)

198. SASSETTA: *The Meeting of Saint Anthony and Saint Paul* (Samuel H. Kress Collection)

199. ALBRECHT DUERER: *Portrait of a Clergyman* (Samuel H. Kress Collection)

200. GRUENEWALD: *The Crucifixion* (Samuel H. Kress Collection)

201. TITIAN: *Venus with a Mirror* (Mellon Collection)

XXI. GIOVANNI BELLINI: *The Feast of the Gods.* Washington, National Gallery of Art (Widener Collection)

202. RAPHAEL: *Alba Madonna* (Mellon Collection)

204. GIORGIONE: *The Adoration of the Shepherds* (Samuel H. Kress Collection)

206. EL GRECO: *Laocoön* (Samuel H. Kress Collection)

207. REMBRANDT: *Portrait of a Lady with an Ostrich-Feather Fan* (Widener Collection)

208. JAN VERMEER VAN DELFT: *A Woman Weighing Gold* (Widener Collection)

209. FRANCISCO DE GOYA: *Señora Sabasa Garcia* (Mellon Collection)

210. GEORGE ROMNEY: *Mrs. Davenport* (Mellon Collection)

211. PIETRO LONGHI: *Blind Man's Buff* (Samuel H. Kress Collection)

212. FRANCESCO GUARDI: *View on the Cannaregio, Venice* (Samuel H. Kress Collection)

213. GILBERT STUART: *The Skater* (Mellon Collection)

214. JEAN-BAPTISTE CAMILLE COROT: *Rocks in the Forest of Fontainebleau* (Chester Dale Collection)

215. ALBERT RYDER: *Siegfried and the Rhine Maidens* (Mellon Collection)

216. THOMAS EAKINS: *The Biglen Brothers Racing* (Mr. and Mrs. Cornelius Vanderbilt Whitney)

217. JOSEPH MALLORD WILLIAM TURNER: *Venice: Dogana and San Giorgio Maggiore* (Widener Collectio.

218. AUGUSTE RENOIR: *Bather Arranging her Hair* (Chester Dale Collection)

219. PAUL GAUGUIN: *Self-Portrait* (Chester Dale Collection)

220. GIORGIONE: *Portrait of Antonio Broccardo*

221. GIOVANNI ANTONIO BOLTRAFFIO: *Madonna and Child*

222. GIOVANNI BATTISTA TIEPOLO: *Saint James of Compostela*

223. FRANCISCO DE GOYA: *Girl with Jug of Water*

224. MASTER OF THE ANNUNCIATION OF AIX: *The Prophet Jeremiah*

225. DIRK BOUTS: *The Justice of Emperor Otto*

226. HANS MEMLING: *Portrait of Guillaume Moreel, Mayor of Bruges*

227. FRANÇOIS SNYDERS: *Stag Hunt*

228. PIETER BRUEGEL: *Landscape with the Fall of Icarus*

229. RUBENS: *The Bearing of the Cross*

230. LOUIS DAVID: *Marat Stabbed in his Bath*

231. ALBRECHT DUERER: *The Apostles Paul and Mark*

232. FRANCESCO FRANCIA: *Madonna and Child in the Rose Garden*

233. MASTER OF THE ST. BARTHOLOMEW ALTARPIECE: *Saint Agnes*

234. ALBRECHT ALTDORFER: *The Battle of Alexander*

235. PIETER BRUEGEL: *Head of a Peasant Woman*

236. EL GRECO: *The Disrobing of Christ*

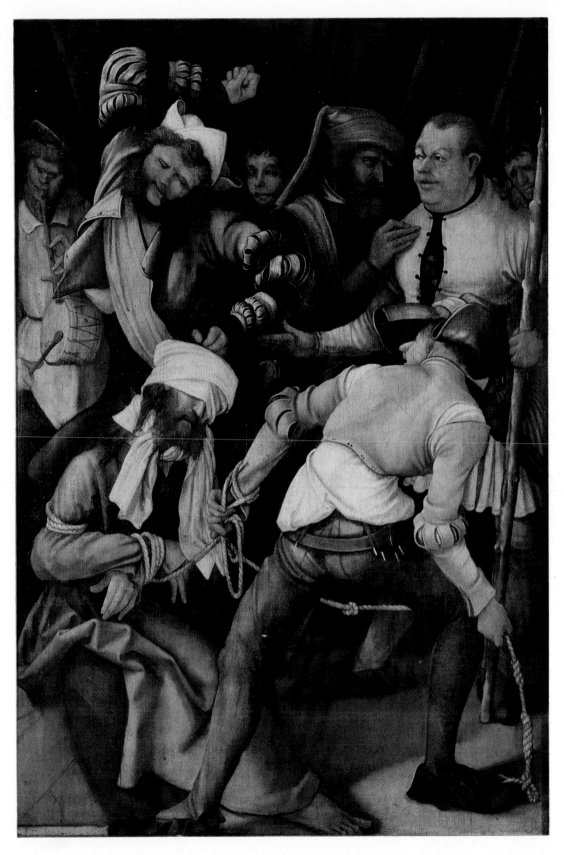

XXII. GRUENEWALD: *The Mocking of Christ*. Munich, Picture Gallery

237. REMBRANDT: *The Descent from the Cross*

238. Van Dyck: *Self-Portrait*

239. RUBENS: *Self-Portrait with his first Wife in the Honeysuckle Arbour*

240. RUBENS: *Bathsheba Receiving King David's Letter*

241. REMBRANDT: *The Rape of Ganymede*

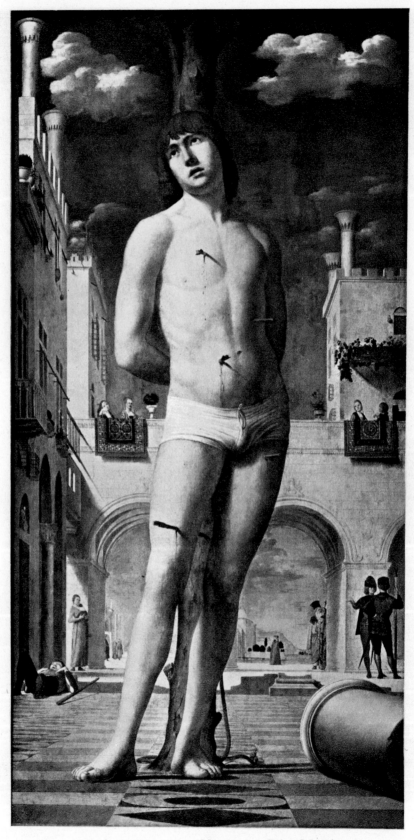

242. ANTONELLO DA MESSINA: *Saint Sebastian*

243. RAPHAEL: *The Sistine Madonna*

244. CORREGGIO: *Holy Night*

XXIII. Titian: *The Tribute Money*. Dresden, Gallery

245. GIORGIONE: *Venus Reclining in a Landscape*

246. JEAN-ÉTIENNE LIOTARD: *The Chocolate Girl*

247. Francesco del Cossa: *Saint John the Baptist*

248. BRAMANTE: *Christ at the Column*

249. PIERO DELLA FRANCESCA: *Madonna and Child Enthroned with Angels and Saints,*
Adored by Duke Federigo of Urbino

250. GIOVANNI BELLINI: *Pietà*

251. BERNARDINO LUINI: *The Soul of Saint Catherine Borne by Angels*

252. JACOPO TINTORETTO: *The Finding of Saint Mark's Body*

253. Jacobello del Fiore: *Paradise*

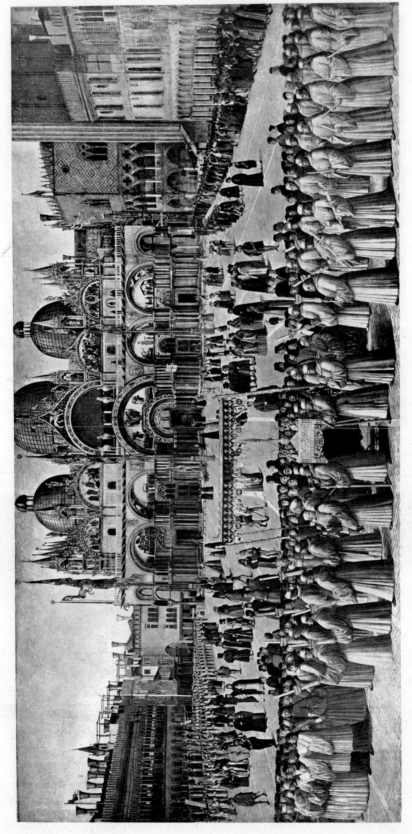

254. GENTILE BELLINI: *The Corpus Christi Procession in the Piazza di San Marco*

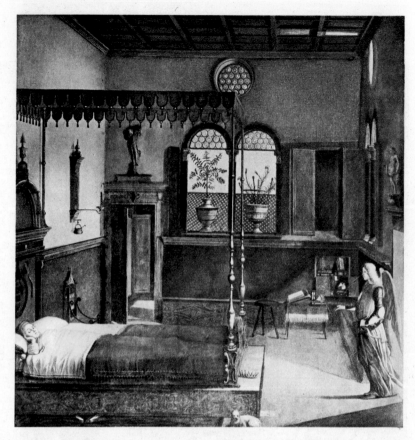

255. VITTORE CARPACCIO: *The Dream of Saint Ursula*

256. GIOVANNI BELLINI: *Madonna and Child between Saints Catherine and Mary Magdalene*

257. GIORGIONE: *The Tempest*

258. TITIAN: *The Presentation of the Virgin in the Temple*

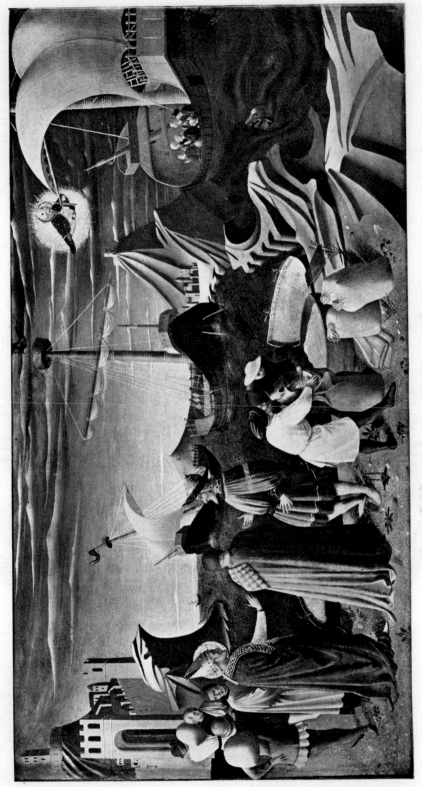

259. FRA ANGELICO: *Two Miracles of Saint Nicholas of Bari*

260. RAPHAEL: *The Transfiguration*

TEMPLA DOMVM EXPOSITIS; VICOS FORA MOENIA PONTES:
VIRGINEAM TRIVII QVOD REPARARIS AQVAM.
PRISCA LICET NAVTIS STATVAS DARE COMMODA PORTVS:
ET VATICANVM CINGERE SIXTE IVGVM:
PLVS TAMEN VRBS DEBET: NAM QVAE SQVALORE LATEBAT:
CERNITVR IN CELEBRI BIBLIOTHECA LOCO

261. MELOZZO DA FORLI: *Pope Sixtus IV and his Court*

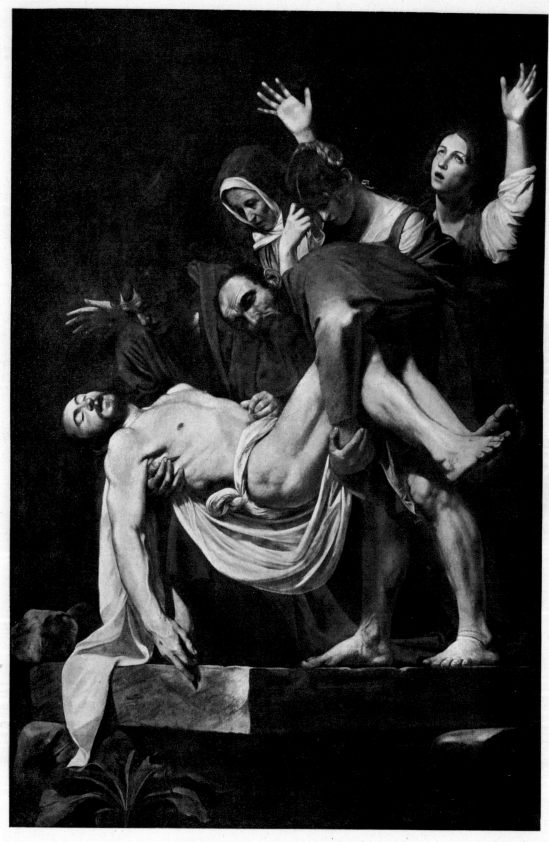

262. CARAVAGGIO: *The Entombment*

XXIV. EL GRECO: *View of Toledo*. New York, Metropolitan Museum of Art

263. JEROME BOSCH: *The Adoration of the Magi*

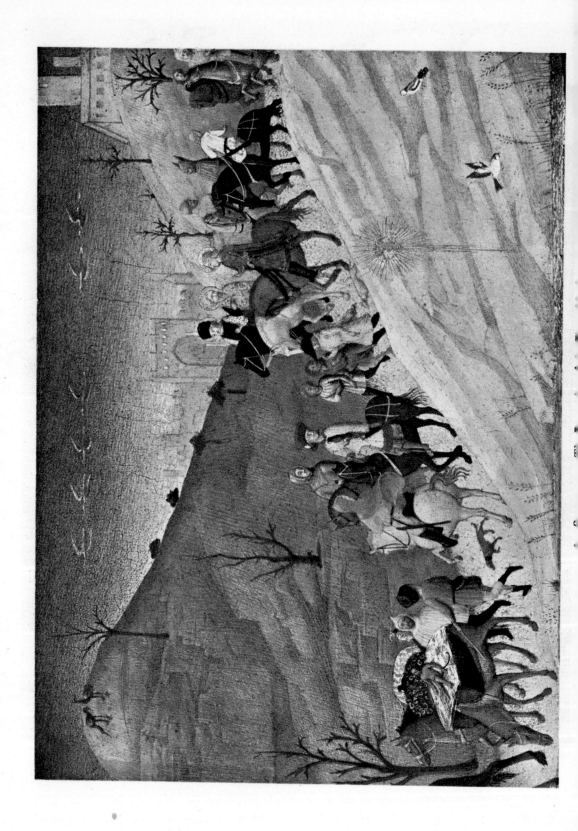

265. VITTORE CARPACCIO: *Meditation on the Passion*

266. REMBRANDT: *Man with a Magnifying Glass*

267. EL GRECO: *Portrait of the Grand-Inquisitor Fernando de Guevara*

268. JOHN SINGLETON COPLEY:
Portrait of Joseph Sherburne

269. JEAN-HONORÉ FRAGONARD:
The billet-doux

270. HONORÉ DAUMIER: *In the Third Class*

271. FRANCISCO DE GOYA: *Women on a Balcony*

272. EDOUARD MANET: *Woman with a Parrot*

INDEX
OF PAINTERS AND PAINTINGS

ACKNOWLEDGEMENTS

SINCERE THANKS are due to the authorities of the following Galleries for according permission to reproduce pictures in their collections and for providing the necessary photographs: The National Gallery of Art, Washington, D.C.; The Metropolitan Museum of Art, New York; The Kunsthistorische Museum, Vienna; The Rijksmuseum, Amsterdam; The Hessische Treuhandverwaltung, Wiesbaden, administering the Berlin pictures; The National Gallery, London; and the Alte Pinakothek, Munich.

Pictures in other Galleries have been reproduced from photographs taken by Archivo Mas, Barcelona; Gustav Schwarz, Berlin; Walter Steinkopf, Berlin; A.C.L., Brussels; Alinari, Florence; Soprintendenza alle Gallerie, Florence; Archives Photographiques, Paris; Anderson, Rome; and from material in the publishers' archives. The illustrations on pp. 30 and 68 are reproduced by courtesy of Exclusive News Agency, London.

INDEX

CIMABUE (c. 1240–1302). Italian
The Virgin and Child Enthroned. *Florence.*
Pl. 27

CLAUDE see Lorrain

CONSTABLE, John (1776–1837). English
The Cornfield. *London.* Pl. 193

COPLEY, John Singleton (1737–1815). American
Portrait of Joseph Sherburne. *New York.*
Pl. 268

COROT, Camille (1796–1875). French
Rocks in the Forest of Fontainebleau.
Washington. Pl. 214

CORREGGIO, Antonio (c. 1489–1534). Italian
Jupiter and Io. *Vienna.* Pl. 18
Leda and the Swan. *Berlin.* Pl. 151
Holy Night. *Dresden.* Pl. 244

COSSA, Francesco (1435–1477). Italian
Allegory of Autumn. *Berlin.* Pl. 156
St. John the Baptist. *Milan.* Pl. 247

COURBET, Gustave (1819–1877). French
Funeral at Ornans. *Paris.* Pl. 78

CRANACH, Lucas (1472–1553). German
Stag Hunt. *Vienna.* Pl. 6
Rest on the Flight into Egypt. *Berlin.* Pl. 152

CRISTUS, Petrus (active 1446–1467). Netherlandish.
Portrait of a Girl. *Berlin.* Pl. 146

CRIVELLI, Carlo (1430/5–1495). Italian
The Annunciation. *London.* Pl. 172

DAUMIER, Honoré (1808–1879). French
In the Third Class. *New York.* Pl. 270

DAVID, Louis (1748–1825). French
Three Ladies of Ghent. *Paris.* Pl. 81
Marat Stabbed in his Bath. *Brussels.* Pl. 230

DEGAS, Edgar (1834–1917). French
Ballet Dancer on the Stage. *Paris.* Pl. 87

DELACROIX, Eugène (1798–1863). French
The Massacre at Scios. *Paris.* Pl. 80

DOU, Gerard (1613–1675). Dutch
Self-Portrait. *Amsterdam.* Pl. 141

DÜRER, Albrecht (1471–1528). German
The Adoration of the Trinity. *Vienna.* Colour
Pl. II
Portrait of the Emperor Maximilian. *Vienna.*
Pl. 4
The Adoration of the Magi. *Florence.* Pl. 30
Self-Portrait. *Madrid.* Pl. 98
Portrait of Hieronymus Holzschuher. *Berlin.*
Pl. 153
Portrait of a Clergyman. *Washington.* Pl. 199

The Apostles Paul and Mark. *Munich.*
Pl. 231

DYCK, Anthony van (1599–1641). Flemish
Marchesa Paola Adorno and her Son.
Washington. Colour Pl. VII
Portrait of an Officer. *Vienna.* Pl. 19
Portrait of King Charles I of England. *Paris.*
Pl. 68
Portrait of Prince William II and his Young
Wife. *Amsterdam.* Pl. 129
Self-Portrait. *Munich.* Pl. 238

EAKINS, Thomas (1844–1916). American
The Biglen Brothers Racing. *Washington.*
Pl. 216

ELSHEIMER, Adam (1578–1610). German
Landscape with St. Mary Magdalen.
Berlin. Pl. 165

EYCK, Jan van (died 1441). Netherlandish
Portrait of Cardinal Albergati. *Vienna.* Pl. 3
Madonna and Child Adored by Chancellor
Rolin. *Paris.* Pl. 58
Madonna in the Church. *Berlin.* Pl. 144
Portrait of Giovanni Arnolfini and his Wife.
London. Pl. 170
The Annunciation. *Washington.* Pl. 195

FOUQUET, Jean (1420–1481). French
Portrait of King Charles VII of France.
Paris. Pl. 56
Portrait of Etienne Chevalier with his Patron
Saint Stephen. *Berlin.* Pl. 145

FRAGONARD, Jean-Honoré (1732–1806). French
The Music Lesson. *Paris.* Pl. 74
The Billet-doux. *New York.* Pl. 269

FRANCIA, Francesco (1450–1518). Italian
Madonna and Child in the Rose Garden.
Munich. Pl. 232

FRENCH SCHOOL, c. 1460
The Pietà of Villeneuve-lès-Avignon. *Paris.*
Pl. 60

FRENCH OR ENGLISH SCHOOL. c. 1395
The Wilton Diptych. *London.* Pl. 169

FROMENT, Nicolas (c. 1450–1490). French
The Raising of Lazarus. *Florence.* Pl. 39

GAINSBOROUGH, Thomas (1727–1788). English
Portrait of Mrs. Siddons. *London.* Colour Pl. I

GAUGUIN, Paul (1848–1903). French
Self-Portrait. *Washington.* Pl. 219

GEERTGEN tot Sint Jans (c. 1465–1495).
Netherlandish